For my wife, Linda, from whom I've learned so much, and from whom I'd learn a lot more if I were less stubborn.

And for Mike Abourezk, who led me to many of the insights in this book, sometimes by the ear.

The sincerity of a true heart is the only requirement of effective advocacy. No one wants to know that, because a true heart is so much harder to acquire than a few advocacy techniques.

— JAMES MCCOMAS

PRAISE FOR LAWYERS, JUDGES & SEMI-RATIONAL BEASTS

"You can spend the next 5 years reading every good book published on persuasion, or you can read this one elegantly written book by Dan Holloway. But this is more than a summary of what others have written; it is a brilliant integration of what others have written into a powerful perspective on persuasion for the trial lawyer."

— **Richard H. Friedman**, Inner Circle of Advocates; co-author of *Rules of the Road*; author of *Polarizing the Case* and *On Becoming a Trial Lawyer*

"Lawyers spend their careers attempting to persuade judges, jurors, clients, adversaries, and the press to adopt their positions — without giving sufficient thought to what would motivate those audiences to do so. Dan Holloway has drawn together a fascinating analysis of the inner workings of the human mind and how lawyers can apply that knowledge to persuade different types of thinkers. A valuable analytical tool for any attorney's arsenal."

— **Robert J. Dwyer**, Boies Schiller Flexner LLP

"In easy, engaging prose, this book provides indispensable light for anyone engaged in the foggy, mysterious work of persuasion. Every law firm should provide a copy to each of its lawyers."

— **Lawrence B. Schlachter**, MD, JD, Neurosurgeon (retired); medical malpractice attorney (active); author of *Malpractice: A Neurosurgeon Reveals How Our Health-Care System Puts Patients at Risk*

"Crossing back and forth through the permeable membrane between the conscious and the unconscious realms where decisions sprout, Dan Holloway guides us on a meticulous, no-stone-unturned quest to reveal what determines how jurors or judges hear or read what the advocate speaks or writes. As Dan explains, persuasion is a matter not of proof, but of people:

> No one should be disappointed or disturbed to realize how little the "I" yammering away in your head actually controls. It's mainly the unconscious self we love — the way you wear your hat, the way you sip your tea, the way you grin when your niece walks in . . . all the things you do without thinking about it. Those define you most. Those are the reasons people like you (or don't).
>
> You hardly need me to say that all of this holds true as much for judges and law clerks and jurors as it does for you. Their responses to your brief or your trial presentation will derive largely from unconscious processes.

Actually, Dan, we *do* need you to say it, and particularly in the depth and breadth of observation with which you have considered it in this book."

— **Joshua Karton**, communication and trial consultant; co-author of *Theater for Trial* with David Ball

"Full of surprising facts and strikingly original observations, this book manages to combine sound practical advice for lawyers with a profound meditation on human thought, motivation, and behavior."

— **Louis Michael Seidman**, Carmack Waterhouse Professor of Constitutional Law, Georgetown University Law Center

"A comprehensive study of the science and art of persuasion — boiled down to effective tools for winning over judges and juries (and your spouse and teenage child too)."

— **Mauricio Gonzalez**, DLA Piper

"The lessons and information Holloway provides would be valuable in any law school classroom. In particular, this book could serve as a key text in a stand-alone class on persuasion. It could also be a valuable supplemental resource in a variety of legal writing, clinical, and other courses that merge theory and practice."

— **Ann Mallatt Killenbeck**, Professor of Law, University of Arkansas

"This book distills a library of cognitive science literature into a concise description of how human beings think and decide. Dan Holloway's book provides the bedrock foundation from which all lawyers should work. It is required reading for anyone who wants to persuade."

— **Lloyd N. Bell**, medical malpractice attorney and member of the Inner Circle of Advocates

LAWYERS, JUDGES & SEMI-RATIONAL BEASTS

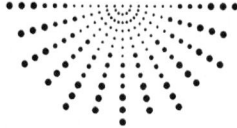

SUMMARY TABLE OF CONTENTS

Part III

COMMUNICATION AND PERSUASION

Part IV

JURORS AND JUDGES

Part V

KEY PRINCIPLES & IMPLICATIONS

DETAILED OUTLINE

What follows here is a detailed outline of this book. Reading the outline will not, of course, substitute for reading the book itself. But for anyone who has read the book, the outline may provide a useful summary for review. It's hard to put knowledge into practice, when the information is buried in hundreds of pages of paragraphs. But a concise list of main points — *that* you can keep at hand and refer back to as the occasion arises. Better yet, you can adapt it into a reference source customized for your own practice and needs.

1. THE BRAIN-CENTRIC VIEW OF HUMAN NATURE

1.1 Our brains consist of many specialized circuits operating in parallel, without a command center.

1.2 Our brains run on cells and molecules, physics and chemistry.

1.3 Mental processes correspond to processes in the physical body.

1.3.1 Brain chemistry affects how we think and feel
1.3.2 The rest of our bodies affect our thinking and feeling, too.
1.3.3 A special example: We empathize by simulating in our own brains the experience of others.
1.3.4 What we learn gets etched into our brains, more or less literally.

1.4 Our brains aim to do well enough, efficiently — not to achieve perfection.

1.4.1 Our brains (and thus our minds) operate with limited energy.
1.4.2 Our brains create coherence out of bits and pieces.
1.4.3 Our brains make systematic errors.

1.5 Our brains run our lives unconsciously for the most part, with our conscious selves playing a vital managerial role.

1.5.1 Unconscious processes drive most of our lives.
1.5.2 Conscious processes play a limited role in moment-to-moment decisions.
1.5.3 The conscious self does little or nothing without heavy assistance by unconscious processes.
1.5.4 We barely know ourselves.
1.5.5 The conscious self participates in joint projects.
1.5.6 Through its influence, including mere thoughts, the conscious self affects the physical brain.
1.5.7 Despite its limitations, the conscious self plays a role of earth-shaking importance.
1.5.8 Scarce energy and mental sloth limit the scope and power of the conscious self.

1.6 Our brains guide us through life largely by means of emotion — as an efficient form of cognition.

1.6.1 Unconscious thought sometimes expresses itself physiologically.

1.6.2 We respond affectively to more or less everything, for good reason.

1.6.3 We depend on emotion for information.

1.6.4 We depend on emotion in order to make decisions and take action.

1.6.5 We can't even distinguish clearly between thought and feeling.

1.6.6 We can and should reason seriously. We can and should distinguish between appropriate and inappropriate emotion.

1.6.7 The rational-man distinction between reason and emotion makes us stupid.

1.7 Our brains are built for society and behavioral flexibility.

1.7.1 Our brains are wired for behavioral flexibility — and thus for culture, to guide flexible behavior.

- Behavioral flexibility, within bounds
- Cultural variation
- Culture, behavioral control, and the slow-maturing brain
- Culture as nature (sort of)

1.7.2 Our brains are tuned to the problems of living with other people.

1.7.3 We think and feel the way our culture tells us to — largely.

1.7.4 There are lots of cultures, subcultures, sub-subcultures, and so on.

1.7.5 We get smarter over time, as cultures and as individuals.

1.8 Our brains come pre-loaded with some content, probably including social and moral content.

1.9 Some of our differences go all the way down, and we have no transcendent arbiter of who's right.

2. SEEING, FEELING, THINKING

2.1 General processes

2.1.1 We evaluate anything new by means of an existing worldview — a catalog of preexisting thoughts and feelings.
2.1.2 We think and feel by activating networks of associations.
2.1.3 We judge by tangential cues as much as by actual merits.
2.1.4 We think in sensory, especially visual, terms.
2.1.5 We think by analogizing, and we revise (or ignore) concepts, standards, and rules when they don't seem to fit the specifics.

2.2 Perception and memory

2.2.1 We see the next, new thing in the light cast by what we already believe and feel.
2.2.2 We see nearly everything by comparison to something else.
2.2.3 We consciously see what we pay attention to, and not the rest.
2.2.4 We see what we expect to see, often wrongly.
2.2.5 We remember a little, often wrongly.
2.2.6 A list of things that make us remember

- Simplicity
- Concreteness
- Emotion
- Stories
- Context, coherence, relating new to old
- Imagery
- Repetition with variation
- Numbering
- Poetry

- The first, the last

2.3 Immediate responses, conscious reasoning, ultimate judgments

2.3.1 We form judgments in a snap.

- Intuition volunteers answers automatically and confidently.
- We "decide" only occasionally, and economize even then.

2.3.2 We think largely in stories.

- Stories organize information and carry powerful implications.
- Stories structure emotional responses.
- Imagining a thing makes it real.
- We spot narrative incongruities easily.
- Too many facts can hurt imagination and plausibility.

2.3.3 We navigate life largely by means of snap judgments, but very imperfectly.

- We believe what comes to mind easily.
- Familiarity feels like truth.
- Intuition doesn't get statistics.
- We extrapolate from likes and dislikes.
- Fast judgments aren't necessarily bad judgments.
- Expert intuition rarely or never applies in law.

2.3.4 We believe what we feel inclined to believe — even after hard, conscious reasoning — but it's complicated.

- Coming to believe something and finding justification

for the belief are two different things, and usually occur in that order.

- Things constrain what we feel inclined to believe.
- Ignorance expands our range of potential beliefs.
- We believe whichever possible answer appeals most to the feelings and thoughts working most strongly within us at the time.
- We actively bias our own beliefs. All our reasoning is motivated.
- We believe and feel many contradictory things, but they don't all guide us at the same time.
- We believe what we're told, if it doesn't conflict with our preexisting thoughts or feelings.

2.3.5 We sometimes infer our beliefs from our behavior.
2.3.6 We stick to old, pre-written answers, right or wrong.
2.3.7 We learn when we feel motivated to learn — usually to solve problems.
2.3.8 We moralize intuitively.

- We make moral judgments intuitively and automatically, and then we rationalize them.
- We possess (or are possessed by) an innate moral sense with cultural settings.

2.4 We think and feel the way our language tells us to — to a fair extent.

2.4.1 Words imply a logic that may or may not fit the situation.
2.4.2 More generally, language raises associations that help or hurt your position.

2.5 Some substantive content or leanings

2.5.1 We look for agents, intention, and causation — and often find them wrongly.

2.5.2 We put too much stock in a simplistic view of personal character.
2.5.3 We divide the world into US and THEM, and reserve good feeling and thinking for the former.
2.5.4 We respond more to the bad than to the good.
2.5.5 The moral sensibilities of liberals and conservatives differ in predictable ways.
2.5.6 We enjoy altruistic punishment.
2.5.7 We feel that other people see things as we do.
2.5.8 We need to feel the world is safe, just, understandable.
2.5.9 We blame departures from the norm.
2.5.10 We see race, gender, and class.

2.6 We can improve decision-making a little.

2.6.1 Hard thinking helps, but less than we'd like.
2.6.2 We need good routines for good reasoning.

3. COMMUNICATION AND PERSUASION

3.1 We communicate by evoking thoughts and feelings in someone else's head — always imperfectly.

3.1.1 Communication evokes intellectual, emotional, and physio-logical responses.
3.1.2 The audience is everything (sort of).
3.1.3 Communication always fails, a little or a lot.

3.2 Writing and reading make the problems worse.

3.2.1 Writing and reading are unnatural.
3.2.2 Merely parsing the damned sentence takes work.
3.2.3 Unfamiliar things get in the way.
3.2.4 Different people read differently.
3.2.5 Expectations shape what we read.

3.2.6 Comprehension depends on context.

3.2.7 Readers need coherence markers.

3.2.8 Legal writing and reading are the worst.

3.3 Persuasion works by accommodating the decision-maker's existing values, attitudes, and beliefs.

3.4 When you can get it, thoughtful consideration mitigates irrelevancies, but irrelevancies always matter.

3.5 Trust confers power, so we give it warily.

3.5.1 Trust confers power.

3.5.2 We have a hair-trigger for untrustworthiness, when we're wary.

3.5.3 Trust begins with goodwill.

3.5.4 Emotional kinship serves as a marker of goodwill.

3.5.5 Integrity and competence serve as general markers of trust-worthiness.

3.5.6 An appearance of high competence can backfire.

3.6 Social dynamics pull us thoughtlessly and automatically.

3.6.1 We care about our reputation and want others to like us.

3.6.2 We want to agree with people we like.

3.6.3 We reciprocate.

3.6.4 We want to be normal.

3.6.5 We look to authority.

3.6.6 We agree more readily when we're in a good mood.

3.7 A decision-maker's feelings toward an advocate — and the advocate's feelings toward the subject — make a big difference.

3.8 We actively resist changing our beliefs.

3.8.1 We don't like being told what to think or do.

3.8.2 We don't want to change our beliefs. Inertia grounds us.
3.8.3 Inertia operates with special power when we've publicly committed to something.
3.8.4 We look for faults in ideas we don't already accept.

3.9 We can build resistance to the other side, by preempting counterarguments.

3.10 We get sucked in, and maybe suckered, by stories.

3.11 Stories, not arguments, evoke moral feeling.

4. JURORS AND JUDGES

4.1 Jurors make decisions as groups of strangers — under stress, about mostly unfamiliar issues, according to rules they often don't understand.

4.2 Judges make decisions as semi-dictators or in small groups, under a mixed bag of circumstances, with minimal account-ability.

4.2.1 On fact questions, the judge's individual worldview largely drives the decision. And all questions are fact questions.
4.2.2 Then there are all the normal corruptions of human judgment.
4.2.3 The legal setting supports good decision-making.
4.2.4 The legal setting impedes good decision-making.
4.2.5 Bench rulings carry the greatest risk.
4.2.6 You're right to worry about the inescapable subjectivity of judge (or jury) decisions.

KEY PRINCIPLES & IMPLICATIONS

Preliminaries

- Fight the temptation to think of persuasion as a matter of proof. Think of it as a matter of people.
- Don't get carried away with any particular insight. Think of yourself as spinning plates.

Principles for Persuasion

1. EARN TRUST.

1.1 Respect and value the person you're talking to.

1.2 Take positions you believe in.

1.3 Tell the truth — including the essential bad parts.

1.4 Bring your whole self — but a decent, restrained version of it.

1.5 Engage your listeners on a human level.

1.6 Keep your emotional pitch in tune with your listener's.

1.7 Don't try to hide your agenda or shine it up.

1.8 Know what you're talking about, and look like it — without putting on airs.

1.9 Abide by values you share with the decision-maker — and beware the hair-trigger for distrust in high-suspicion contexts.

2. ENLIST EXISTING ATTITUDES, TO MOTIVATE THE DECISION.

2.1 Find what will motivate this person for you, and against you.

2.2 Find the stories, scenes, and details that feed helpful motivations and starve harmful ones.

2.3 Find the language that evokes the values and motivations you're appealing to and leads away from contrary ones.

2.4 Use comparisons and framing, thoughtfully.

2.5 Make yourself and your client an Us to the extent you authentically can.

2.6 Identify likely counter-motivations and do something about them.

2.7 Sequencing: Story first, then analysis. And maybe begin with the harm, to motivate scrutiny of bad conduct.

2.8 Sequencing: Address essential negative points after the decision-maker has begun to see things your way. And put the negative point in your opponent's mouth.

3. JUSTIFY THE DECISION.

4. MAKE IT INTERESTING, CLEAR, AND EASY.

4.1 Use the basic tools of effective, efficient communication.

- Simplicity with accuracy
- Clear, intuitive organization
- One thing at a time
- Thesis statements and topic sentences; conclusions that relate back; transitions
- Short, simple sentences — mostly
- Concrete particulars
- Visuals and tangibles

4.2 In responding: First lay out the truth, then deal with their nonsense.

4.3 Talk conversationally and concretely, like a person interested in connecting with the listener.

4.4 Make it no longer than it needs to be.

5. STEER AROUND RESISTANCE, AND BUILD COUNTER-RESISTANCE.

5.1 Earn permission before anything that sounds like advocacy or overt emotion.

5.2 Don't get pushy or strident. Avoid subjective characterizations. State argumentative conclusions only when you have to, and present them as your views, not divine truth.
5.3 Preempt and inoculate against powerful negative points.
5.4 Offer choices, where you can.

Principles for Putting Knowledge to Work

1. NOTES, BEST PRACTICES DOCUMENTS, AND INSTITUTIONAL ROUTINES

2. DELIBERATE PRACTICE

INTRODUCTION

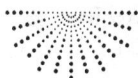

You can't write a brief to a judge or address jurors at trial — or talk to your spouse or kids — without some understanding of how people work: how we think, decide, and come to be persuaded. This book summarizes what we know about those processes from empirical study, and the book distills first principles of persuasion. The discussion here focuses on the concerns of lawyers, but of course the same points apply in many other contexts, too.

We should inform our work with the reliable, useful findings of cognitive science. This business of persuading people is hard, tricky, baffling. There's a blizzard of advice on how to persuade judges and jurors — much of the advice conflicting, much of it nonsense, much of it mere taste-mongering, much of it slivers of ad hoc insights drawn from some striking thing that happened once to some lawyer in some confluence of circumstances that will never recur. In the blizzard, you can lose the landmarks. The cognitive science literature helps you find them.

I'm using the term "cognitive science" loosely to sweep in all the sciences bearing on human cognition, communication, and decision-making. These studies include various forms of psychology, sociology, anthropology, and their bio- and neuro- versions (bioanthropology and neuropsychology, for example).

In recent years cognitive science has swept across the culture, but unreliable, headline-grabbing findings proliferate. The more extravagant the claims, the more attention they draw. Some of what passes for science is just crackpottery with a sciencey veneer. And of course the movies and TV shows include a lot of fantasy. Furthermore, even where we do run across reliable findings, they may be interesting, even fascinating, feel rich with potential in some vague way — and yet have little practical application in the context of legal work. *Want to feel powerful? Strike a Superman pose!*

This book pulls together a summary of the cognitive-science findings that appear both reliable and useful, and the book tries to assemble those findings into a coherent, more or less complete (if general) model of human minds.

The value of cognitive science lies less in novelty than in sepa-rating *reliable*, familiar insights from *unreliable*, familiar insights. Most of the insights of cognitive science have roots in what we might call the "wisdom literature" stretching back millennia. People have been observing themselves and each other for as long as there have been people, and it's a safe bet that in one way or another, someone somewhere has observed pretty much anything that can be observed. When a psychologist offers an insight that feels radically new, turn on your flim-flam detector. But it's nothing against cognitive science to sniff, "Well, Voltaire said that 250 years ago." Maybe he did. Keen observers have made all sorts of keen observations, but many of those observations are marginal, or misleading, or too narrowly specific to bother with. It helps to know which fenceposts you can lean on without falling over.

This book focuses on the general principles that should (but often don't) underlie any practical advice for lawyers. Any general principle will apply in different ways in the multitude of different contexts lawyers work in — civil, criminal, administrative; brief-writing, cross-examination, closing arguments, etc. This book does not focus on any single type of lawyerly task. To illustrate a point, I occasionally suggest how this or that principle might apply in this or that situation. But this book does not try to work through practical applications in satisfying scope or detail. That would take shelves of books. This book lays out general principles and tries to explain them.

This is not, therefore, a how-to book. Indeed in one sense, this is an *anti*-how-to book. Some of the practical-advice literature seems to promise that if only you understand the advice well enough, if only you follow the advice diligently enough, then you're all but guaranteed to win your next case. (Or maybe we just read that promise into the advice, because we so badly want it to be true.) In any event, the promise is false. One broad lesson from cognitive science (if we needed the lesson) is that we human beings are massively complicated, mysterious, and stubborn. There is no magic bean, no love potion, no secret code that will bring you guaranteed success. The science *can* help you find ways to increase your chances, ways to nudge the odds a little in your favor, ways to avoid tripping over your own feet. That's powerful stuff, and well worth having, but it's not magic. Those hoping for magic will be disappointed by this book (and by every other book, and by life itself).

A poor working lawyer digging into the literature on cognitive science can't avoid fantasizing shamefully about occult secrets of mind control. *Maybe neurolinguistic programming will put the witness in a trance and make him tell the truth.* Reality mostly disappoints the desire to manipulate. For selling t-shirts online, we really do have ways to manipulate people, a little. But legal disputes present a special context, designed precisely to minimize the potential for anything we'd consider manipulation. The insights from the science center on the ordinary, legitimate — even boring — means of persuasion. The science gives us nothing remotely like "mind control."

Indeed, I'm a little surprised at how moralistic this book has turned out — more Sunday School teacher than litigator. Several of the "key principles and implications" toward the end deal more or less explicitly with personal character. This book is less a B.F. Skinner manual than George Washington's *Rules of Civility and*

Decent Behavior in Company and Conversation. Personally, I find this more a relief than a disappointment. I'd rather be thrown back on decency and honesty than on cynical stratagems.

THE MAJOR SECTIONS of this book close with suggested readings, but the book mostly does not provide sources for specific points. The discussion here remains general enough that a curious or skeptical reader can easily vet the discussion in the suggested readings. Further, most of the points here have been told and retold many times. So I have mostly felt no need to credit particular writers. The suggested readings do, however, include the authors who have especially influenced what I say here.

I WISH I'd had a book like this when I started as a lawyer. For all its limitations, the cognitive science literature can give us principles to understand how persuasion works generally. With those principles, we can grope our way through the blizzard a little more confidently, with better odds of success. And what's the alternative? The alternative is just to do whatever happens to come to mind, or to follow some piece of advice picked more or less at random from the mass of conflicting advice, with no way to know whether it holds up in general or applies in this particular situation. That's no alternative.

PRELUDE: OF RATIONAL MEN & SEMI-RATIONAL BEASTS

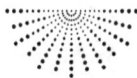

M ost of us have at least two models of mind. We all have an implicit sense of human minds that guides our day-to-day actions. We'd have trouble articulating this model, but we have it. We also have an explicit model of minds that influences our more conscious, intellectual conduct. The dominant model endorsed by intellectuals began before Plato, and it's still going strong millennia later. It goes something like this:

> We are rational beings with animal passions. However, by strict application of rational thought, we can apprehend reality as it is and attain truth with certainty. We should therefore isolate mere animal emotion and submit serious matters to rational reflection.

This idea carries some intuitive force. We do feel like rational spirits that stand separate from, but somehow enmeshed with, our animal bodies. We feel like a sort of angel/animal hybrid.

The rational-man idea must have been a radical insight when it first occurred to some proto-thinker in a tribe that just emerged from the wilderness. The idea carries a good measure of truth, and the habits of mind it tries to foster — calm down and think things through — have done great good in human history. (Probably great harm, too, but that's how these things go.) Flying off in a rage almost never works as well as calm consideration. Picking a president on the basis of a square jaw and an aura of strength works out badly. Nonetheless, the rational-man model gets things only half right. While we should hold to the good half, I focus here on the other half.

No one believes the rational-man model of mind entirely. In day-to-day life, none of us consistently base our actions on that model. Skeptics, cynics, and misanthropes have always scoffed at it. Finley Peter Dunne's "Mr. Dooley" reviewed the Supreme Court's decisions in the insular cases and drew the moral that "No matther whether th' constitution follows h' flag or not, th' Supreme Coort follows th' election returns."[1] Mocking the rational-man ideal more broadly, Ambrose Bierce offered the following definitions in *The Devil's Dictionary*:

> LOGIC, n. The art of thinking and reasoning in strict accordance with the limitations and incapacities of the human misunderstanding. The basic of logic is the syllogism, consisting of a major and a minor premise and a conclusion—thus:
>
> *Major Premise*: Sixty men can do a piece of work sixty times as quickly as one man.
>
> *Minor Premise*: One man can dig a posthole in sixty seconds; therefore—
>
> *Conclusion*: Sixty men can dig a posthole in one second.
>
> This may be called the syllogism arithmetical, in which, by combining logic and mathematics, we obtain a double certainty and are twice blessed.
>
> RATIONAL, adj. Devoid of all delusions save those of observation, experience and reflection.
>
> REASON, v.i. To weigh probabilities in the scales of desire.
>
> REASON, n. Propensitate of prejudice.
>
> REASONABLE, adj. Accessible to the infection of our own opinions. Hospitable to persuasion, dissuasion and evasion.

Discussing trials for witchcraft, Bierce commented that:

The judges' decisions based on [the admissible evidence] were sound in logic and in law. Nothing in any existing court was ever more thoroughly proved than the charges of witchcraft and sorcery for which so many suffered death. If there were no witches, human testimony and human reason are alike destitute of value.[2]

Bierce got carried away in his ultimate conclusion, but he made a mostly fair point.

In more scholarly criticism, intellectuals of varying stripes have attacked different aspects of the rational-man model. These thinkers, too, have proposed a more deflating view of human minds as cognitively messy, with intuition, thought, and feeling entwined and tending as much toward bias and partiality as toward transcendent truth. Philosophers and scientists as diverse as David Hume, Friedrich Nietzsche, William James, Stephen Toulmin, Antonio Damasio, and Daniel Kahneman (among many others) have contributed in various ways to this line of thought.

In law, the rational-man model expresses itself largely as formalism. Legal formalism says we can pin down the law on the basis of governing language and apply the law to the facts rationally — all in a process that does not depend on who the judge happens to be. Anti-foundationalist legal critics say formalism fails as a description of what we actually do, of what we could do, and of what we should try to do. (Anti-foundationalists don't necessarily agree on anything else.)

Even for those of us who reject the rational-man model, though, it still pulls us. It does so in part because the model has embedded itself in all of Western intellectual culture over thousands of years. The model is, after all, partly true. The text of a statute really does constrain interpretation. You can't turn "nothing in this section shall be construed to create a private right of action" into "this section creates a private right of action" — at least not if you have any integrity.

The rational-man model and legal formalism also pull us because they express norms and values that most of us accept — impartiality, consistency, limits on a judge's role in setting public policy, incremental change in law, predictability of law, and so on. We modern Westerners all hold those values to one degree or another. That makes formalism tantalizing: The heaven of impartial, objectively correct decisions is at hand, if only the right sort of people (your sort of people) run the show. The model flatters. It assures you that you're smart, and those who disagree with you are stupid. You're pure; your opponents aren't. Emotion clouds their eyes, while yours remain clear.

In any event, we fall into trains of thought driven by the rational-man model. We forget its failings and act on its advice even though in certain moods we'd scoff.

As a practical matter, though, can we improve our actions by refining our model of the human mind? Whatever the technical faults of our models, haven't we been getting along fine with them?

Our models of mind work well enough for many purposes. We've lived in large societies for millennia. We communicate and cooperate on a massive scale, which requires having a good idea of what's going on in each others' heads. Thousands of people on nearly all continents combine their efforts to produce airplanes that carry hundreds of people across oceans in hours — and rarely fall from the sky. We have the internet, mega-churches, smartphones, and pizza with cheese stuffed into the very crust itself. Much of the time, judicial decisions seem to go the right way. We couldn't accomplish any of this without a pretty good understanding of how people work.

On the other hand, we suffer daily failures, some big, some little — probably in part because we don't understand well enough our own or other people's minds. You say the wrong thing to your daughter, and mysteriously the weekend is ruined. You brief a simple issue, and it never occurs to you the judge could get it wrong, but then it happens. You see that something hit the wing of your space shuttle, your engineers send you a report, you send the shuttle back to space, and on return to Earth it burns up, killing all seven crew members. You somehow fall into a world war that slaughters 60 million people, a gruesome defeat for everyone. We fail all the time, in ways trivial and world-historical. Part of that — of course not the whole of it — has to do with not understanding ourselves or each other well enough.

We need to act based on how people actually work. We should not design human institutions based on assumptions about a make-believe race of rational actors who never existed. Nor should we write legal briefs to make-believe judges built on the rational-man model, or try cases to make-believe jurors.

None of this is to say that if only we understood each other, we would all join hands and dance to Shangri-La. We would still have contrary beliefs and plain cussedness and intractable conflicts and theft and rape and murder and all the rest. It would still be true that when you file a motion with a judge, at least one side is going to lose. But so what? No one refuses to fix a leaking toilet just because that won't fix the car brakes, too.

Over the last century, researchers have amassed an inventory of findings that show we are *not* capable of rational certainty so long as we cordon off mere emotion. Science keeps going, and broad areas of ignorance remain, but it now seems clear that the age-old wisdom of cynics and misanthropes hits closer to the truth. It seems clear enough that we are semi-rational beasts operated by brains tuned to the practical challenges of life; brains that guide us by means of emotions and mental shortcuts, some of which are inborn in us; brains that care little for disinterested truth but can perform rational thought in limited doses; brains that pick a path forward by the twin means of emotion and rationality.

This view of the mind should neither surprise nor sadden us. It shocks no one to learn that we're emotional creatures, that we make systematic mistakes, or that it takes work to prevent or correct them. We knew that all along. If it turns out that nature has baked these limitations into our brains and that they place out of reach the prospect of transcendent truth and universal agreement — well, we learned to live without those blessings long ago. People have been getting by without universal agreement for as long as there have been people. Nor does the semi-rational beast model say, or even hint, that we must give up hope of improving our decision-making. To the contrary, cognitive science points the way toward at least modestly better decision-making — and more usefully than by telling us to wait for transcendent Truth, by commanding us to "be rational," or by assuring us that we're *so* right and those deluded others are *so* wrong.

PART I
THE BRAIN-CENTRIC VIEW
OF HUMAN NATURE

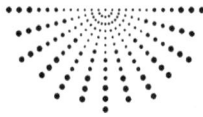

Let's start with a brief description of the brain-centric theory of human nature. This discussion relates to persuasion in important but indirect ways. It also adds depth to more directly relevant ideas in later sections.

Until recent decades, people widely believed that the conscious, experiencing self that feels pain when your tooth aches was a sort of ghost that sat astride and somehow controlled the physical brain. Many of the same folks tended to think the brain was essentially a single big computer that started out empty at birth and learned everything from experience. A lot of us still believe some of that. The idea of the mind as a soul-like thing separate from the body feels compelling. But it now seems discredited by empirical evidence.

It now seems tolerably clear that the feeling, thinking, wanting "I" arises as an effect of the operations of the body — largely but not entirely the brain. That is, you are "your" body. You are not some ghost who wears your body like a coat and could in theory take it off and put on another body. With plastic surgery, you can shave and shape your nose with better or worse results, but even in principle you can't swap out your whole body. You *are* your body, and especially your brain.

1.1 OUR BRAINS CONSIST OF MANY SPECIALIZED CIRCUITS OPERATING IN PARALLEL, WITHOUT A COMMAND CENTER

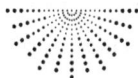

Research in neuroscience so far seems to indicate that the brain consists of a multitude of circuits that connect to each other but perform discrete functions. It's still early days, and scientists debate what exactly counts as a neural circuit, what circuits exist, how independently various circuits operate, and so on. It probably varies depending on the function in question. Recognizing a triangle drawn in black ink on white paper involves different brain processes than answering a four-year-old girl who asks what happened to her friend who was kidnapped. Maybe different brain circuits operate by different rules. So far, however, there does not seem to be any central control room that sits atop a neural hierarchy and integrates or controls the various brain functions. Rather, the brain seems to be a complex system with many discrete parts that give rise to a more or less orderly collective, like a traffic pattern, a weather system, or a kibbutz.

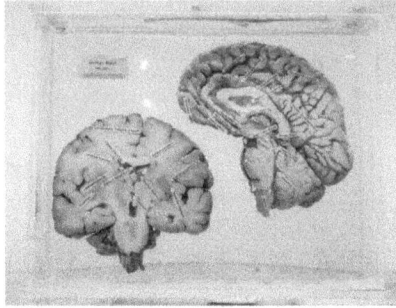

(Image credit in notes.[1])

Patients with neurological damage furnish the most compelling evidence that the brain consists of more or less discrete functional areas. Brain damage may arise in the womb, or from stroke or disease, or from other head trauma. Damage to one part of the left hemisphere of the brain causes Wernicke's Aphasia. The poor souls afflicted with that syndrome lose some of their ability to understand words, or to find them. They pepper otherwise fluent speech with nonsense words, without recognizing that they're nonsense. Damage to a different part of the left hemisphere causes Broca's Aphasia. That leaves comprehension and word recall intact but impairs your ability to make grammatical sentences out of the words. So you tend to speak in short, ungrammatical bursts.

Other brain injuries show connections between other specific areas and particular functions — including functions you wouldn't think are "functions" at all. Damage one area, and you can't recognize individual faces anymore. Damage a different area, and you lose all awareness of one side of your body, and of the world on that side. A guy doesn't shave the left side of his face, he bumps into walls on his left, ignores people standing to his left, and so on. Hurt a different area of the brain, and you don't recognize your left arm. Maybe it belongs to your niece. Maybe it's that guy's over there. Damage another area, and you know you're sitting in your house in Freeport, even though to the rest of us you're in a hospital room in New York City. You have no idea who put elevators outside your living room door, but you're in your Freeport house all the same. Separate the left and right hemispheres of the brain, and the left hemisphere starts making up stories — reasonable guesses by an observer, but false all the same — about things the other side of your body did without the involvement of the left hemisphere. Damage to other areas impairs emotion, empathy, self-control, moral judgments, short-term memory, long-term memory, recognition of social norms, and so on.

These injuries are as poignant as they are bizarre. People who suffer damage to a particular area generally retain the abilities associated with undamaged areas. So the speech expert who can't find words anymore retains his intelligence and desire to talk, but he can't. The woman still loves her fiancé; she just can't recognize his face anymore.

What these injuries show, though, apart from sorrow, is that specific parts of the brain do specific things. When you injure the brain, you don't just reduce overall computational power, as if you removed one processing chip from a computer with eight processors. Nor does the injury just damage random knowledge or memory, as when you damage certain sectors of a hard drive. Rather, the brain seems to have a great many specific functions assigned in more or less the same way to specific parts of all our brains — subject to some potential for change or reassignment.

1.2 OUR BRAINS RUN ON CELLS AND MOLECULES, PHYSICS AND CHEMISTRY

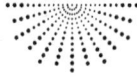

The physicality of the brain has bite: At bottom, the brain is built of biological cells that grow and function according to the laws of physics and chemistry. The neuron serves as the basic unit of the brain. A neuron puts forth an axon, a tendril through which the neuron can send a chemical or electrical charge to another neuron. A neuron also sprouts dendrites, a different kind of tendril, which reaches out to connect with the axon of another neuron, to receive chemical or electrical charges. The body of a neuron contains multiple chemicals that contribute to the functioning of the neuron. The axon and dendrites contain chemicals within them, too.

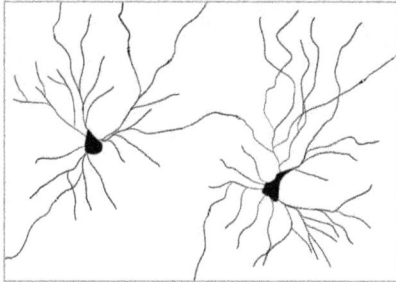

Neural connections operate according to the laws of physics and chemistry. Electrically charged molecules in the brain act in accordance with the same physical laws that govern electricity in your TV set. Molecules interact with one another in and around neurons according to the same physical laws that govern chemistry when you bake up a tray of chocolate chip cookies.

Even a single pair of neurons — operating according to dumb, mute physics and chemistry — can do real work. In a sea snail, for example, a single sensory neuron receives a stimulus from the outside world. The molecules inside that neuron act as chemistry requires. That sends a charge through the axon, to a motor neuron. The motor neuron acts as chemistry requires, and it sends a charge to the muscles that control the snail's gill. The gill closes.

The human brain, like the snail's, is built out of neurons that act according to physical laws.

With 100 billion neurons or so, and trillions of interconnections, in a multitude of discrete but connecting and overlapping circuits, the human brain is unfathomably complex and wonderful. The extraordinary complexity leads to magic — including sentience, conscious thought, self-reflection. It might be too much to say the brain "reduces" to cells and molecules, physics and chemistry. Presumably, many properties of the brain arise from large, interacting neural circuits, and disappear when those circuits or their connections vanish. It is not too much to say, though, that all the magic of the human mind arises from cells and molecules governed by physical laws. How? Who the hell knows.

1.3 MENTAL PROCESSES CORRESPOND TO PROCESSES IN THE PHYSICAL BODY

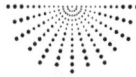

O ur inability to answer that profoundest of questions — how does a grayish meatloaf in your skull give rise to wonderful, glorious *you*? — tempts us toward dualism. *There must be a magic ghost floating around inside my skull. That's where subjective mental experience comes from.* Well, we can sort of picture that, but there's no reason to think it's true.

So far as we can tell, every mental process corresponds to some process in the physical brain. At the most fundamental level, general anesthesia temporarily deletes consciousness altogether. A doctor puts chemicals into the body, they make their way into the brain, they block the processes that give rise to the "I," and a surgeon cuts into the living body from which the conscious self has mercifully taken leave. All the discrete particulars of our mental lives seem to arise from the physical brain, too. A few years ago neuroscientists discovered that a person's recognition of Jennifer Aniston relates to the sparking of a single particular neuron in the subject's brain. It seems that every recollection, every moment of pondering, every recording of a new memory, every jolt of pain or pleasure, every sensation of filial or fraternal or romantic love, every recognition of Jennifer Aniston — it all stems from some physical event in the brain.

Of course science has not yet pinned down the connection between each aspect of mental life and some particular neural circuit. So if you'd like to think there's a ghost in the machine, you can hold out hope for that. But neuroscience has moved far enough along that the spirit hypothesis seems unlikely. Maybe at the end of time, when neuroscience has exhausted itself, there will be some residual element of mental life that can't be pegged to physical operations of the brain — why people care about Kim Kardashian, for example. Maybe it will become safe to assume *that much* at least arises from pure spirit and has nothing to do with the physical body and brain. For now, though, it seems likely the body and brain do it all, even the Kardashian obsession.

For anyone hoping to persuade someone else of something, it matters that the mental events in the other's mind — and in your own — depend on physical events in the brain. Our brains run up against limits you want to be aware of, because they can dramatically limit the effectiveness of your efforts.

1.3.1 BRAIN CHEMISTRY AFFECTS HOW WE THINK AND FEEL

Neurochemicals in the brain affect the actions of neurons, and thus affect our mental lives. Extreme cases throw this into relief. Heroin, cocaine, and other psychoactive drugs addle the brain and poison one's thoughts and feelings and behavior. More therapeutic psychiatric drugs, too, change brain chemistry and, with it, mental life.

Brain chemistry works in subtler ways, too. Some random examples: A guy in love produces higher amounts of oxytocin, and as a result he pays less attention to women other than his girlfriend. A woman who produces less of the neurotransmitters serotonin and GABA will tend to suffer depression, anxiety, and lower impulse control. A pregnant woman gets changing levels of estrogen and progesterone that appear to cause better stress management and caretaking. Fathers-to-be seem to gain fluctu- ating hormone levels, too, which reduce their sex drive and contribute to caretaking.

Brain chemicals don't just affect feelings. Increasing the level of the steroid pregnenolone, for example, improves memory in people with memory problems and increases clarity of thinking. Testos- terone improves spatial and mathematical reasoning. Lead depresses general intelligence and impairs impulse control. Dopamine affects attention and decision-making. And so on. Neuronal structures and brain chemicals, interacting with experi- ence and the outside world, cause our mental lives.

Normally, of course, you can't know what's going on with the brain chemistry of a judge or law clerk or juror, and usually not of yourself. But in your work, you're speaking to individual human beings with peculiarities and idiosyncrasies. Many or most of those features probably arise from physical forces beyond the control of the people you're talking to. That emphasizes the need to respect, and maybe fear, the characteristics of the audience, and your need to accommodate those characteristics.

1.3.2 THE REST OF OUR BODIES AFFECT OUR THINKING AND FEELING, TOO.

It's not just the brain that creates our mental experience. The rest of the body impacts the brain and mental activity, too. Some effects of the body on the mind seem obvious and maybe trivial. If your heart stops beating, your brain dies along with the rest of the body and, it appears, the light of your "self" flickers out. Similarly, you respond mentally if you feel something crawling up your leg. Also obvious: If you're trying to work in sweltering heat, you have a hard time focusing. And so it goes with cold, dehydration, hunger, exhaustion, and so on, even without getting to extremes.

Concerning emotional feelings, the brain and the rest of the body participate in a complicated relationship. When we feel some- thing we'd call an emotion, it usually involves both (a) physiolog- ical sensations and actions in the body (a racing heartbeat, sweating, brow-furrowing, whatever) and (b) "feelings" that seem purely mental (fear, joy, etc.). The causal path between bodily feeling and mental feeling runs both ways. Something may happen in the brain and then flow down to the body. The brain generates mental feelings and sends out signals to the body to act out the feeling — to smile, scream, grimace, flinch, kick, or whatever.

Causation can run from the body to the brain, too. A reaction or gesture may happen first in the body. The brain then interprets the bodily action and generates mental feelings to go along with it. Laugh for the hell of it, though nothing is funny or happy, and you'll feel better. Stand with better posture, and you feel marginally more confident. People who have Botox injected into their faces, paralyzing some facial muscles, may feel emotions less intensely. Quadriplegics sometimes report a reduction in the intensity of their feelings because their bodies can't react as before.

How the body feels in the moment affects what the mind does with whatever the mind is attending to right then. Waft a little fart spray in someone's direction when they're making a moral judgment, and they'll judge more harshly. That sounds odd, but we've known about similar effects all our lives. The little boy knows not to ask his dad for a new toy, when dad has a headache. All of us, not just toddlers, grow cranky, lazy, or thoughtless when we're tired, hungry, or overworked. Famously, some research has indicated that sentencing judges and parole boards decide more harshly just before lunch than right after breakfast. We didn't need that study to know to fear the hungry, tired judge.

The brain is a physical, organic machine, and this implies some moderately uncomfortable facts. The brain runs on chemicals — blood, sugar, neurotransmitters, and so on. The body makes those chemicals, mostly out of stuff we eat or drink. So it shouldn't surprise us much to hear that nutrition affects our thinking and feeling. Nor does it sound too odd to hear that chemicals that get into our bodies through air or water — lead from gasoline, for instance — might affect cognition and feeling. But past these still nearly-banal facts, the brain/body relationship gets creepy.

In a sense, our brains and minds get enmeshed in other organisms, not just our own bodies. Rabies, a virus, causes wild aggression in humans. Hookworms attaching themselves inside a human intestine cause laziness and a desire to eat dirt. Other parasites, too, affect how we think, feel, and act, at least in subtle ways. Some parasites are associated with a small increase over our baseline risk of suicide, probably because they reduce our fear of physical harm. Less maliciously, it appears that microbes normally living in the human gut produce neurotransmitters and other chemicals that pass to the brain and affect our mental activity in normal, healthy ways. Our minds lie deeply entwined with our bodies, other organisms, and still other physical stuff in the world.

And of course every unique brain inhabits a unique body with a unique ecology of micro-organisms inside it, and interacts in a unique way with a unique combination of things in the outside world, including other unique human bodies.

These facts hold profound meaning for the great question, "What manner of beast are we?" But they also say something about the grubby little business of legal work. The life of the mind is the life of a body — a body that sweats and eats and gets a crick in the neck, a body whose stomach growls, whose eyes grow heavy. Judges and jurors and lawyers do mental work, but it gets done by a particular body in a particular environment — say, a hard chair in a hot room, with jackhammers pounding the street outside. When we forget that, we stack the deck against ourselves. We keep going on about an issue, long past the time when the jurors have checked out or the judge has started shuffling papers. We write briefs that require too much work, too much time, too much energy.

We can't control whether the judge or law clerk or juror will come to the task tired or hungry, or with hookworms in their intestines (unlikely, now we have indoor plumbing). But we control some things, and should give thought to the physical setting and condition of our decision-makers.

1.3.3 A SPECIAL EXAMPLE: WE EMPATHIZE BY SIMULATING IN OUR OWN BRAINS THE EXPERIENCE OF OTHERS.

Empathy and its cousin, compassion, play a special role in law. It tentatively appears that empathy involves running a sort of simulation in our own brains of the processes going on in the other person's brain. This suggestion arises from the discovery of mirror neurons. When one monkey watches a second monkey grab a banana, neurons related to the physical grabbing of bananas fire in the *observer monkey's* brain. The same sort of thing happens in the brains of humans and in a range of other animals.

The importance of mirror neurons has yet to be worked out fully, but it at least tentatively appears that we empathize by simulating in our heads what's happening with the other person or beast. When you see someone else yawn, you tend to yawn, too. Yawn contagion exists in primates, and brain imaging studies show mirror neuron activity when yawn contagion goes to work. This research suggests that the feeling of empathy corresponds to a physical reality: What happens to the other person also happens, in a shadowy way, to us.

This process also occurs in response to imagined actions. When you hear a vividly told story about a hero clinging to a rope over an abyss, neurons related to hand-clenching probably fire in your brain. Your hands may clench in sympathy with the hero. When you read *Les Misérables* and poor Fantine receives Tholymyes' break-up letter, the neurons in your brain related to emotional pain light up. Real tears might well up in your own eyes.

Empathy grows in rich, complex folds, but it starts from sensory detail. The subtleties of empathy for Fantine stand atop simple bodily empathy based on sensory detail.

These considerations lend force to an old truism about writing and speaking: Details matter — sensory details especially. We imagine a child reach for a toy. We see the little hand grabbed by a tight adult fist. The child's head snaps to the side as a hand slaps the face. Everything entailed in our empathy begins from the root-level sensory detail.

Much of our work involves far less emotional content, but empathy is not just about high emotion. Empathy is understanding. You can't fully understand even a breach of a commercial contract without imagining yourself in the shoes of the parties. If you haven't stood in the right place, you haven't seen the right picture. If you don't give the sensory details, the judge or juror won't stand in that place.

For legal work, the right details make the difference between annoyed dismissal and passionate engagement. You've seen this at hearings or trials. You talk for half an hour, and from the decision-maker's face and body-language you know you couldn't bore them more with a Yanni album. But then you mention some new detail, and the judge or juror or commissioner tilts their head, gives a little surprised look, and leans forward. You gave them the right detail, the one that hooked them, the one that connected with something in their brain and struck a spark of engagement. Now, you can make headway. Figuring out what the right detail is, though — that takes imagination, insight, empathy, research, and a little luck.

The considerations we've been talking about — empathy and the importance of physical context — go far toward explaining the importance of being "fully present" for live events like trials or hearings. We speak in vague, almost hippie-esque terms about "being in the moment" for such occasions. Sometimes we make that sound like a mystical state, but it comes down to something very concrete and practical. You cannot know what's going on with your audience at a live human event unless you pay close attention to your audience. If you're not tuned in, if you aren't making eye contact, if you aren't leaning in and at some level registering their expressions, gestures, posture, then you cannot know or respond to what's going on with them. That is, you can't empathize with the audience if you're not "fully present" "in the moment." And you can't know how they're receiving what you're trying to show them; you can't know where they need more explanation, or less, or something else entirely. Physical context exerts enormous influence, and you can't register and respond to it (or other forces) without empathy.

1.3.4 WHAT WE LEARN GETS ETCHED INTO OUR BRAINS, MORE OR LESS LITERALLY.

When we learn something, it gets etched into the physical brain. When we learn, specific neurons spark and connect with each other. An axon from neuron A and a dendrite from neuron B reach out to each other. The axon sends a little chemical signal across the synapse separating the two outreached hands. With repetition, the connection becomes solid. The axon and dendrite hold together across that little gap.

As related experience recurs, more connections form and the neural circuit may expand from one little connection to millions. By the time a pianist attains mastery, the related neural network has grown large and long-lasting. Similarly, by the time a Christian, or a Republican, or a vegetarian, or a civil libertarian has grown mature in their worldviews, the neural circuitry involved has grown extensive and durable.

The brain remains "plastic," changeable to one degree or another; so we can learn new things and unlearn old things. Unlearning involves changing the existing wiring of neurons in the brain. Learning anew means new wiring. We don't know the limits of brain plasticity or the full potential of it, but it's clear enough that learning takes time, unlearning is hard, and it all gets harder as we get older. Still, some potential for change in the brain continues throughout life.

For any form of persuasion, these facts emphasize the old wisdom that you don't get far by swimming upstream. Most often, you either get there by means of the judge's or juror's existing beliefs, or you don't get there. Try hard to accommodate those beliefs and work within them. If you can't win within the decision-maker's existing worldview, think twice about pressing the issue at all.

∾

To head off a misunderstanding: This discussion does not suggest a crude biological determinism. We become who we are through the interaction between our bodies and the world. It might be better, if annoyingly Heideggerian, to say we *are always becoming* who we are, to say that *being is becoming*, because we constantly change as the interaction of our brains with the world continues as time moves on and things keep happening.

It helps, though, to keep in mind that inside the heads of judge and juror there are brains sparking in a chemical soup, according to a long history that has created durable neural circuits. How you frame and present a case will affect how the brain does its work. You may connect up with the existing circuitry, or your ideas may find nowhere to lodge, and get sloughed off. Your case may activate a sort of felt-in-the-bones understanding, or it may leave the listener cold. It all depends on these particular brains in these particular bodies in these particular chairs with these particular histories, and how your case fits into that system.

1.4 OUR BRAINS AIM TO DO WELL ENOUGH, EFFICIENTLY — NOT TO ACHIEVE PERFECTION

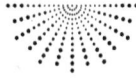

God or nature did not design our brains for Truth. Our brains are designed to let us navigate the world well enough to keep out of the mouths of crocodiles, to catch crickets or blackberries to eat, to get laid and produce kids, to keep them alive and fed, too, and so on. Our brains have to do all this with the limited organic material we can carry around on our skeletons. That's a tall order, and it requires some compromises in the design and engineering of our bodies generally and our brains in particular.

1.4.1 OUR BRAINS (AND THUS OUR MINDS) OPERATE WITH LIMITED ENERGY.

All mental activity involves your physical brain doing physical work and consuming physical energy. Recognizing faces, forming sentences, forming judgments, exercising self-control, reasoning logically, recalling words, responding emotionally — the physical brain does all these things, and consumes energy in order to do them. An adult human brain only weighs about 3 pounds, but it uses about 20 percent of the energy our bodies consume. The brain's energy mainly comes from glucose, blood sugar.

The more mental work you've already done, the less energy your brain has left, and the worse it performs until the energy gets replenished. Performance degrades across the board. If you cross-examine a witness while tired, you'll misspeak more often. If you've been working on a puzzle and someone asks you to analyze a tricky piece of contract language, you're more likely to screw up. If you try to hold a seven-digit number in memory for five minutes, your self-control weakens. If you drive home at the end of a wearying day and someone cuts in front of you, you're more likely to give them the finger. All this means that the more work you make a judge do to understand your brief, or make a juror do to understand your case, the more likely the judge or juror will make a mistake, and perhaps react against you in annoyance.

1.4.2 OUR BRAINS CREATE COHERENCE OUT OF BITS AND PIECES.

We possess a more complete image of the world than we're entitled to, because the brain stitches together a seamless picture from scraps of data. This stitching-together operates at the lowest level of sense perception and the highest level of cognition. The brain does this by making amazingly efficient use of information collected by our limited sense organs, and by making assumptions to fill in the gaps. This cobbling together enables us to navigate life well enough, usually.

At the sensory level, you see a seamless visual field around you, in high resolution. Your brain creates that rich visual image by using patchy, low-resolution images gathered by your eyes. The current iPhone contains a 12-megapixel camera. Each of your eyes captures about a 1-megapixel image, at around 60 "frames" per second. As you read this text, your peripheral vision extends out, and you see in good detail even well out to your side. Except you don't. As you can demonstrate to yourself, you only see detail if an object is almost directly in front of your eyes. To demonstrate this, get a pack of cards or write symbols on a few scraps of paper. Then stand in front of a mirror, look into your eyes, and keep them there.

As you stare into your eyes, move a random card, facing you, from the far edge of your peripheral vision, slowly toward the center of your visual field. If you hold your eyes steady, you won't be able to identify the card until you've brought it almost directly in front of you. Furthermore, contrary to your sense of fluidly looking around, your eyes don't move smoothly like a camera on a tripod tracking a bird. Your eyes jump, pause, jump, pause. Yet you don't live in a jumpy, low-resolution visual field that blurs everything outside a tiny cone. Your brain stitches the limited images captured by your eyes into a rich, detailed, seamless visual field. It performs this intricate operation so effortlessly and automatically that you feel like a ghost just peering out at the world through glass eyeballs.

In creating your image of the world from limited information, your brain makes assumptions. You thus "see" a good many things you don't really see, and you "know" a good many things you don't really know. You see a pencil on a desk, partly blocked by a stapler. You don't entertain the possibility that you're looking at two fragments of pencil, with empty air between them, arranged behind the stapler. That doesn't even occur to you. You see a single pencil. You "know" there's one pencil there. If asked about it later (if you remember it at all), you'll just remember seeing a pencil. This perceptual process, "good continuation," reflects just one sort of assumption your brain makes in constructing your image of the world.

In higher cognitive realms, too, your brain automatically fills gaps with plausible assumptions. Consider this sentence from Daniel Kahneman:

> After spending a day exploring beautiful sights in the crowded streets of New York, Jane discovered that her wallet was missing.

Your brain contributes plausible assumptions, probably involving a pickpocket. If you were to read that sentence and move on to something else, and someone later asked you about it, you might well remember the story as being about a pickpocket, although the story doesn't mention that and you could easily supply other explanations for Jane's missing wallet. As with sensory perception, so with cognition.

Our brains' penchant for gap-filling assumptions — to the point of outright confabulation — goes deep, extending even to self-knowledge. Neurological research with split-brain patients reveals that the left hemisphere of the brain contains what Michael Gazzaniga calls "The Interpreter." Some circuit in the left brain spins out a web of autobiographical narrative, explaining to ourselves what we're doing. The left brain continues spinning out the story even when it can only guess.

Here's how we know that. The two sides of the brain connect to each other through a thick bundle of nerves, the corpus callosum. When that connection is severed, the two brains can't communicate with each other, though they still both connect to the body through the brain stem.

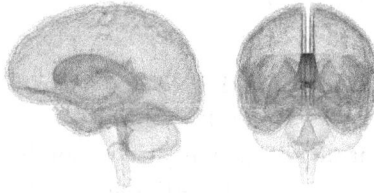

(Image credit in notes.[1])

Each side of the brain controls the opposite side of the body. Split-brain patients often get through life more or less normally. In a laboratory setting, though, researchers can present different information to the separate brains. So you can ask the right brain to pick up a key, while muffling the left brain's ear so the left brain doesn't know what's going on. With both eyes open, though, the left brain can see "its" body pick up the key. Afterward, you muffle the right brain's ear and just ask the left brain why it picked up the key. The left brain couldn't hear the instruction and therefore doesn't know why the body picked up the key. But the left brain will make up a story to explain the action. That most elementary bit of self-knowledge is false, confabulated. The left brain spins a story of the self, what the self is up to and why, with gap-filling assumptions. The left-brain interpreter works in all of us. This suggests that we all create partly fictionalized self-narratives as we go through life, and indeed if you've been paying attention you can probably recognize some of your self-fictions. If you don't see any, just ask your spouse or kids.

The brain makes sense of the world through abundant, efficient use of assumptions to fill in the blanks, before we've even seen the blanks. It may be slight exaggeration, but only slight, to say we *always* see more than is there to be seen. We *always* make gap-filling assumptions. We *always* add to the bare phenomena our senses pick up. Exactly what we add depends on the ideas and associations stored in our heads. Take a look, for example, at one of the lowest forms of art — so low it seems pretentious to even call it "art" — the mere stick figure.

These aren't even good stick figures, but you see more — far more — than the mere lines. You see human forms, yes, but more than that, you see action, intention, relationships, emotional states. You see caring, love, and security; joy; sadness; confidence. That's a lot to get from a handful of lousy stick figures. Or more accurately, that's a lot to *bring to* a handful of stick figures. And you don't bring extra information just to stick figures, of course.

This discussion holds important implications for advocacy. We talk about "reading between the lines." That's because we see so much more than the bare information given to us. In reading a brief, judges and clerks will fill in unstated words, facts, ideas, feelings. In listening to witness testimony, jurors will do the same.

They'll see a larger, fuller, more detailed reality than you put on the page or than comes out explicitly through testimony.

The way the judge or clerk or juror fills out the story will depend on the interaction between the explicit information given and the listener's expectations and stock of assumptions. Sometimes what the judge or juror brings to the matter will help you (in which case we say "less is more"). Sometimes what the judge or juror brings will hurt you (in which case we say "more is more"). Sometimes you'll be able to fill out the picture with enough information to beat back any harmful assumptions the judge or juror brings. Sometimes what they bring will overwhelm anything you say: You might as well whisper at a rock concert.

Much of the art and frustration of persuasion lies in making educated guesses about how the audience will add to and fill out the contents of the page, and figuring out how to make the river flow with you rather than against you.

1.4.3 OUR BRAINS MAKE SYSTEMATIC ERRORS.

The brain's reliance on assumptions, shortcuts, and gap-fillers produces systematic errors. We see this most easily in visual illusions. Vision scientists have identified many illusions that consistently recur, even though you know they're illusions. One of the simplest, discovered in 1889 by Franz Carl Müller-Lyer, will do for our purposes. The two horizontal lines below have the same length. You can measure them, you can know they're the same, but it doesn't matter. The first looks longer than the second, and it always will. (Unless, that is, you have an unusually large visual cortex, in which case you may not see the illusion.)

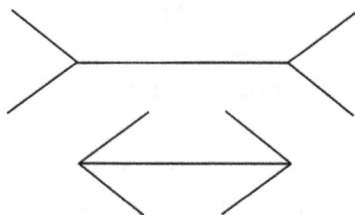

Your brain serves to solve problems within constraints imposed by your body and the physical world. Those constraints include the size of your skull, the number of neurons and connective filaments that will fit into it, the resolution of images produced by your eyes, the varying lengths of nerve fiber running from different parts of your body to your brain, the need to suppress information to allow focused attention, and a million other considerations.

Your brain exists to solve problems that came up often enough in the ancestral environment to justify the cost of carrying the problem-solving gear around inside your head. Accurately perceiving the relative lengths of two horizontal lines with fins pointing in opposite directions apparently didn't make the cut. So you systematically err in perceiving the Müller-Lyer lines.

So it is with a multitude of other things, as well — many of which we now deem quite important. To take one example: We have great natural talent for caring about people in a small, intimate circle around us, and cooperating with them. But we find it much harder to care about or cooperate with people remote from us. So violence on scales small and large, from bar fights to world war, accompanies us all through history. Awe-inspiring as our brains sometimes seem, God or nature did not design them for Truth and Happiness. In many ways we are profoundly, tragically stupid.

∿

WE SHOULD NOT FEEL TOO much exuberance about our extraordinary brains, nor too much despair over our proclivity to err. Our brains build models of the world in our heads, though some of the pieces are missing. Those models will of course misrepresent reality in some respects. That's what models do. But they match reality well enough, usually, that we can keep ourselves whole and fed.

1.5 OUR BRAINS RUN OUR LIVES UNCONSCIOUSLY FOR THE MOST PART, WITH OUR CONSCIOUS SELVES PLAYING A VITAL MANAGERIAL ROLE

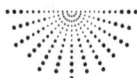

The brain performs most of its work unconsciously, without our awareness. As all that activity goes on below the surface, though, our conscious minds stay busy. We pay attention to this and that, our inner voice chats away, we make conscious decisions endlessly, or seem to. We identify with the conscious self, and our conscious selves seem to control our decisions and actions. That's almost comically wrong. It's true, though, that the conscious self — though limited in scope and power — does play a profoundly important role in managing our selves and our lives.

1.5.1 UNCONSCIOUS PROCESSES DRIVE MOST OF OUR LIVES.

To start with basics, our brains control autonomic processes without even conscious awareness, much less with conscious control or effort. We breathe, pump blood, digest food, etc. on auto-pilot. What's going on in your pancreas right now? You have no idea, but it's doing something, and your brain participates in regulating it.

Moving up toward consciousness, we do a lot of things we're consciously aware of, but for which the mental work occurs magically behind the curtain. You reach for the coffee cup, and you control your body with perfect thoughtlessness. You walk across the street, avoiding the pothole. You don't have to think, or focus, or experiment to get the right muscles to move together in the right way. It took years for your growing brain to gain this effortless control over the multitude of muscles recruited to get you to the other side of the street alive. A whole industry of scientists and engineers spent decades trying to get robots to move as fluidly as a bumbling toddler, and they've only recently started to get there. Certain forms of brain damage take away this automatic control of one's body. People with such disabilities must plan, focus, calculate every movement. For them, walking a few steps requires heroic, exhausting effort. The rest of us don't even realize that getting up from the couch or taking a sip of gin and tonic requires mental work.

Similar unconscious magic happens in what we do think of as mental work. We walk down the street, and we recognize fellow humans as humans, dogs as dogs, street lights as street lights. We recognize them instantly. With few exceptions, you don't work to puzzle out what those things are, and you can't choose not to know. You just know, like it or not. It's the same with language. You hear two guys plotting to kill the mayor, and you instantly know you've heard intentional human speech. With no work at all, you know it's English, you retrieve the words, parse the syntax, and understand the meaning. You wish you didn't understand it, because now you know too much. This sort of task may seem trivial, but it wouldn't work at all if the guys were speaking Pirahã. The task only seems trivial because your brain is designed for it and grew up with English. That instant, effortless understanding is powered by an unfathomably sophisticated organic computer. Despite decades of research, man-made computers still stumble over face and language recognition. And all this vastly complicated work happens in your brain with no conscious effort on your part.

1.5.2 CONSCIOUS PROCESSES PLAY A LIMITED ROLE IN MOMENT-TO-MOMENT DECISIONS.

We become consciously aware of the results of many unconscious processes, but that doesn't mean the conscious self participated in the process in a meaningful way. All day long, thoughts, feelings, inclinations, judgments pop into our heads from we-know-not-where. Like a vending-machine swami spitting out answers on cards, your unconscious hands out responses to most any question you have, any dilemma you confront, any fact you run across — pretty much anything at all. You might suppress the instinctive response as uninformed and unqualified, but the unconscious serves up responses shamelessly. Indeed, we conduct the bulk of our lives by means of intuition, with our conscious thought occasionally vetoing or correcting it.

In fact, it seems our unconscious selves drive even much of the behavior that feels consciously chosen. At least for simple actions like taking a drink of water, neuroscientists can identify the point at which the brain decides you're going to take a drink, and then, up to several seconds later, the point where you consciously "decide" to take a drink. We should avoid extrapolating wildly from that data point, but at least for relatively simple acts, it seems our unconscious self decides what we're going to do and then tells the conscious self what the plan is — perhaps in time for the latter to veto the plan, perhaps not.

The conscious self plays a real role, however, in creating habits — after which the unconscious takes over. That is, some mental tasks require conscious effort to learn but, once learned, the work gets shuttled to another part of the brain to be done unconsciously. You execute learned routines without thinking about them. You know you're tying your shoes, but you don't have to think about it. Indeed, if you paused to talk yourself through the process, you'd screw it up. You know it so well you can't remember how to do it. We have thousands of routines like this. To begin at the start of day: You have routines for brushing your teeth, for shaving, for showering, and all the other tiny steps of your morning rituals. These routines run on auto-pilot. Now and then that causes a little trouble, when you want to change the routine. So you're going on a trip, and you intend to leave your deodorant out on the counter after using it, so you can pack it. When you arrive at the hotel that afternoon, you realize you've left the deodorant at home. What happened? When you put on the deodorant, your brain switched on the auto-pilot, and you unthinkingly put the deodorant back in the drawer, violating your conscious intention. These unconscious routines drastically reduce the demands on our time and attention. If you had to think consciously about every damned thing you do, you'd have no time or energy to think about anything important. In that world, you might as well have no conscious mind at all, for all the good it would do.

1.5.3 THE CONSCIOUS SELF DOES LITTLE OR NOTHING WITHOUT HEAVY ASSISTANCE BY UNCONSCIOUS PROCESSES.

When are you not at the mercy of your unconscious? When does the conscious self ever do anything on its own? Rarely or never. How could it be otherwise? Conscious thought works slowly. We can't hold many things in mind at once. Thinking consciously about one thing means you can't think about other things. Besides, conscious thinking is often hard, unpleasant. You dislike getting drawn into thinking seriously about what variety of latte or vacuum cleaner or fabric softener or stationery or olive oil or external hard drive you want. Who wants to think about every damned thing? No one, that's who.

Conscious thought operates within tight limits, and remains heavily dependent on the unconscious. For example, when you speak extemporaneously, you rely on your unconscious to feed you the words you speak. Words float up from below. You have a split second to reject or revise them. But you can't speak — to anyone, ever — if you insist on much conscious thinking about your words.

Even the slowest speakers among us do very little in-the-moment word-choosing. Compare conversation to writing. You might spend an hour on half a page in the initial composing, and then revise it several times later. No one talks like that, because no one would listen. Oral speech comes to us mostly from the unconscious, with the conscious mind's veto and deliberation limited to a few key words here and there.

Even when we mull something over consciously, we don't have much control over our thoughts. You puzzle over some point in Heidegger or Harry Potter. You direct your attention to this or that aspect of the problem, but how consciously controlled is that attention-focusing decision, really? What faculty within you decided that you should focus on this thing rather than some other thing? It's hard to say that this attention-focusing faculty itself is fully conscious. As for the ideas that come into your head when you do control your attention, you mostly take what you get, whatever floats up from below. Conscious thought seems to consist mainly of some influence over attention, then stirring the unconscious and looking over whatever floats to the surface.

Genius seems to come from nowhere — that is, from the unconscious. "Genius," like "muse" or "daemon" originally meant a spirit who attends you and gives you inspiration. "Inspiration" itself originally meant divine guidance. Just so: Ideas good and bad come to us more or less unbidden, at will, from the depths of our unconscious. Famously, a dream led Einstein to the principle of relativity. Another gave Coleridge the lines of *Kubla Khan* ("In Xanadu did Kubla Khan / A stately pleasure-dome decree: / Where Alph, the sacred river, ran / Through caverns measureless to man / Down to a sunless sea") until, in writing it down after waking, Coleridge lost the thread.

Conscious thought seems to act in a strong form only in following an algorithm of some sort — solving a quadratic equation, following step-by-step instructions to assemble a crib, going over a checklist at the grocery, applying a formula to make nitroglycerin, and so on. In those sorts of activities, and maybe only in them, can we say conscious thought runs with the ball while the unconscious mostly sits on the sidelines. Even there, we're probably overlooking some crucial, pervasive contribution by unconscious processes.

Hooray, then, for the unconscious. No one should be disappointed or disturbed to realize how little the "I" yammering away in your head actually controls. It's mainly the unconscious self we love — the way you wear your hat, the way you sip your tea; the way you grin when your niece walks in; the jokes you let slip when you've had a few drinks; all the things you do without thinking about it. Those define you most. Those are the reasons people like you (or don't).

You hardly need me to say that all of this holds true as much for judges and law clerks and jurors as it does for you. Their responses to your brief or your trial presentation will derive largely from unconscious processes. Maybe a brief or trial case works fine as a sort of rational, algorithmic manipulation of legal rules and putative facts. But if that's all the brief or case does, you should worry.

These considerations also hold implications for your own thinking about the issues, and for your approach to your case. How you stock your unconscious with information and insights, and how you train it with habits and routines, will determine how you do your work. You can increase your creativity by making a conscious habit of taking in a wide range of experiences — a wide range of intellectual, cultural, artistic, physical, practical experiences and influences. By doing that, you stock the unconscious with ingredients, which later pot-stirring can make use of. This is an old insight, but an important one.

1.5.4 WE BARELY KNOW OURSELVES.

The vast scope and power of the unconscious imply one piece of wisdom we'd all do well to get through our heads: We barely know ourselves. Tim Wilson titled his book on the cognitive unconscious "Strangers to Ourselves." The title does not seem exaggerated. Experiments show that we are deeply ignorant of who we are and how we work. When asked to explain ourselves, we wouldn't go wrong by just shrugging, "How am I supposed to know how I feel?" How am I supposed to know what I think — or what I want, or what I believe? Sometimes, trying to figure it out and put it into words only corrupts self-knowledge. When we say why we like something, we may end up getting it wrong, half-believing what we say, and under the influence of this sloppy self-knowledge, making poorer choices in the future, and ending up unhappier. To some extent, the Heisenberg uncertainty principle applies to self-knowledge: By peering in at ourselves, we change the thing we're trying to observe. Or to invoke another German: Our selves exist in the world of noumena, beyond the reach of our perception, which extends only to phenomena.

This means we can never get the real truth about a person — from others or from ourselves. When asking about another, the fundamental uncertainty problem deepens because of display rules: Depending on the circumstances and whatever cultural rules apply, we're not supposed to reveal all of our thoughts and feelings. Does she love me or does she not? Does he really like the present I gave him, or is he just sparing my feelings? Do they want to come for a visit, or are they being polite? You can ask, but they may not know their own feelings fully, and may feel constrained to withhold full candor even if they do.

We obey display rules even with ourselves. Some thoughts, some feelings, we dare not admit to ourselves. I'm ashamed to admit even to myself that I want this total stranger to think I'm smart. I'm supposed to be a grown-up and be past pointless vanities like that. So I bury that little truth in mounds of pretense. We try to maintain appearances even to ourselves. Alone by ourselves in the dark, we blush.

We'll get by, but to some irreducible degree that now and then agonizes us, we remain always strangers to ourselves and to each other. Our limited knowledge leads us into error, and occasionally into heartbreak. Keeping this sad truth in mind, however, can sometimes help by prompting useful caution when we do make conscious decisions.

1.5.5 THE CONSCIOUS SELF PARTICIPATES IN JOINT PROJECTS.

Conscious thought does, of course, play an important role in many things. Conscious thought gives the ability to check our intuition, to censor our words and other actions. It lets us pursue hard, algorithmic thought — like finding the cube root of 7.29. Lengthy mental processes (like writing a brief) involve interaction between unconscious and conscious processes. No one ever wrote a brief, a poem, or a short story wholly unconsciously — not one worth reading, anyway. The unconscious contributes ideas, and the conscious, critical mind pays attention, sets tasks for the unconscious to perform, reviews the results, and may send the matter back for the unconscious to take another stab.

1.5.6 THROUGH ITS INFLUENCE, INCLUDING MERE THOUGHTS, THE CONSCIOUS SELF AFFECTS THE PHYSICAL BRAIN.

Mental experience corresponds to physical brain activity, including the development of neural circuits. The conscious self affects the physical brain both by influencing the experiences the body has as it moves about the world, and through mere thoughts themselves.

Things that happen to you through life affect the physical structure of your brain — each change too tiny to notice, but there all the same. When your teenage son yells at you, or hugs you (?), that affects the physical happenings in your brain. When you jump out of a pickup and land on your face in the mud, that affects your brain. Hopefully, you'll encode some new insight about slippery boots on a muddy tailgate and the proper angles for jumping.

Thus, your conscious decisions feed back on the physical events within your brain. That is, you have some influence over whether your son will yell at you or hug you. Do the right thing and hold your ground, and he'll punish you with sulking. Give in and buy the damned thing, and he'll reward you with a fake hug. Your choice. In that way, you have some influence over what neurochemicals will get released in your brain, what neural circuits will light up, what axons will link up with what dendrites. Of course, you also influence what happens in your son's brain, so hold your ground and take the punishment, so he won't develop the brain of an entitled brat.

The experience that affects your brain includes mere thoughts themselves. The brain is a feedback machine. Conscious thought activates neural circuits, releases chemicals, strengthens or weakens specific neural connections. When you spend hours ruminating on how your dad mistreated you, your thinking causes physical activity in your brain that may produce long-lasting changes in neural circuits. Similarly, you can create sticky memories of wholly imaginary things. Make a list of 20 random nouns and, with about three minutes of visualization, you can create a memory of them that will stick in your head for weeks or months. (Google the phrase "memory linking technique.") Through conscious thought alone — with no direct involvement of the world outside your head — you've etched memories into neurons and the tendrils that connect them to each other. Almost literally, treading paths of thought wears grooves in your brain.

1.5.7 DESPITE ITS LIMITATIONS, THE CONSCIOUS SELF PLAYS A ROLE OF EARTH-SHAKING IMPORTANCE.

The unconscious is unruly. The notion of an "individual" is misleading. You're not a coherent unity. Our basic schizophrenia is obvious, once you look past the physical appearance of a single skin-wrapped container. We feel the furious toddler demanding a donut, while the conscious self wants to eat right and shrink the bulging belly. The self is a bunch of monkeys in a bag, shoving wildly this way and that. The conscious self is a chaperone managing kids on a field trip.

Conscious thought provides the great lever we have to govern ourselves. Conscious mental processes increase our ability to apply behavioral flexibility — to govern conflicting inclinations in the moment to match the particulars of a complex situation. Our elaborate capacity for conscious thought probably explains why humans, and not our ape relatives, have adapted to nearly every climate on earth.

I've mentioned how conscious mental effort can train the unconscious to acquire habits and new behaviors — piano playing, table etiquette, gratitude, and so on. Indeed, we consciously direct our lives not so much by in-the-moment self-control, but more by forming good habits — that is, by directing the unconscious to put on the show in the way we want the show to run. Success in life stems largely from the conscious self's role as coach, trainer, director to the unconscious performer.

Conscious thought can also help to control behavior through pre-planning and pre-commitment. Ulysses had his crew lash him to the mast, so he couldn't obey the siren call and kill himself and his crew on the crashing boulders. I try to keep ice cream out of my house, so I won't eat it. In ways big and small, the conscious self can look ahead to circumstances in which the unconscious will act poorly, and plan to avoid the problem.

The conscious self can influence the broader unconscious through various forms of mere exhortation. Cognitive Behavioral Therapy works on the premise that what we consciously think affects the rest of our selves. If you sit around thinking about how sad you are, you'll feel sad. But you can consciously force your thoughts onto something else — cat videos, or tending your herb garden, or reading Mark Twain, or whatever. Similarly, through the ways we consciously talk to ourselves, we can change how we behave. This is the principle behind the weirdness of Eastern meditation, cringing hippie stuff like self-hypnosis or recitation of mantras, and solid normal-guy stuff like Sunday sermons and prayer. By such means, the conscious self talks to the unconscious self. Weirdly, it works. Such methods can re-shape the stories that form our identities and guide our conduct. Such methods can influence our preferences, in accordance with our preferences about our preferences.

Conscious mental life — effortful thought, self-control, willpower — constitutes a small part of our selves, but it's the glory of human life and our main source of hope for improving the lives of ourselves and others. Then again, it's also the means by which we create crueler new forms of torture. But let's you and me use it for good.

For a working lawyer, the influence of conscious thought offers some consolation, some hope for circumstances in which the judge or jurors will want to go against you. Judges, and to a lesser extent jurors, generally feel committed to the idea of enforcing laws they disagree with. If you can engage judges or jurors and convince them that the law mandates the outcome you want, even if they don't want it, then a commitment to the idea of law might — just might — overcome all the forces working against you. You shouldn't place too much hope in this, but it's something at least.

～

THE IMPACT of conscious thought means we should not accede to a fatalistic determinism about mental qualities and abilities. We operate within hard, biologically determined constraints. You can't recognize 50 names shouted at you in five seconds any more than you can grow an eyeball in your neck. You can't learn a new language in 60 days, despite the breathless promises of YouTube clowns. But we can change and grow within the hard limits of brain plasticity, wherever they are. And we don't know where they are. We don't know the boundaries of improvement (or degradation). So fatalism makes no sense. We should assume we can attain significant improvement in this or that aspect of life, unless incontrovertible evidence says otherwise.

For legal work, this suggests some modest hope of nudging judges off the ground they currently stand on, slightly. For a particular judge reading a particular brief, this potential remains tiny, but it grows over the course of an entire case, or a course of years, through many cases. Radical conversions happen rarely, but we all change significantly over long stretches of time. This matters particularly for lawyers who practice in the same jurisdiction for many years, and especially for those with a niche practice. Take that into account in deciding how to frame the dispute, what issues to raise, how modestly or aggressively to form your position, and so on. For jurors, though, the potential for changing attitudes over the course of a trial probably hovers close to zero. If a jury's preexisting attitudes can't accommodate your case, you probably can't win. (But it's complicated, and in the complexity lies some hope.)

1.5.8 SCARCE ENERGY AND MENTAL SLOTH LIMIT THE SCOPE AND POWER OF THE CONSCIOUS SELF.

To make the most of our chances to influence people, we need to understand the tight limits on conscious effort. We possess shockingly limited faculties for conscious thought. For example, any conscious mental operation depends in the first instance on working memory. We can only hold about seven pieces of simple information in memory at once — though we can squeeze more power out of the system by chunking small pieces into bigger pieces, through visualization, and so on. Even the memory strain from merely parsing a sentence can wear us down. That's one reason you never hear people say, "I can't get enough of Henry James." This sentence from James doesn't bother you, taken by itself: "There are circumstances in which, whether you partake of the tea or not — some people of course never do — the situation is in itself delightful." But a few hundred of those packed together punish the reader. In his essay "The Awful German Language," Mark Twain makes a related point. In German syntax, the verb frequently appears toward the end of the sentence. The reader must hold the subject in memory until the verb appears. Twain provides a literal translation of a sentence from a German novel and then comments:

"But when he, upon the street, the (in-satin-and-silk-covered-

now-very-unconstrained-after-the-newest-fashion-dressed)
government counselor's wife *met*," etc., etc.

. . .

You observe how far that verb is from the reader's base of
operations; well, in a German newspaper they put their verb
away over on the next page; and I have heard that sometimes
after stringing along the exciting preliminaries and parentheses
for a column or two, they get in a hurry and have to go to press
without getting to the verb at all. Of course, then, the reader is
left in a very exhausted and ignorant state.[1]

We have trouble holding things in memory.

We also have trouble switching tasks and working under time
pressure. Daniel Kahneman describes a simple-sounding task
called "Add 1." The task requires you to switch between short-
term memory and simple addition, under time pressure:

> To start, make up several strings of 4 digits, all different, and
> write each string on an index card. Place a blank card on top of
> the deck....
>
> Start beating a steady rhythm (or better yet, set a metronome
> at 1/sec). Remove the blank card and read the four digits aloud.
> Wait for two beats, then report a string in which each of the
> original digits is incremented by 1. If the digits on the card are
> 5294, the correct response is 6305. Keeping the rhythm is
> important.

Kahneman writes that this exercise "should bring you to the
limits of your cognitive abilities within 5 seconds," but he adds that
you can make the task harder by adding 3 instead of 1 to the digits.
Kahneman tested many subjects and measured their pupil dilation
in real time. (Pupils dilate when we exert mental effort.)
Kahneman writes that the Add 3 task "is as hard as people can
work — they give up if more is asked of them."[2]

If this seems implausible, try it. Or for an easier challenge, try
reading some other lawyer's discovery requests. Lawyers typically

write document requests in a paranoid style that makes them hard to read. Here's a randomly chosen request (with names changed):

> All documents, including electronically stored information, concerning any representation provided to you by Jim Davis, Brian Howard or any other person at the Erickson, Harp & Ward law firm from the first date of that representation through the date of the last activity by Mr. Davis, Mr. Howard or the Erickson, Harp & Ward law firm, excluding documents concerning the pursuit of bad faith or punitive damage claims against The Old Connecticut Fire Insurance Company as set forth in Plaintiff's First Amended Complaint.

And that's not even a sentence. It's just a noun phrase — an 83-word noun phrase. Of course you can parse it, but it takes attention and effort. Imagine having to read 10 or 15 requests like this as a judge, in order to rule on a motion to compel discovery. That task alone could burn through your patience. We tolerate this nonsense in our own requests because they're ours. We crafted them so cleverly. But try reading someone else's requests. You'll quit. We have little capacity for hard thinking, and the threshold for "hard" thinking lies low.

Capacity aside, as for our willingness to think hard, consider this question: *Together, a bat and ball cost $1.10. The bat costs $1.00 more than the ball. How much does the ball cost?* The number that popped into your head — 10 cents — is wrong. It takes just seconds to check the answer, to see if "10 cents" is right or wrong. But when the question is posed to undergraduates at Harvard, only half bother to check the answer before giving it. At lesser colleges, only 20% of the students stopped to check. We avoid conscious thinking, because it takes work.

Again, this suggests a special urgency about making our cases — briefs, oral arguments, witness testimony, etc. — easy to understand and digest. You should assume the judge and clerk and juror will avoid effortful thinking, just like the rest of us. Again, this is an ancient insight, but we kid ourselves into thinking it doesn't matter so much *here*. We lie to ourselves precisely because we, too, are cognitively lazy. It would take too much hard work to make the argument simple, clear, and accurate. So we go to jurors and judges with arguments they can't follow without hard work of their own. No surprise, then, that we lose.

1.6 OUR BRAINS GUIDE US THROUGH LIFE LARGELY BY MEANS OF EMOTION — AS AN EFFICIENT FORM OF COGNITION

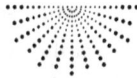

F eeling plays a far larger role in cognition than we usually recognize — a necessary and unavoidable role, a right and proper role.

1.6.1 UNCONSCIOUS THOUGHT SOMETIMES EXPRESSES ITSELF PHYSIOLOGICALLY.

We possess a category of mostly unconscious mental activity that includes what we might call bodily or emotional cognition. The cognitive work occurs unconsciously, and it produces physical responses. Sometimes we become consciously aware of the physical response, sometimes we don't. When you read the word *vomit*, your body recoils slightly, imperceptibly. You react in ways that would register on monitoring devices, if they were hooked up to you. When you pass someone in the grocery store, you respond bodily to them, usually too subtly to notice. That emotional response reflects a cognitive process — an immediate, unconscious sizing-up. Will this person harm you, help you, ignore you? Should you approach, avoid, or ignore? In the ancestral environment, you wouldn't often meet a stranger, and when you did, it would present a moment of high danger. Today strangers surround us continually, and close to 100% of them present no danger. But your brain still scans the environment continuously to make micro-judgments that affect your behavior.

These judgments rise to conscious awareness only when they grow relatively strong. People play a computer betting game requiring them to find hidden, complex regularities to increase how much they win. Their bodies show signs of recognizing the regularities before the people become consciously aware of either the physiological responses or the regularities in the game. The players just have vague, hard-to-articulate feelings about where the good bets are. When we say we "feel" that something is wrong or right, that's not just a metaphor. We really do have physiological feelings that arise from the brain's taking in of information, processing it, and forming judgments. This occurs fast, effortlessly, unconsciously. Our intuitive judgments often get it wrong, but then so do our slow, conscious judgments. More amazingly, our intuitive judgments often get it right.

An advocate — particularly an advocate working in a live human event like a hearing or a trial — should keep aware of these ancient, unconscious feelers we all possess, this machinery for unconscious sizing-up. Judges and jurors will take in far more information than they're aware of. They won't pay conscious attention to everything, but the multitude of circuits in their brains will silently register more or less everything in the environment — faces, tones of voice, body language, gestures, actions, clothing, artifacts, numbers of people, relationships, everything. The judges' and jurors' brains will silently evaluate it all and produce feelings that influence judgment. Those feelings may work subtly, so that judge or juror could not say quite what they're feeling; or these feelings may scream with urgency. However strongly they work, they'll work, and they'll influence judgment to one degree or another.

An advocate may bear all this in mind easily enough, but knowing what to do about it presents a different problem. I discuss that problem at greater length toward the end of this book, but for now it's enough to say advocates should behave themselves. They should take care to be honest, decent, and reasonable. It may seem easy and cost-free to take stupid or dishonest positions in writing, but when you show up for a live hearing or trial, with decision-maker eyeballs quietly scanning you, the unreasonable positions may not seem so easy and cost-free. Similarly, an experienced oral advocate should not put too much faith in his or her acting ability. Lawyers typically don't have much *general* acting ability, but some lawyers do develop skill in pretending to assert stupid or dishonest positions with sincerity and genuine conviction. Some lawyers pride themselves on that. That's risky. We should adopt a working assumption that we'll somehow give ourselves away, that the ancient, unconscious feelers will register the little details — a micro-expression, a moment of awkward body language, etc. — that betray the pretense of sincerity. Of course this is just a working assumption. Maybe the act will work this time. But over the run of cases, over the run of a career, the safer assumption is that bullshit will somehow unknowingly betray itself.

1.6.2 WE RESPOND AFFECTIVELY TO MORE OR LESS EVERYTHING, FOR GOOD REASON.

As the preceding point suggests, our emotional responses guide us more pervasively than we know. One bizarre neurological defect throws this point into relief. A man suffers injury to the emotion centers in his brain. His wife comes into the hospital room. He tells the staff to get rid of her, because she's an impostor. He recognizes everything about her — her face, voice, posture and gait, every-thing. They test the wife's knowledge, and she knows things only the two of them could know. The man can't find a single respect in which the supposed wife differs from his actual wife, but he knows with certainty that she's an impostor. He knows this, it seems, because his emotional response to her is gone. A brain injury has jammed the emotional machinery, with heartbreaking results. Conscious and unconscious emotional responses pervasively inform our judgments, knowledge, beliefs.

Legal arguments spur emotional reactions, too, of course. Often the judge or juror reacts so strongly that the emotional response dominates, at least temporarily. Read the literature on writing legal briefs, for example, especially the books and articles by judges, and you'll see an abundance of emotional responses to briefs — mainly anger and contempt: *too long, too burdensome, too confusing, too much lying, too nasty, too much cry-babying*, and so on. Read a random sample of judicial opinions, and you'll often see these and other emotional reactions peeking out, despite attempts to conceal them.

1.6.3 WE DEPEND ON EMOTION FOR INFORMATION.

As we've already glimpsed, emotional reactions often constitute cognition. We experience conscious emotion as good or bad in itself, and we value it for that. But affective responses include much more than the big emotions we think about when we talk about "emotion." Emotions represent your brain taking in data, making calculations, forming quick judgments, and sending out conclusions in the form of feelings.

In legal disputes, emotion provides much of the basic information we need. Most of what we ask a judge or jury to do requires weighing the credibility, meaning, and importance of facts, and weighing the desirability of the alternatives the parties argue for. Those sorts of judgments come to us primarily as emotion. Why do you find this person credible and the other one not? Why do you take this conclusion from this pile of evidence, rather than some other conclusion? Usually, the judgment comes to you emotionally and often unconsciously — perhaps augmented by some sort of conscious rational process, perhaps not.

Often we can't say much about our judgments themselves. We can recite the facts about the doctor's actions during surgery, the facts about how other surgeons behave, and how much this doctor departed from the norm. But deciding whether that departure goes too far or doesn't, is reasonable or unreasonable, negligent or not — that's just a feeling. We don't have much to say about it. We can't dissect the feeling or trace out the "logic" of the feeling. At bottom, many if not most judgments in legal disputes come down to mute, inarticulate feeling — however surrounded by talk about preliminaries.

1.6.4 WE DEPEND ON EMOTION IN ORDER TO MAKE DECISIONS AND TAKE ACTION.

We depend on emotion in order to make even trivial choices — what clothes to wear, what kind of potatoes to buy at the grocery, what tasks to perform at work. Emotion controls our ability to set priorities. Emotion assigns value and motivates action. Antonio Damasio has demonstrated that when the emotion circuits in the brain suffer damage, the victim's ability to make decisions suffers. Damasio describes one patient who struck him as smart, pleasant, and knowledgeable. The patient had surgery to remove a brain tumor, and the surgery damaged the areas controlling emotion. Afterward, the patient couldn't run his own life. Still smart and knowledgeable, at work he couldn't make minimally competent decisions. He still had his skills; he just didn't know what to do with them.

> The tragedy of this otherwise healthy and intelligent man was that he was neither stupid nor ignorant, and yet he acted often as if he were. The machinery for his decision making was so flawed that he could no longer be an effective social being. In spite of being confronted with the disastrous results of his decisions, he did not learn from his mistakes. He seemed beyond redemption, like the repeat offender who professes sincere repentance but commits another offense shortly thereafter. . . .
>
> [He was] fallen from social grace, unable to reason and decide in ways conducive to the maintenance and betterment of himself and his family, no longer capable of succeeding as an independent human being.[1]

A robot might know that some proposed action would destroy

all human life, but so what? Without something like emotions that reflect human values and that make the robot care about the potential outcomes, the robot couldn't distinguish the extermination of all human life from the extermination of the split infinitive. The robot could not feel any motivation to avoid a global holocaust.

Emotion gives the values and motivation necessary to decide between courses of action. Values or priorities come to us as fundamental data, as postulates we feel. We think *about* values, but we don't think them *up*. Even the simplest of choices — say, between getting punched in the face and not getting punched in the face — depends on whether you feel a higher value in avoiding pain than in experiencing pain. Not everyone does. Boxers, for instance. Masochists and self-mutilators also stand outside the norm in this face-punching respect, and they throw into relief the emotional commitments that underlie even the most elementary choice — to avoid pain or to seek it.

The value-setting role of emotion applies in law, as everywhere else. Law codifies moral and practical values. The principles of contract law embody a particular set of values. So do procedural rules and the principles of how to decide legal disputes. Any legal analysis starts with, and serves, some set of values. Judges and jurors can't make reasoned decisions that comport with the law, unless they feel the values enshrined in law and understand how the issue at hand implicates them. A eunuch can't understand lust. A psychopath can't understand shame. We want judges to *feel* the offense of misconduct. We want judges to *feel* what counts as appropriate in the situation. We want to avoid calling jurors to service if they don't feel the values embodied in the law.

It's feeling the values embodied in law that motivates the application of the law. Intellectual understanding is not enough. Judges face lots of demands on their time, and any particular issue may draw slight notice, even for diligent, conscientious judges. If an issue generates no feeling, it doesn't matter. An issue may have a clear answer, but finding the right answer usually takes work, effort, inconvenience. Who will bother, if it doesn't matter? Even more than judges, jurors need some reason to pay attention over days of often-boring, unfamiliar discussion with frequent annoying interruptions, then to deliberate late in the night, perhaps over days, to apply the law properly. If jurors don't feel the values enshrined in law, they won't do the hard work.

In the ways we've discussed so far, emotion holds sway in the background, but in some areas of law, emotion governs explicitly. We explicitly make feelings the ultimate criterion for many legal questions. We ask whether the damages award shocks the conscience, whether the conduct was so outrageous that no civilized society should tolerate it, whether the appellate court has a firm and definite conviction — a feeling — that the trial court erred, whether the defendant had an evil mind, whether an action serves the interests of justice, whether the wrongdoing counts as reprehensible. More generally, we judge the severity of offenses, the degrees of unreasonableness, the degrees of doubt, the clarity of error, the extent of prejudice to substantial rights. We decide whether a trial court abused discretion, whether the verdict clearly went against the evidence. In these and a multitude of other ways, law routinely relies explicitly on feeling.

Moral feelings, of course, play a particularly important role. Moral feelings largely decide what counts as "reasonable" for a grocery store's efforts to maintain shelves that won't tip over and crush little kids, or in deciding whether the public should have access to papers filed in court, or in deciding whether a punitive damages award grossly exceeds the egregiousness of the misconduct. In each case, the decision-maker draws on a sense of right and wrong, a sense of the relative weights of competing values. And those moral values largely decide how much urgency the judge feels about the dispute. Emotion pervades law. Emotion drives judicial decisions. It could not be otherwise.

1.6.5 WE CAN'T EVEN DISTINGUISH CLEARLY BETWEEN THOUGHT AND FEELING.

I've been talking about thinking and feeling as if we can neatly separate the two. We can't. Thinking and feeling entwine each other. They fade into one another. When you try to pick apart the mental events that go by "thought" and those that go by "feeling," you reap only frustration for your trouble.

For one thing, we have feelings about our thinking, and those feelings influence our thinking. We don't trust ideas that make sense rationally but don't feel right. We may not be able to put our finger on it; we may not be able to explain why the idea is wrong, but it feels wrong, so we reject it — like the neurological patient rejects his wife as an impostor.

One semi-famous example: Lawrence Summers signed a memo as Chief Economist of the World Bank in 1991, arguing that "The economic logic behind dumping a load of toxic waste in the lowest wage country is impeccable and we should face up to that."[2] Summers and a subordinate later said they intended the memo only as satire. But whether satire or crackpot rationalism, the memo does make rational economic arguments. Indeed, libertarian economists still defend the memo.[3] Most of us reject the memo's conclusion before we can articulate why it's wrong. Indeed, most people who reject that conclusion (or any conclusion, on any subject) reject it well before bothering to think it through. We have jobs to hold down, kids who want dinner, and other things more pressing than untangling some guy's nutty logic. Usually, the feeling ends the discussion. Even if we do give thought to the matter, the feeling comes first and guides whatever thought we expend. The feeling represents a sort of nascent thought, a judgment we haven't figured out how to articulate.

Often, feeling provides the only "thinking" a situation allows, even in theory. Expert intuition often operates this way. A veteran firefighter is inside a flaming house. With his team, he's in the kitchen when he somehow senses danger. He couldn't say why, either in that moment or even perhaps later. It's just a feeling. He yells at his crew to get out of the room. Shortly after they do, the floor collapses. In this and other examples Gary Klein discusses, the brain makes immensely sophisticated judgments unconsciously and delivers the judgment in the form of inchoate feeling. Later, the expert may try to explain the feeling, but the explanation may have little to do with the actual mental process that formed the judgment.

Our mental events occur on a continuum from pure rationality to pure feeling, and from wholly conscious to wholly unconscious. At the purest rational end, we have math and logic. Finding the cube root of 109 likely won't involve feeling in any noticeable way. At the other end, your response to a vanilla cupcake with pink frosting and white sparkles, floating in a pool of feces, doesn't involve rational thought in any meaningful way. But practically everything in life stands between these extremes. Most of what matters in life (and in law) occurs in the vast middle zone where we can't really say what is rational and what is emotional, and where some but not all of our cognition occurs consciously.

> Should we accept refugees from war zones? Which of these lawnmowers should I buy? Should the Fed raise interest rates? Should I move in limine to forbid that argument they keep insinuating? Should I let my daughter go out with this kid? Should I buy Tesla stock? Should I accept that we're causing climate change? Does this discovery request reflect the importance of the issues at stake? What's a just sentence for this burglar? Did the insurance company know the policy afforded coverage when they told the insured otherwise? How fast should I drive on this stretch of road?

And on and on. Each of these questions draws on rationality and feeling, and on conscious and unconscious cognition, in different ways, in different proportions.

Feelings play a particularly large role in selecting and inter-preting phenomena to establish elementary facts. Rationality largely deals with whether a conclusion derives logically from given premises. But the premises rest on facts, and facts don't just lie around like stones to be picked up. To find facts, you select from the mass of phenomena pouring in through your eyes, ears, etc., and you interpret it. For the most part, you do so automati-cally and unconsciously — largely aided by emotion.

In particular, with almost any question about people, inter-
preting evidence relies heavily on feeling. To decide whether the
insurance company knew they owed coverage when they denied it,
you sift through a pile of stuff including testimony, denial letters,
internal claim notes, and so on. The evidence can logically bear
three interpretations. But which of them is most believable? Your
answer will largely come down to feeling.

As with premises, so with conclusions. Rationality alone carries
limited power to distinguish between sound and unsound conclusions from given premises. We can check the formal logic of an
argument easily, but formal validity doesn't mean the conclusion
really follows from the premises. A syllogism never proved
anything interesting enough to bother talking about. The relationships among premises get more complicated than logic textbooks
suggest. Recall Ambrose Bierce's satirical syllogism:

> *"Major Premise*: Sixty men can do a piece of work sixty times as
> quickly as one man.
>   *Minor Premise*: One man can dig a posthole in sixty seconds;
> therefore
>   *Conclusion*: Sixty men can dig a posthole in one second."

The logical argument is spoken in words, and the meaning of
words is never entirely explicit. Every statement (and every
premise of every argument) invokes unstated information. With
Bierce's syllogism, the conclusion immediately sounds absurd, and
that sends you back to think through the premises. But notice that
the premises each seemed sound enough at the start, and Bierce's
absurd syllogism follows the rhetorical rules of logic. Not all
mistakes of reasoning declare themselves as openly as Bierce's
flagrant example. Frequently, you only have a vague feeling that
the validly-derived conclusion doesn't sound right.

Similarly, rationality takes an agnostic view toward much
nonsense that you reject quite properly on grounds of feeling.
"Maybe I'm just a brain in a vat, being fed electrical impulses that
make me feel I'm in a body moving about the world." "Maybe I'm

the only conscious being in the world; my mom, dad, sister, and everyone else are all just vastly sophisticated robots without sentience." Or any number of other improvisations by bored pot smokers. A strict rationalist would say we have no choice but to keep an open mind as to these questions. But that's crackpot rationalism. We don't keep an open mind to this nonsense, and there's no reason we should. We should not, for example, entertain the thought that torture victims don't really experience pain; that à la Descartes, their wails signify no more than the rasping of a rusty hinge. Nonsense like that never enters our heads. But it's our feeling of reality, not our rationality, that shuts the door to preposterous ideas we can't disprove. Apart from utter nonsense, we also close the door on many ideas that may have something to say for themselves, but not enough to bother with. So most of us don't entertain the possibility that 9/11 was an inside job, that faith healing works, or that financial crises would be a thing of the past if bankers could just break free of regulatory requirements.

Purely rational thought covers only the tail end of cognition. Emotion necessarily participates in one degree or another in almost all reason. And we can't readily dissect our mental processes to separate thinking from feeling. It all blurs together.

1.6.6 WE CAN AND SHOULD REASON SERIOUSLY. WE CAN AND SHOULD DISTINGUISH BETWEEN APPROPRIATE AND INAPPROPRIATE EMOTION.

None of this is to valorize intuition, emotion, or the unconscious. None of this is to value gut feelings over thoughtful consideration. Obviously, feelings can get it wrong. The unconscious is not God. We make mistakes nonstop, and we do so through all forms of cognition, conscious and unconscious, rational and emotional. But we get a lot of things right, too, and all forms of cognition play a part in that as well. Like rationality, emotion can play its role well or poorly, constructively or destructively, but one way or another emotion will play a role.

Feelings don't all bear the same weight, any more than

thoughts do. Some bear on the issue, some don't. When a doctor accused of malpractice moves for summary judgment, we don't want judge or jury to be moved by sympathy for the patient or the doctor because one of them is a Methodist. We do, however, want the judge to consider the situation the doctor acted in, what risk a course of action presented to the patient, and what could count as reasonable conduct in that situation. We want the relevant facts to elicit some appropriate emotional response from the judge, because only then can the judge decide whether any reasonable jury could weigh the evidence and find the doctor liable.

Some feelings arise from sound perception; some don't. Some feelings improve decision-making; some degrade it. Some feelings, we might say, are true; some, false. A girl feels she can never be loved, that she is unlovable. A boy feels himself to be worthless, beyond redemption. Those feelings are lies, and they'll guide that girl, that boy down destructive paths.

We can and should think about our feelings. We should think consciously, critically, rationally. We should judge our feelings thoughtfully. We should not dissolve clear-eyed analysis in a puddle of tears or throw out hard thinking in favor of group hugs. Without feeling, law is vapor. But that doesn't mean we should embrace stupidity.

1.6.7 THE RATIONAL-MAN DISTINCTION BETWEEN REASON AND EMOTION MAKES US STUPID.

The rational-man model misses the distinctions between emotions relevant and irrelevant, appropriate and inappropriate, "true" and "false." If you buy the rationalist's reason/emotion distinction, you'll find it harder to identify the emotions affecting your own thinking. You'll view emotions as weak or stupid. And because you don't want to think of yourself as weak or stupid, you'll avoid recognizing the emotional components of your own thinking. That makes it harder, not easier, to spot the ways in which emotion leads you astray. Demonizing emotion makes it easier to shower contempt on someone for being moved by sympathy, while failing to notice that you've adopted an ideal of antiseptic rationality out of a child's desire to win the approval of Professor Kingsfield, or whatever.

Buying into the reason/emotion distinction also causes trouble in understanding other people — other people like judges and jurors. The rational-man model predicts naively. You start thinking of people as making rational calculations from value premises that seem self-evident to you. You ignore factors that do influence others. You overestimate how much your ideas will appeal to them. You become a little delusional.

The reason/emotion distinction hides the role of feeling in establishing facts. The distinction encourages the beguiling sense that we apprehend reality as it is in itself. That fosters false confidence in our own sense of the facts. It instills false confidence that a judge or jury will see the facts we see. It leads us away from alternative interpretations we need to grapple with.

The *rhetoric* of rationality clouds our thinking. That rhetoric signals that we're engaging in rationality now, and emotion has to leave the room. We usually employ this rhetorical gimmick to gain sham credibility. Maybe that effort works, maybe it doesn't, but it impairs our thinking.

~

WE'RE NOT RATIONAL CREATURES. We're semi-rational beasts. We operate largely by emotion or feeling, and without them can't operate at all. Emotions are to human reason like fins are to a dolphin. We can use them well or poorly, but you don't make a better dolphin by hacking off its fins.

1.7 OUR BRAINS ARE BUILT FOR SOCIETY AND BEHAVIORAL FLEXIBILITY

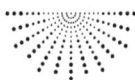

Humans lack the specialized organic tools of other species (claws, horns, super-long tongues for digging ants out of anthills, etc.). Yet humans inhabit a greater range of climates, conditions, and cultures than any other species. Humans have created civilizations, and technologies as good as magic. To do all this, we have to live socially, with enormous behavioral flexibility. That requires special brains — brains built for culture.

1.7.1 OUR BRAINS ARE WIRED FOR BEHAVIORAL FLEXIBILITY — AND THUS FOR CULTURE, TO GUIDE FLEXIBLE BEHAVIOR.

It may seem premature to address culture in Part One, which focuses largely on hardware — neurons, chemicals, etc. — and the most elementary characteristics of mind. But culture is that elemental to the human brain and mind.

BEHAVIORAL FLEXIBILITY, WITHIN BOUNDS

More than any other animal, the human individual can adapt to different conditions and regulate behavior according to a multitude of considerations. We can live today in frigid tundra, tomorrow in hot savanna, and adapt our behavior instantly. We can turn from negotiating a temperamental dog that doesn't want to get off the couch to negotiating a temperamental lawyer who doesn't want to produce documents. We can deal with mountain lions and with long lines at Starbucks. We can vary our physiological, emotional, and cognitive responses rapidly. Faced with a dozen conflicting impulses, we can suppress Set A in this situation, while acting on Set B, and reverse the controls in that other situation.

Of course, behavioral flexibility notwithstanding, human bodies and brains do follow certain patterns highly fixed by the genome. We learn to walk with our feet, for instance, not our hands. Not even carnies walk with their hands more than occasionally. That's genetic, not cultural. The genotype constrains human brains even as to more flexible traits: Behaviors and beliefs are not infinitely malleable. Cultural universals exist. So far as we can tell, all human cultures, everywhere, over all time, use names for individual human beings. All use language. Fear of snakes predominates everywhere. And so on. A government or a social movement can't get a culture to embrace just any damned thing — like universal celibacy, or complete obliteration of personal property, or whatever. An individual can learn a wide range of beliefs and practices, but wide as that range is, it doesn't stretch to infinity.

CULTURAL VARIATION

Despite a long list of universals and constraints, cultures still vary tremendously. The exotic differences include, for example, widow burning, eating one's dead, and Balinese trance — which involves people "biting off the heads of living chickens, stabbing themselves with daggers ... performing miraculous feats of equilibration, mimicking sexual intercourse, eating feces, and so on" and which people enter into "rather more easily and much more suddenly than most of us fall asleep" and emerge from "five minutes to several hours later, totally unaware of what they have been doing and convinced, despite the amnesia, that they have had the most extraordinary and deeply satisfying experience a man can have."[1]

More subtly but maybe more strikingly, cultural differences can extend even to simple perception of the physical world. Richard Nisbett has studied cultural differences in cognition. He reports that people from more collectivist cultures (like Japan) will look at a picture and primarily notice the relationships among the things in the picture, whereas people from more individualist cultures (like the US) primarily notice the separate things themselves.[2]

CULTURE, BEHAVIORAL CONTROL, AND THE SLOW-MATURING BRAIN

Our adaptability to varying conditions arises from the enormous variability and flexibility in our mental apparatus — and from our capacity for executive control, which allows us to suppress the desire to grab the candy bar and run out of the store when we don't have enough of the little green paper.

Humans are unique among animals for our extraordinarily long period of immaturity, which relates directly to variability of behavior. Most animals attain maturity quickly — some of them completely mature at hatching or birth — and their mature brains or nervous systems guide them through life with fixed action patterns. A human brain, by contrast, takes decades to mature. In that time, the individual acquires a culture that guides everything from perception of the physical world, to the categorization of other humans, to complex beliefs and value systems and intricate behavior patterns.

The human infant is born with a nervous system mature enough for basic operation of lungs, kidneys, and so forth, but with vast areas of mental life immature, even the "mental life" involved in operating much of the body itself. Unlike a worm or a minnow or even a foal, the human nervous system is too undeveloped for the infant to contribute even minimally to his or her own survival. Within an hour of falling to the ground, a foal can stand and walk. The human takes a year or more before the brain has mapped the body to enable enough control to walk with a toddler's competence. Forget walking, though. A new human can't even control peeing and pooping. That, too, takes years to master.

It takes many more years for the human to acquire any of the mental apparatus necessary for what we would call human life. Being human involves more than walking, picking berries, and shitting outside the cave. Human life involves living in society among other humans. To do that requires a vast store of skills and knowledge that the brain comes prepared for but which require years of learning — about who counts as family, how we treat non-family, how to work a can opener, what property is and what rules govern it, what gods to pray to and what manner of beast to kill in order to placate this or that god, how to stay out of trouble with the government, and on and on.

It takes years of *cultural* learning for the infant to acquire all this skill and knowledge. Cultures exist in part to provide guidance in the exercise of executive control, in the selective suppression and release of impulses and desires. Culture teaches us, for example, how to speak and act toward this or that group of people, what characteristics of individuals are salient and create a basis for group identity, and so on. Cultures and sub-cultures vary tremendously in the rules they instill.

To facilitate this enormous store of cultural learning, the human brain remains immature — especially plastic, especially receptive to learning — into the individual's twenties. Different parts of the brain mature at different rates, and the longer the delay in maturation, the greater the influence of culture in shaping that aspect of the individual's mental life. For example, the dorso-lateral prefrontal cortex is a recently evolved chunk of brain at about the top front left of your head. If your right-handed brother faces you and slaps you on the top of the head, that'll probably mark the spot. The dlPFC gets involved in executive functions and abstract reasoning. The dlPFC is rational, unsentimental, controlled. It doesn't fully mature until your twenties. So the dlPFC is heavily influenced by what happens in the life experiences of the young individual — the formative years in which the young person is taught and disciplined and scolded and educated; the years, in short, in which the young person is enculturated. So the ways in which the individual reasons, the lines of thought that do and don't make sense, will be heavily influenced by culture. The same goes for other brain regions involved in other functions and maturing at other rates. So, for example, "subjects from individualist cultures [like the United States] strongly activate the (emotional) [medial] PFC when looking at a picture of themselves, compared to looking at a picture of a relative or friend; in contrast, the activation is far less for East Asian subjects" from more collectivist cultures.[3]

CULTURE AS NATURE (SORT OF)

The preceding discussion implies a slippery point: Despite certain universals, there is no generic human being — no *complete* generic human, anyway. A feral child abandoned in the woods and kept alive by a pack of dogs will not become recognizably human. The child's physical form will look human enough, but if not rescued while the brain is still in the highly plastic, immature state of early childhood, the child will never be more than a tragically stunted dog-person.

Every culture, and thus every full human being, is its own particular thing. There is no complete generic culture. There's early 21st-Century New England upper middle-class culture, and the lower middle-class variants, and 19th Century Balinese culture, and 1980's Birmingham, England youth culture, and so on. Wherever you draw the lines between a full culture and mere sub-cultures, there's no ideal type of the human culture, and thus no ideal type of the human being. There's only the range of particulars, with various commonalities among them.

More profoundly, without culture, human beings as we think of them cannot exist. As Clifford Geertz wrote,

[T]here is no such thing as a human nature independent of culture. Men without culture would not be the clever savages of Golding's *Lord of the Flies* thrown back upon the cruel wisdom of their animal instincts.... They would be unworkable monstrosities with very few useful instincts, fewer recognizable sentiments, and no intellect: mental basket cases. As our central nervous system — and most particularly its crowning curse and glory, the neocortex — grew up in great part in interaction with culture, it is incapable of directing our behavior or organizing our experience without the guidance provided by [culture]. [I]n the Ice Age [] we were obliged to abandon the regularity and precision of detailed genetic control over our conduct for the flexibility and adaptability of a more generalized, though of course no less real, genetic control over it. To supply the additional information necessary to be able to act, we were forced, in turn, to rely more and more heavily on cultural sources.... Without men, no culture, certainly, but equally, and more significantly, without culture, no men. [4]

1.7.2 OUR BRAINS ARE TUNED TO THE PROBLEMS OF LIVING WITH OTHER PEOPLE.

We're an intensely social species, and our brains reflect (and create) that fact. Different areas of the brain serve various functions relating to social life — assessing what others think of us, assessing what we think of others, assessing what we think of ourselves in light of what others think, and so on. When the brain has no immediate task at hand, it turns on the circuits that analyze social life. That seems to be the default system. When the brain has time on its hands, it thinks about our life among other people.

The importance of social life should be obvious, so it should not surprise anyone that the brain is built for it. But our social nature can become invisible because we're so thoroughly immersed in it. Fish don't notice water. From birth to death, we move among other people continuously. We play by the rules, because we have to. The "mavericks" among us stand out because they comply with social rules only 98% of the time, rather than 99.8%. The "self-made man" eats food grown by others, wears clothes made by others, lives in a house built by others. We have a handful of truly rugged near-hermits who probably amount to less than 0.0001% of the population. Some of them build their own dwellings. Most probably do so with tools made by others, and raw materials harvested or created by others. If a hermit owns a gun, he didn't make it himself from steel he forged in his own kiln. Even the hardiest hermit was brought up by others, taught a language by others, and lives largely by the education he received from others. Even feral children owe their survival in part to dogs or wolves — other social animals. The truly self-reliant human being dies in infancy.

1.7.3 WE THINK AND FEEL THE WAY OUR CULTURE TELLS US TO — LARGELY.

Culture shapes nearly all aspects of mental life. Culture shapes beliefs about how the physical world works. Get born in one place and time, and you believe that leeches can suck the illness out of you. Get born in another place and time, and you believe a pantheon of minor gods control the weather, and that you can propitiate them by menstruating indoors or leaving a hunk of goat meat to rot on that flat rock by the river, or whatever.

More importantly here, different cultures endow people with different values, different ideological commitments, different senses of right and wrong. A couple years after moving to Indiana, my Bulgarian friend got pulled over for speeding. As the cop walked up, my friend pulled out a $20 bill. He was confused when his girl-friend told him to put it away. In Bulgaria, corruption occurred as unremarkably as tap water flows out of spigots. In that respect, Americans and Bulgarians live in different moral/political/emo-tional worlds.

Culture also influences the shape and contour of emotions, how we understand and experience them. At least much of the time, emotion begins with interoception — keeping track of the physical feelings inside the body. Something happens in the world, a snake slithers onto the path or your boss scowls at you or a voice on the phone says, "I'm sorry, but there's been an accident." The sensory stimulus runs to your brain. Your brain signals your heart to beat faster, your lungs to breathe faster, your muscles to contract. Your interoceptive apparatus registers these bodily changes. Your brain then interprets these interoceptive signals and bestows meaning on them — fear, anxiety, dread, nervousness, terror, anger, rage, angst, aggression, whatever. Your brain's interpretation depends on the entire context, everything about the situation, not just the internal body signals.

We can interpret and experience a given situation and set of physical feelings in more than one way. The same moment can make us scared or angry. We usually see only one way to interpret our feelings, and we interpret them so immediately and thoughtlessly that we don't even experience any moment of "interpretation." But we have more flexibility and control than we know. Timothy Wilson and others have shown for example that you can sometimes transform nervousness to excitement simply by telling yourself you're excited, not nervous.[5] Obviously, there are limits to interpretive flexibility. When the snake slithers out, you probably couldn't interpret your feelings as *relief*, however much you try.

Our cultures teach us how to feel emotionally — how to interpret interoceptive feelings in context — and what to do about it. Parents may teach children explicitly that "you're feeling angry because she hit you." But even without explicit teaching, culture shapes how we understand and experience our feelings. Culture does so in part simply by making certain words and concepts available to us through language. The Czechs, for example, have *litost*, an emotional concept Americans don't have. Milan Kundera describes *litost* as a spiteful desire for revenge caused by the contemplation of one's own misery. Kundera tells a story of a child ridiculed by a violin teacher. Fueled by *litost*, the boy deliberately infuriates the teacher until the teacher throws him out the window. As the boy falls to his death, he delights in the knowledge that the teacher will go to prison for murder.[6] Part of the meaning provided by the cultural interpretation of feelings includes ideas about what to do, how properly to respond to particular feelings. An American pupil lacking the idea of *litost* would have been less likely to provoke his own murder.

Despite cultural differences, all humans share much in common — similar bodies, brains, needs, problems. Those bland commonalities suffice to let us attain some meaningful understanding of another's emotional response to a thing. An Amazonian tribe member experiencing *liget* may respond to the death of a father with a frenzy of howling and wailing, and then by killing someone. I would not respond that way, but I sort of get it. Foreign as it is, it's not so foreign as to be wholly incomprehensible to me.

Our cultures don't just teach us how to interpret feelings. They also help determine what we feel — even bodily — in the first place. Culture does this by instilling us with values, by telling us what matters and what we should care about. For example, Richard Nisbett and Dov Cohen have shown that Southerners and Northerners react in very different ways to insults — ways that show up in measurements of stress hormones minutes after the insult, and ways that show up in murder rates.[7] The things we care about, will fight and suffer for — come to us mostly from culture.

1.7.4 THERE ARE LOTS OF CULTURES, SUBCULTURES, SUB-SUBCULTURES, AND SO ON.

There is no complete set of neatly identifiable cultures that we can label. In his book *American Nations*, Colin Woodard describes 11 broad regional cultures in the United States — cultures rooted in centuries of history. Each of those could be further sub-divided indefinitely. Cultures multiply into subcultures, sub-subcultures, and so on, far down past any hope of creating a neat, comprehensive taxonomy. My family has a culture of its own. So does yours.

It's important to keep in mind, therefore, that any discussion of a particular culture helps our thinking only if we guard against sliding into simplistic, reductionist impressions. We can usefully state some broad generalities about, for example, Turks — *"they make disgusting coffee*" — but any Turkish individual participates in dozens of other cultures or subcultures we could usefully speak of. In this or that situation, some of those subcultures will be salient and some won't.

If we put too much stock in the common labels for cultures — Southern, Texan, New Yorker, Protestant, Catholic, Black, White, Feminist, Chauvinist, etc. — we can slide into a delusional reductionism. Of course we all know not to indulge crude stereotypes, but even smart, sensitive people like you and me slide unwittingly into reductionist impressions, because words have an almost mystical power to make things seem real. If we label this guy a Protestant and that one a Catholic and the other an Athiest, it comes to seem, without any intention or even awareness on our part, that the three must differ deeply, and then the follow-on impression may settle silently over our thinking, that those differences are salient for whatever purposes matter in the present situation. The impression may be true, but then again it may be false. It needs guarding against.

⁓

ALL THIS TALK of slow-maturing brains and cultural rules may seem remote from legal work, but it's not. This discussion contributes to two massively important points for any advocate.

First, people vary in their perceptions, emotional responses, and ideas much more than we can remain aware of as we go about our work. We each swim in our own cultural worlds, and it's simply not possible for us to have much detailed awareness of how things are in the subtly or not-so-subtly different worlds the individuals around us swim in. We can of course understand at some level of bland cognition that differences exist — I've been yammering about it for pages, after all. But there simply is no way to fully appreciate the particular differences in detail, as we go about our business moment to moment. We are ever and always largely oblivious to how things look from behind different eyeballs. But we can try to appreciate these differences.

Second, other people's ways of seeing and feeling are baked into them, and you can't change those ways to any significant extent — at least not any time soon. The infuriatingly wrong-headed judge, the juror off of whose back your arguments run like water — they've been made that way by titanic forces working over decades if not centuries or millennia. You can't change them through your advocacy, however great your genius. But maybe you can work with these people's ways of seeing and feeling, if you can see and understand and empathize with them. (Then again, maybe you can't work with them. Life isn't fair, or easy.)

1.7.5 WE GET SMARTER OVER TIME, AS CULTURES AND AS INDIVIDUALS.

Individuals and cultures do learn and change gradually over time. In part, we get smarter because discoverers or inventors stumble on new insights. The broader language community then makes those ideas available to the rest of us through new words, new concepts. At the level of culture, the development of the ideas of gravity, germ theory, radio waves, crop rotation, fertilization, immunization, etc. have changed life dramatically. Civilization grows up on the back of steadily increasing cultural knowledge, embodied largely in new words and concepts.

More importantly for our purposes, individuals can learn over time. Once you understand the concept of sunk costs and see how it applies to your own life, you're permanently smarter. It's not just that you can drop a new phrase in conversation to impress your friends. You now have a new insight that can permanently help you make decisions that make you happier.

Similarly, a judge or juror may see a self-evaluation by an insurance adjuster who argues for a year-end bonus by saying "I employed creative solutions to achieve a 10% reduction in claim payouts over last year. In multiple cases, I was able to maintain a claim denial despite outside counsel advising that the claim should be paid." The judge or juror only needs to see that once, to gain a lasting insight into how compensation systems influence claim handling.

While we waste time and energy when we try to change someone's baked-in ways of seeing and feeling, we *can* hope and expect to show them new things. And we can hope (and sometimes expect) that the baked-in attitudes, applied to these new facts or concepts, will lead the judge or juror to a conclusion that happily aligns with our own conclusions.

1.8 OUR BRAINS COME PRE-LOADED WITH SOME CONTENT, PROBABLY INCLUDING SOCIAL AND MORAL CONTENT

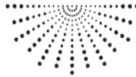

It seems well-established that the brain comes with certain content pre-loaded. This innate mental content ranges from the seemingly simple to the sophisticated. It includes mere potentials that have to be triggered by experience, as well as specific, hard-wired action patterns. For example, at the low end we come with pre-programming for the brain to control the autonomic systems of the body (breathing, heart-beating, digesting, etc.). At the high end, it seems we innately possess a generic capacity for language, but the specific settings (words and syntax) have to be given by the language environment we grow up in. More surprisingly, perhaps, certain social and moral predispositions seem to be soft-wired or pre-wired into the brain — innately there in a generic form, but influenced by experience.

Until recently, one semi-popular theory held that the mind is a blank slate at birth, that we gain all knowledge and traits by learning them from the environment. For a time, some hoped we could therefore mold human "nature" more to our liking — an alternately glorious or monstrous ambition. The broad public probably never adopted this view much, and few probably ever bought it entirely. All the same, the blank-slate hypothesis carried a lot of weight in the intellectual and political history of the 20th century. It probably still discreetly influences many of us.

The blank-slate hypothesis sprang largely from the shocks of cultural anthropology and history. Research in those fields does indeed show that human nature permits a broad range of phenomena, including very strange ones — trances, shamans, cannibalism, vision quests, mind-blowing sadism and stoicism, treating infants as tiny adults and letting them play with knives, etc. Awed by reports of human diversity (some of those reports apparently bogus), some intellectuals extrapolated that *everything* is culture, and *nothing* innate. Extrapolating to infinity in a state of shock usually leads you wrong, and so it did here.

Evidence for innate knowledge has accumulated from a variety of sources, including experimental psychology, animal studies, neurology, and anthropology itself. For starters, it's hard to imagine you had to learn how to recognize your left arm as yours. Yet it turns out that's an "ability" you can lose — an ability apparently hard-wired into the normal brain. It also turns out that laboratory mice that have never been exposed to a cat react with fear when you put cat fur into their cage. Even tiny-brained mice thus seem to have a wired-in fear of cats. Similarly, as I've mentioned, despite amazing variety it appears that all cultures share an impressive list of universal traits. Given the number and variety of cultures through history, with widely varying circumstances, exhibiting wild variation in many of their aspects, cultural universals suggest that God or nature has cooked at least some of these traits into our brains.

More importantly, we have good reason to think our brains give to us (in soft-wired or hard-wired form) even higher-order attributes like language, logical thought, temperament, social and moral sensibilities, and basic knowledge of the natural world. Thus, even newborns seem to know, or expect, that things fall down, that one solid object can't pass through another in ghostlike fashion, and so on. Equally striking, many of our personal traits resist all efforts to change them. Gender and sexual orientation seem to reside in our blood and bones. Children born with both male and female genitals turn out to have a particular gender, and no effort by parents to raise the child as a girl will work, if the gender switch in the brain has been turned to "boy." Decades of efforts to change homosexuals into heterosexuals by creative and appalling means, even with eager would-be converts, have succeeded mostly in creating not cures and converts, but sorrow and suicide.

Language, social sensibilities, and morality all seem to involve our brains natively providing a sort of generic content system, for which the cultural environment then dials in specific settings. For language, this mechanism seems well established. It appears the child's growing brain naturally possesses a proto-language. The linguistic environment dials the knobs to make the child a Mandarin speaker, or English, or Urdu, or whatever. The evidence suggests this kind of system also creates the social and moral codes we live by — at least at a high but meaningful level of generality. Thus, experiments indicate that infants innately understand social and moral concepts like helping and harming another. Infants feel drawn to those who help, rather than harm, third parties. Identical twins separated at birth and raised in different families find, in adulthood, that they possess eerie similarities not only in their favorite colors and clothing styles, but in their temperament, politics, and religion.

The wired nature (hard or soft) of some contents of the mind makes sense in light of the co-evolution of brains, bodies, and societies. Our predecessors did not sit quietly in caves until they finished evolving, and only then emerge to build cities, form religions, and invent the internet. Non-human primates, the early proto-human species, and eventually *homo sapiens* evolved into ever more social creatures, and their bodies and brains kept evolving throughout that process. That is, we evolved in response to, and thus also in reliance on, social life. That helps explain why we carry within us a generic social and moral code, wired into our brains.[1]

1.9 SOME OF OUR DIFFERENCES GO ALL THE WAY DOWN, AND WE HAVE NO TRANSCENDENT ARBITER OF WHO'S RIGHT

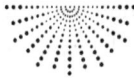

The importance of biology to our identities gives the lie to the dream that we're all the same underneath, and that a Truth exists that we can all acknowledge and share in common. After 10,000 years of civilization, we haven't gotten very close to a consensus on Truth. But the dream dies hard. So does the fantasy on the flip side of the coin. As you go about your day-to-day business, you tend to feel that those who disagree with you would see the truth if only they would open their stupid eyes. In a few limited domains (what 5x8 equals, how a carburetor works), that's true. But the sense of certainty grips us in the rest of life, too. That conviction keeps us from communicating, from persuading, and even from simply understanding. It drives disputes deeper and makes them shriller. Appreciating the limits on our mental lives can help moderate our self-righteousness and help us deal with people more effectively. This knowledge won't turn dissension to ashes and grow a great flower of unity from them, but it can help.

Important parts of our identities do seem to arise from our biology and remain fairly durable. I've mentioned the shocking similarities between identical twins separated at birth. In another field, psychopaths seem to have brain abnormalities that cause an enduring lack of empathy and of moral feelings like shame and compassion. Men and women appear often to feel and think in different ways, seemingly as a result of different brain chemistry (although that conclusion remains highly contested). Conservatives seem to be more alert to potential threats, in part because of the mix of neurotransmitters in their heads. Liberals seem to seek new experiences more, in part because of their neuro-chemical cocktails. Both dispositions serve valuable functions, and a diversity of outlooks probably helps a large society.

Differences in brain biology likely cause subtler hard-wired differences from one individual to another. If the brain contains a multitude of specific functional areas; if brains vary so greatly from birth as to include congenital brain defects; if brain development varies with individual experience; then it seems likely that the more or less permanent settings of individual adult brains vary in innumerable subtle ways. How trusting I am, how curious, how adept at logical thinking, how compassionate, how religious, how creative — all may derive in substantial part from peculiarities of my brain biology and personal history that lie beyond my control.

Despite plasticity, brain biology tends to remain relatively stable over time. We don't careen wildly from one personality to another, from one set of basic beliefs to another. The ideas I've discussed here can provoke anxiety and outrage that something as momentous as *Who I Am* depends on something as changeable as the composition of fluids in my skull. The more important implication, though, may be that the particularities of *Who I Am* resist change so stubbornly.

The problem is less that we change so rapidly, but that we change so slowly, even when we want so badly to change. Mental illness can provoke rapid changes, as when a bipolar person ascends into mania, his personality morphing surreally before your eyes. Psychoactive drugs can work similar effects. Ordinarily, though, changes in brain chemistry or neuronal structures move slowly. This suggests that important attributes of each of us — attributes that determine how we see the world, how we feel and think about things — will stubbornly resist efforts to change them. That goes for me and you, and also for judges and jurors.

The brain-centric view of human nature puts a new twist on two lessons your kindergarten teacher tried to teach you.

First, adopt a little humility. The morons who see things so wrongly are working under the influence of brain biology and personal histories that shape their sense of things. But then so are you. Outside a few tiny domains like arithmetic and how a screw-top works (and maybe not even there), no one has a clear window to transparent truth. No one has the view from God's throne. We should tone down our certainty and self-righteousness. We should tone down our frustration with people who stubbornly resist our obviously correct view of things.

Second, try to appreciate the views of other people. Consider what it really means that other people see through other eyes, that other brains stitch the world together with other machinery. If you want to persuade them, you have to understand how their eyes see, how their brains work. We all share profound similarities, so we can imagine at least a little what it's like to stand in another's shoes. Imagination can be aided by research, which includes just listening.

That other people have other eyes and other brains doesn't just mean they get things wrong that you get right. It also means they see things you don't. The old story of the blind men and the elephant is clichéd because it carries real insight. The beauty of the jury system is not just a civic fairy tale. For all his metaphysical nonsense, Plato hit on a solid truth with his cave metaphor. Reality doesn't pour into our eyes, pure and true. We take in evidence of it, like shadows on the cave wall, and construct an idea of the world from that imperfect evidence. Other people, standing elsewhere, taking in other evidence, feel and sense things you can't. Henry Beston referred to animals "gifted with the extension of the senses we have lost or never attained, living by voices we shall never hear." That insight gave Beston a respect for animals that we'd do well to apply to other people: Speaking of animals, Beston wrote, "They are not brethren, they are not underlings: they are other nations, caught with ourselves in the net of life and time, fellow prisoners of the splendour and travail of the earth."

The judge who doesn't get it, the juror devoid of compassion, the neighbor with oddball views — they may be wholly wrong, but then they may be responding to something you could understand, sympathize with, and accommodate or even appropriate, if only you listened for it. C.S. Lewis got at this point in discussing the value of literature:

> The man who is contented to be only himself, and therefore less a self, is in prison. My own eyes are not enough for me, I will see through those of others. Reality, even seen through the eyes of many, is not enough. I will see what others have invented. ... Literary experience heals the wound, without undermining the privilege, of individuality. ... [I]n reading great literature I become a thousand men and yet remain myself. Like the night sky in the Greek poem, I see with a myriad eyes, but it is still I who see. Here, as in worship, in love, in moral action, and in knowing, I transcend myself; and am never more myself than when I do.[1]

1.10 FURTHER READING, ETC.

We have an overabundance of print, audio, and video on cognitive-science topics — books, magazines, newspaper coverage; podcasts; TV shows, documentary movies, and other streaming video. The following list is not remotely exhaustive, but the items listed here provide a good starting point. These materials bear on the issues discussed above.

I list these materials (and all later recommendations as well) in the order in which I would suggest reading them for purposes of the discussion in this book.

BOOKS

- David Eagleman, *The Brain: The Story of You* (2015).
- Robert Sapolsky, *Behave: The Biology of Humans at Our Best and Worst* (2017).
- Antonio Damasio, *Descartes' Error: Emotion, Reason, and the Human Brain* (2005).
- Michael Gazzaniga, *Tales from Both Sides of the Brain: A Life in Neuroscience* (2015).

- Eric Kandel, *In Search of Memory: The Emergence of a New Science of Mind* (2006).
- Matthew Lieberman, *Social: Why Our Brains are Wired to Connect* (2013).
- Steven Pinker, *The Language Instinct* (1994).
- Jonathan Haidt, *The Righteous Mind: Why Good People are Divided by Politics and Religion* (2012).
- Timothy Wilson, *Strangers to Ourselves: Discovering the Adaptive Unconscious* (2002).
- Stephen L. Macknik and Susana Martinez-Conde, *Sleights of Mind: What the Neuroscience of Magic Reveals about Our Everyday Deceptions* (2010).
- Oliver Sacks, *Musicophilia: Tales of Music and the Brain* (2007).
- Patricia Churchland, *Touching a Nerve: The Self as Brain* (2013).
- Daniel Dennett, *Elbow Room: The Varieties of Free Will Worth Wanting* (1984).
- Roy Baumeister, *The Cultural Animal* (2005).

OTHER MATERIALS

The new world of streaming video and audio has produced a seemingly unlimited amount of material — of greatly varying quality — on every subject, from erotic whispering to funny cats to surgical operations to neuroscience. Searching on "neuroscience" or "mind and brain" in the various streaming services will return thousands of hits. I mention here only a handful of sources, with no claim to have canvassed the whole universe of relevant materials:

- *The Brain*, a 2015 TV series hosted by David Eagleman (author of the book of the same title).
- The World Science Festival has a YouTube channel that contains a "Mind and Brain" playlist.
- The TED Talks series has collected a variety of short

lectures on topics in neuroscience, at this link (as of 2020): https://www.ted.com/topics/neuroscience.

For podcasts, the best shows discussing the issues explored above seem to come up in general science productions — not those focused specifically on neuroscience. Some examples:

- NPR's *RadioLab* podcast.
- NPR's *Invisibilia* podcast.
- Brain Science with Ginger Campbell, MD.

PART II
SEEING, FEELING, THINKING

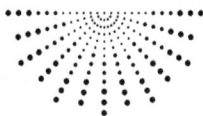

If you wanted to boil down to a bumper sticker the major findings of cognitive science, you might settle on this old scrap of cynical wisdom: *We see what we want to see and believe what we want to believe.* Simplistic and exaggerated, but true enough, and more useful than a rationalist bumper sticker. Anyone who thinks facts and logic win every time — or could, if only judge and juror did their jobs — is in for a lot of frustration.

2.1 GENERAL PROCESSES

We have so far focused on the most elementary and general characteristics of human cognition, starting from the physical brain and body. Here, we move to a more specific, but still quite general, discussion of cognitive processes.

2.1.1 WE EVALUATE ANYTHING NEW BY MEANS OF AN EXISTING WORLDVIEW — A CATALOG OF PREEXISTING THOUGHTS AND FEELINGS.

By the time we emerge from toddler-hood, and perhaps even from infancy, we've built up a store of usually-unconscious thoughts and feelings, a worldview. We keep adding to it as we keep on living. This mass of mental stuff includes scripts, schemas, ideas, beliefs, expectations about how the many things in the world work — how, for example, cops treat pretty blonde girls, what happens to a sock left out on the porch, where dogs run when they grab a hot dog off the counter, how insurance adjusters treat claimants, how judges talk to criminal defendants, and an indefinitely large list of other things.

At each new moment, at each encounter with new information or a new situation or a new question or a new task, various presumably relevant or quasi-relevant threads from this massive quilt of mental stuff come into play and discretely affect how we see and feel in the new encounter — how we perceive what's going on, what bits we remember and how we remember them, how we feel about it, what we think or assume about it, how we act.

For an advocate, this may be the most important aspect of our mental life. We'll revisit this general process in more specific discussions below.

2.1.2 WE THINK AND FEEL BY ACTIVATING NETWORKS OF ASSOCIATIONS.

Our minds create networks of associations. When anything in a network floats toward the surface, it tugs other associated things up toward the surface, too, other things tied to it in a vast, loose net. Those other things become more available or active, so they can influence us.

Networks of associations exist physically, in the neural structure of the brain. When the environment repeatedly presents things together, the related neurons connect to each other. In this way, neural networks grow and expand. The network of associations thus operates both as a metaphor and as a physical reality in the brain.

The most consistent connections provide natural, embodied metaphors. From the moment of birth, babies are held by their mothers. They feel physical warmth and affection at the same time. That pattern recurs throughout life. So warmth serves as a natural metaphor for affection. Neural connections embody the metaphor.

When one element in a network presents itself to us, it activates the larger network. It primes us to be influenced by the other elements. Researchers have shown, weirdly, that if you evaluate someone while holding a warm drink, you do so in a measurably kinder way. The mere warmth of a cup makes you feel, and give, more affection. Researchers have documented a variety of similar effects.

The effect holds for words, too. If you think of a drink right now, for most readers, it'll be coffee. I didn't mention coffee earlier, but I referred to "a warm drink." For most Americans, coffee is the most common warm drink, so the idea of coffee was probably floating just below the surface of your awareness. Here's another example: Memorize the following word pairs: Ocean, waves. Snail, shell. Cloud, wind. Now say the first automobile that comes to mind. Now say the first laundry detergent that comes to mind. The car question was a distractor. The real question was the detergent. Drew Westen uses this example when he gives speeches, and he reports that a large majority of people call out Tide. All the words in the pairs relate to oceans and waves and thus to tides. Priming easily becomes a parlor game. Mind-reading acts rely heavily on priming (usually with fallback techniques).

We prime ourselves. You consciously direct your attention to something, and it brings other things to mind. It affects your mood, maybe even your posture and how fast or slow you walk. Your stream of consciousness flows according to the activation of associations in your own mind. This gives you one of your greatest powers to govern yourself. You can choose something to think about, to dwell on, to spend time with. And that will influence the other things that come to mind. It will influence how you feel. It will influence how you behave. This simple but profound insight forms the basis of cognitive behavior therapy.

Priming, including self-priming, affects you in every domain, including legal argument. The objects in your office, what you've been reading, what you've been thinking about, what you heard on the radio — it all influences your thinking about the issues and the way you write about them. And everything you say in a brief contributes to the ideas, feelings, attitudes that float up in the minds of the judge and clerk.

This suggests, obviously, that we should be thoughtful about everything — or about as much as possible. Everything going on at trial will influence jurors in subtle ways. Those things, even if wholly irrelevant, may matter. Everything going on in a brief — word choice, pacing, metaphors, etc. — will bring associations. The associations you generate will affect how juror or judge or law clerk interprets ambiguous statements, facts, and laws. The associated emotions will affect their mood, their expectations, their behavior. The associations may exert only subtle force, but small effects matter in close games.

Associations vary from person to person. Any given person's state of mind at the moment depends on an unfathomable multitude of factors. In guessing about what associations you'll prime with this or that word, or example, or metaphor, or whatever, you can only make probabilistic predictions. But many associations occur commonly enough that you can make some predictions with fair confidence.

2.1.3 WE JUDGE BY TANGENTIAL CUES AS MUCH AS BY ACTUAL MERITS.

When we stop to consider the abstract merits of a question, issue, problem, etc., we can separate relevant from irrelevant factors, and valid from invalid inferences. But while the conscious mind lumbers along this path of tedious thought, the unconscious scans the environment and feels its way to an answer based on all manner of factors, including comically "irrelevant" ones. In doing so, the brain draws all manner of inferences, including idiotic ones. Our gut feelings, first impressions, leanings or inclinations, instinctive judgments arise from this not-quite-rational process.

This sort of quick-response judgment largely runs our lives. Most of our judgments don't merit the time or effort for slow, conscious thought. Even when we do spend the effort to think something over deliberately, the quick-response judgment machine still keeps running, its answers get in first, its answers usually come with a feeling of conviction, and its answers influence our labored, conscious deliberation. Gut feelings always matter. Gut feelings almost always exert strong influence on our ultimate decisions.

This insight breeds paranoia. It means, among other things, that everything — every stupid, irrelevant aspect of any situation — carries the potential to impact the decision. *Even the part of my hair? Even the way I pronounce "voir dire"?* Well, sure, maybe. The paranoia quickly becomes counterproductive, though, even when it's not crazy. You can't worry about everything. You have to prioritize the factors you can expect to exert the most influence. For the minor factors, you don't have time or brainspace to worry about them in the moment. For them, you just have to create thoughtful habits and routines that will probably serve you well most of the time.

2.1.4 WE THINK IN SENSORY, ESPECIALLY VISUAL, TERMS.

The importance of sensory information seems obvious, but lawyers irrationally favor the abstract over the concrete. Like a parasite excreting neurotoxins, this bias makes us choose weak, ineffective speech over presentations with punch. Of course abstractions perform vital work. Abstract thought expands our ability to understand the world, by taking us beyond immediate sensory experience. But everything has a scope. Handy as thumbtacks are, we don't use them to brush our teeth. The glories of abstract thought don't render sensory detail unnecessary.

Generally, the more we can relate an idea to direct sensory experience, the easier and more thoroughly we understand it. Abstract thought arises out of and refers back to the multifarious particulars of the world. That's why so many abstract statements consist of dead metaphors. If you don't see how an abstraction (say, *culpability*) relates to concrete things, people, and events in the world, then you don't understand the abstraction. If you write about culpability in a way that prevents a reader from understanding what particulars in the world you're talking about, then the reader won't get your meaning. Abstract thought works best when it brings the senses along — through examples, metaphors, and the like.

Specific, sensory information also carries emotion. The emotion increases as the concepts get lower on the ladder of abstraction: *outdoor entertainment equipment — fishing gear — fishing pole and tackle box*. For those who have fished, at least, the emotion in "fishing pole and tackle box" resonates softly but distinctly. "Fishing gear" carries less emotion, and "outdoor entertainment equipment" virtually none. It sounds like corporate-speak from a Powerpoint slide. Another example: *negligence — design defect — defective airbag system — airbag that went off out of nowhere*. The more specific and concrete the language, the more emotion it carries, and the more impact.

2.1.5 WE THINK BY ANALOGIZING, AND WE REVISE (OR IGNORE) CONCEPTS, STANDARDS, AND RULES WHEN THEY DON'T SEEM TO FIT THE SPECIFICS.

Abstract thought arises from specifics, and well-chosen specifics trump even the firmest-seeming concepts, standards, and rules.

Most concepts aren't as firm as they seem. Concepts get fuzzy at their boundaries. So in developing an argument, we should look out for the misty borders of concepts, standards, and rules. We should look for places where the specifics of the case push the boundaries this way or that.

We're probably born with categories for some primordial things — human beings, maybe snakes, maybe four-legged predators. Most of our concepts, though, we build up through experience. Experience refines even the concepts we're born with.

We develop concepts by analogizing the specific thing in front of us to things we've encountered in the past. Children learn the categories by trial and error, making analogies that the culture accepts or rejects. So a little boy learns the category "mother" by comparing the woman with the other kid to the boy's own mother. Yes, that woman is a mother. The child considers the old man with the other kid and calls him a mother. Then the concept gets refined. The child looks at the big squirrel with the baby squirrel. Can animals be mothers? Yes. What about the big female doll with the baby doll? Well, sort of, if you pretend. Is the boy the mother of his toy truck? No. The child might be surprised to hear that the old lady is a mother, too. Surely she's too old to be a mother. And what do people mean when they say "motherland"? And so on. Over time, with many refinements, the culturally-agreed-on concept "mother" takes shape in the little boy's mind.[1] We follow more or less the same process for most concepts.

From time to time, we invent new concepts. We decide two things resemble each other in some important way, and it would be handy to have a name for them. Take *computer*, for instance. A company hired a woman to solve math problems (relating to insurance underwriting, perhaps). Then they hired another one. Then a whole staff of them. The company called the women "computers," because their job was to compute numbers, and they needed a handy name for the whole class of these employees. Later, someone invented a digital machine to compute numbers. So it seemed right to call that a "computer," too. Similar machines grew far more sophisticated but still operated, at bottom, by computing numbers. So we called those "computers," too. The same general process applies to *contracts*, *slander*, *corsets*, *banana cream pie*, *summary judgment*, *quark*, and on and on.

Concepts grow fuzzy at their boundaries. In defining concepts or words, we try to specify the thing that's common to the entire set of things we apply the name to, the thing that distinguishes them (mothers, say) from everything else (non-mothers). But there is no ideal MOTHER which all actual mothers reflect imperfectly. We can create perfect definitions rarely, if ever. Is the woman who gave birth but abandoned the child a "mother"? Is the woman who didn't give birth but adopted the child a "mother"? Is the sister who did all the mothering a "mother"? You may answer differently on different days, depending on what specifics you have in mind.

Concepts grow fuzzy because we build them on analogies. Usually, we analogize based on several points of comparison — requiring a sort of implicit statistical analysis of the various similarities and dissimilarities among items in the set. In the case of *mother*, that includes biological birthing, caretaking, age, legal guardianship, sex, and gender, among other things. This new person or situation or thing we're looking at may line up with the established set on some comparison points but not others. This happens with most concepts. Is this thing a contract or not? Is it a prior restraint of speech or not? Is it a falsehood or not? Some concepts have fuzzier boundaries than others, but legal disputes often arise where fuzzy conceptual boundaries carry consequences. This all suggests lawyers should stay alert to specifics and question how well a proposed concept really captures the specifics.

Standards and rules try to formalize things and firm up fuzzy boundaries. We create bright-line rules and definitions to eliminate the natural ambiguity of concepts. These efforts do enormous good. They increase shared understandings. They increase predictability of decision-making. We should take rules seriously and apply them in good faith. But they still run up against limits.

Unexpected situations arise. Taken at face value, the rule might apply, but the new case doesn't fit with the cases from which we derived the rule. We could apply the rule as written, but doing so seems impractical, stupid, cruel, or simply impossible. The Congress and President pass a federal statute criminalizing possession of child pornography, with a mandatory minimum prison term of five years. They write the law to allow no exceptions for situations in which the possessor has a good reason for having the child pornography — like police officers who seize it in a raid, prosecutors who present it as exhibits at trial, jurors who review the exhibits, court marshals who supervise the exhibits, judges who review and admit the exhibits.[2] No one intended to criminalize the police or prosecutor for going after child pornographers. On its face, the law does just that, but most of us conclude without hand-wringing that the law doesn't apply to law enforcement efforts. Some hardline rule-followers claim they would still enforce the law even in these cases. Easy to say in an academic context, but I doubt they'd really support imprisoning jurors in a child-porn case. But even if such hardcore rule-followers do exist, we need take no notice of them. They're crackpots. Just don't put them in power.

Exceptions to rules require us to weigh the value of simplicity against the substantive purposes for which we have the law in the first place. That gets tricky. For starters, we disagree about what new situations reasonably fit the rule. And even when we agree that a given situation doesn't fit, we still face the question whether we should apply the rule anyway, for the sake of clarity and simplicity. That will depend on practical effects and our varying value judgments.

2.2 PERCEPTION AND MEMORY

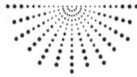

We focus now on immediate perception of whatever new thing or situation appears before us, and how our memory handles whatever it is we perceive.

2.2.1 WE SEE THE NEXT, NEW THING IN THE LIGHT CAST BY WHAT WE ALREADY BELIEVE AND FEEL.

Here we encounter again one of the most important principles in this book — a principle that operates on multiple levels, in multiple domains: The mere fact that we have already come to believe a thing makes us tend to perceive new things to conform with our existing views. The new conforms to the old — or tends to, anyway. Obviously, if your sense of things gets stretched too far, it snaps. Sometimes the new overthrows the old. But as a first principle, the old shapes the new; the new conforms to the old.

This principle reaches down to the level of the most elementary cognition: You learn a thing, and you take it with you into the world. It helps you understand the world. So of course it affects how you see things.

This old-shapes-new effect gains extra power from emotional

attachment. Forming a belief creates a sort of emotional invest-ment. We *are* a patchwork of beliefs, attitudes, and so on. The patchwork creates, constitutes, your identity. We like ourselves (pretty much), and we're invested in our worldview. We may speak very piously about keeping an open mind and deferring to hard facts and being quite ready to throw out old views when they're shown to be wrong. But that's just the PR function of the self. While that part of the self espouses noble Enlightenment values, other parts of the self busily set about arranging facts to confirm the old views we say we're not really that attached to.

So getting in first confers an advantage. If you can be the first to speak or write, take the opportunity. If you can make a compelling showing, and do so first, the cement will start drying. Your opponent will have a harder job if they come second.

This is the "primacy" principle, and it carries hugely important implications for the structure and organization of cases, trial presentations, briefs, and so on.

Often we face bad facts or law that we have to acknowledge. If you just hide from it, your opponent will pull out the bad stuff and pulverize your credibility with it. But how to handle it? Where to put it? The primacy principle gives you the answer: Wait until you've done what you can to get the decision-maker seeing things your way, then looking for reasons to go your way. By then your audience (hopefully) feels motivated to see the potentially negative points in a more generous light. This one little, banal insight can make the difference between a jury rejecting your case right out of the gate, or a jury embracing your client despite her failings.

2.2.2 WE SEE NEARLY EVERYTHING BY COMPARISON TO SOMETHING ELSE.

Most things in life are relative. This principle plays out in a number of ways. First, simple comparisons and contrasts help determine how big or small, good or bad, important or trivial we feel a thing to be. Absolutes — $1,000,000 or $25 — strike us as big or small because we compare them to something else. A 45-

degree basement feels warm if you walk into it from the snowy, frigid outdoors. If you walk in from the upstairs living room, it feels cold. Whether a request seems large or small depends in part on whether it comes after an earlier request that was smaller or larger. Ask people to volunteer as chaperones for a kid's field trip, and most will say no. But make that request after you've just asked them to volunteer every Saturday for a month, and significantly more people will agree to the one-time field trip. Stand next to someone better looking than you, and you look worse than you if you stood by yourself, or by someone less gorgeous than you. Virtually all human judgment reflects implicit or explicit comparisons.

Strangely, and here irrationally, when it comes to numbers, we make implicit comparisons even to obviously irrelevant numbers. Ask people if George Washington lived past 150, and then ask them to guess his actual age at death. They'll guess higher than if you start by asking if he lived past 15. Ask people to write the last four digits of their social security numbers, and then ask them to estimate the number of jelly beans in a jar. People for whom the last four digits form larger numbers will guess higher than others. But they'll scoff at the idea of any such effect. You'd scoff, too; and you'd be wrong, too.

Another relativity effect works more subtly: By paying attention to something, thinking about it, dwelling on it, we make it important. Kahneman puts it nicely: *"Nothing in life is as important as you think it is when you are thinking about it."* Everything in life happens amid a welter of other things. When you think about something, you pick it out of the mass and put it under a spotlight. That makes it more important than it seems in ordinary life. The spotlight effect applies to anything you bring onstage in a brief. And the reverse applies to everything you leave offstage (as long as your opponent and the judge will leave it offstage, too): out of sight, out of mind — and unimportant.

This last point holds an obvious implication for persuasive argument: While you need to do justice to *essential* negative points — the ones you can't ignore without looking dishonest — you also need to give them short shrift. If you give too much attention to the negative points, they loom larger. You end up buttressing your opponent's case even as you think you're undermining it.

The relativity of things doesn't surprise anyone, but we easily overlook the full range of implications for legal work. The listener or reader will make some comparison, if only implicitly. If you don't control the comparison, you lose control of the reader's judgment; you increase your vulnerability to random influences or trains of thought. So compare your request for relief to some bigger potential request. Compare the other side's misconduct to good conduct, or to some less egregious misconduct. Do this gracefully, of course, and maybe subtly. You'll often want to avoid an explicit comparison. But bring the two things onstage so the readers can see the comparison.

The relativity of things (along with the primacy principle) also suggests that, in general, you want to move first. You want to be the plaintiff, the movant, the appellant. With that position, you can set the baselines for comparison, the anchor against which your audience — including your opponents — will automatically compare everything else.

Of course, none of this means you should throw out absurd suggestions, hoping to exploit extreme reference points. Bad faith suggestions backfire. Don't tell the court that you could have demanded every document General Electric produced from 2005 to the present but that you graciously chose not to. That will not make you look magnanimous, but stupid. Say nothing that is unreasonable on its own merits. Within those limits, though, pay attention to implicit and explicit comparisons and make them thoughtfully.

2.2.3 WE CONSCIOUSLY SEE WHAT WE PAY ATTENTION TO, AND NOT THE REST.

Thought and feeling begin with perception and memory. You can't respond to a comment you don't hear. You can't ruminate over an event you have no conscious memory of. Our brains don't just hold everything that pours in through our eyes and ears, like the ocean collecting water from rivers. We register and store only part of what the eyes and ears take in. We consciously remember only a fraction of what the brain socks away in its many-chambered caverns (though unconscious memories still affect our feelings and behavior). And in receiving and storing information, we handle it, massage it, make sense of it, change it. The eyes are not windows to the world. We do not see the world as it is. We see the world as we see it. There's a difference.

In the first place, we limit what we consciously see, by paying attention only to some aspect of what's going on. The brain can consciously register only a small amount of sensory stimulus at once. As you stand on your deck looking out at the yard and the wooded hills beyond, an indefinitely large number of things happen: each bend of each blade of grass, each flutter of each bird, each buzz of each bee, each turn of each ear of each deer, each swaying of each branch of each tree, each breath of wind blowing over each hill, each vehicle humming along each distant road, and so on. Even in this quiet scene with "nothing" happening, far too much is happening for you to take it all in consciously. Even with your mind drifting aimlessly, you limit what sensory information registers. You focus on this piece, then another, and then another. You would say you're not paying attention to anything, but that just means your attention jumps from one thing to the next.

Paying attention to one thing involves actively suppressing awareness of other things. Attention means ignoring everything outside the narrow spotlight we care about at the moment, letting the rest fade to black. The more we focus our attention, the less we see. That's the point of paying attention. It takes work to acquire this ability. Little kids don't have it, so they notice random things we don't. Kids make a tough audience for magicians, because performers can't predict and control a kid's attention as well as they can an adult's.

As adults, we forget how much we miss. You're reading and your wife says something. You don't shift your attention to her immediately. Then you realize in a tiny panic that she's waiting for an answer to some question. Or, semi-famously, you watch a video of kids passing a basketball around; you're asked to count the passes, and you do so. After the video, someone mentions the guy in the gorilla suit waving his arms. "What gorilla guy?" you ask. (See Christopher Chabris' book *The Invisible Gorilla* for this and other cognitive surprises.) You look right at your keys and don't see them; Rule 26(c) states a requirement in black and white and you don't notice it; your boss talks right into your face and you miss key parts of it; someone takes your wallet out of your pocket and you don't feel it.

Multi-tasking doesn't help. There's no such thing as paying attention to many things at once. We can switch attention back and forth quickly. But while we attend to the document requests, we miss the discussion about the brake problem with the car. Our effectiveness with each issue diminishes as attention flashes off and on.

Consciously controlling attention takes work and thus physical energy. When we run out of energy for attention-paying, we still limit the stream of sensation we take in, but in a less directed way. Attention wanders. So the judge worn down by a busy, difficult brief may no longer be able to focus deliberately on anything in particular. A tired or hungry juror looks around the room and notices your opponent's socks, instead of the testimony you're getting right now, on which your entire case turns.

I've been talking about what information we consciously notice, but we take in a great deal more than we notice consciously. But even our unconscious doesn't store everything. There are too many leaves of grass bending in the wind for us to store information about each of them. We have comparatively big brains, with billions of neurons, but they're not infinite.

All these constraints apply to information a judge gains through reading, or a juror gains through sitting in front of the parade of trial. The more that's going on, the less of it we consciously see.

2.2.4 WE SEE WHAT WE EXPECT TO SEE, OFTEN WRONGLY.

When we do see a thing, the thing we see tends to be what we expected to see. Often enough, we therefore see things that aren't really there. This occurs at the level of mere sensory perception and at higher levels as well. Of course this tendency does not govern us inevitably and always. Sometimes we see the unexpected. But the tendency misleads us often enough that we should feel a little paranoid about it.

The context in which we encounter something primes us to recognize this or that, to interpret things in a certain light. Our bodies take in light, sound, smell, and touch. Before we become consciously aware of this flux of sensation, our brains interpret it. Our brains hand it up to our conscious minds not as raw sensation, but as processed, interpreted things with names.

This pre-conscious interpreting of the world proceeds invisibly and automatically — most of the time. You can see traces of the process when it screws up in an immediately noticeable way, when you realize that you've misperceived something. You drive through a seedy part of town, with strip clubs and porn shops. You glance at another strip-club sign with a picture of a woman's face, but a moment later you realize the sign is for a church, and the picture is the Virgin Mary. Why did you see her as some sort of porn queen? The picture contains nothing erotic or suggestive. But you expected to see a strip-club sign, so that's what you saw.

Our unconscious interpretation of things helps us navigate the world, and it usually works well enough to get us by. You're in a restaurant and you hear someone tell a waiter "This sole is not right." You understand the voice to be talking about a fish entrée. You won't even recognize any potential ambiguity. But if you overheard the same comment in a shoe repair shop, you'd understand it differently. And good for you. We want to understand and interpret in light of context. Every day we encounter dozens or hundreds, maybe thousands — who knows how many — theoretical ambiguities, but we never even notice them. If we did not interpret things in light of context, in light of what we've been primed for, we'd be lost. But life being what it is, our interpretive apparatus goes wrong sometimes.

The "context" that shapes our expectations and directs our unconscious interpretation embraces more or less everything. It includes things like what's in the physical environment around us, how we feel physically, our mood at the moment, our history with the person talking to us, our fears and insecurities and anxieties, our background beliefs and values and attitudes, and everything else.

At levels low and high, we see things that aren't there, and miss things that are there, because of our expectations. In any situation interesting enough to talk about, two people looking at the same thing will see different things. A pair of friends hear a news report about a black teenager shot by a cop. The friends shake their heads, look ruefully at each other, and have a flash of shared understanding and feeling. Then the sharing gives way to confusion. It turns out one of the pair heard a news story about a criminal who stupidly threatened a cop, and tragically got himself shot. The other heard a story about a cop who observed ambiguous evidence of a minor crime, overreacted to a sign of disrespect, and killed the kid like a dog. It's as if they heard entirely different stories. Each friend missed elements the other fastened on. What they did hear, they saw in different light. To move beyond frustrated quarreling, the friends need to understand that they really did, in some sense, hear different stories. Any useful discussion will have to take account of all the background stuff in their heads. Of course, these sorts of frustrations arise daily between lawyers and judges, between lawyers and jurors, between jurors and other jurors.

These differences in interpretation arise partly because we slot new information into our existing conceptual frameworks — which differ from person to person. We tend toward what Daniel Kahneman calls "theory-induced blindness" — disregarding facts that don't fit with our understanding of things. That blindness refers not to conscious rejection of a point, but an unconscious filtering-out, a failure even to see the thing in the first place.

We should assume the expected-sight principle applies to every legal brief, every piece of testimony at trial, every argument at a court hearing, everything. To focus on the easier problem of the judge: When a judge or law clerk picks up a brief, they'll always have some conceptual framework, some background assumptions, some expectations about what's going on. If you're not careful (and often enough, even if you are careful), these factors will lead the judge and clerk to miss things, to see things that aren't there, and to misconstrue what is there. You can end up talking past the judge and clerk. Say you write a motion to compel production of documents. The caption page alone may activate a variety of assumptions and expectations by the judge: *The requesting party probably asked for a bunch of junk he doesn't need; the responding party probably served bogus responses; neither side is behaving in good faith;* and so on. Whatever picture comes to mind for the judge (and *some* picture will come to mind), it will influence what the judge sees, doesn't see, and wrongly sees.

We need to tune in to audience expectations and flow with them to the extent possible. We need to make sure that elements of a story or argument that run against the reader's expectations draw attention and can be made to make sense to the audience. We never know enough to do this perfectly. Sometimes we can only grope in the dark, but use what light you can find.

2.2.5 WE REMEMBER A LITTLE, OFTEN WRONGLY.

The limitations of perception and understanding are aggravated by the limitations of memory. A juror can only remember a sliver of what happened in a two-week, or even a two-day, trial. A brief relies less on the audience's memory than a live, oral presentation does — but not *that* much less. A judge or law clerk writing an opinion may look back at parts of the briefs, but even then they will form initial views based on a single reading. If the judge or clerk does look back at the briefs, they'll only look at parts of it, and probably just to support their initial views. You need judges and jurors to remember the overview and highlights without looking back.

We forget almost everything. Of the flecks of information you take in, most wash over your mind without soaking into memory. In rare cases, neurological abnormalities give people access to their full memory (or at least much more than normal), but that abundance of conscious memory can cripple people. So most of us retain conscious access only to a handful of highlights. We've all read articles or books we couldn't remember much about even an hour later. That goes for the contents of legal briefs and trials, too.

When we do remember something, we often skew it. Researchers have identified a variety of systematic memory biases. For our purposes here, we can divide memory mistakes into two broad categories — the mere and the self-serving.

In the category of "mere" mistakes: We confuse sources and misattribute statements. We remember averages better than extremes, and we pull the extremes toward the middle — except that we exaggerate truly dramatic outliers. Obviously, we remember things that matter to us better than things that don't. We remember time frames badly, pushing recent events back in time and pulling distant events closer. More frighteningly, even when we've seen something with our own eyes, we're apt to remember it wrongly if someone describes it falsely. (So do not assume judges or jurors will spot your opponent's falsifications.) We exaggerate things in memory. So a run-of-the-mill mechanized magic trick in which a "rope" rises into the air and stays rigid enough for a boy to climb up gets transmuted into the famous "Indian Rope Trick," in which the rope goes into the clouds, the boy climbs up, and never comes down.[1]

In the category of self-serving mistakes: We remember our decisions as wiser than they were; our accomplishments as harder to achieve and more impressive than they were. We improve on stories when we re-tell them, making them more coherent and more vivid. We remember our past selves as more consistent with our present selves than they were.

To make a bumper sticker out of it: We remember things the way we want to remember them. This is not to say, of course, that we corrupt all our memories. Many of our memories provide tolerable fidelity to fact. And sometimes we make things worse in memory. Some people relive traumatic memories they'd love to forget. Sometimes we exaggerate the negative. But we tend to remember things in a way that validates us and our beliefs, including negative beliefs. Our perceptions don't provide a clear window on the world as it is, and our memories don't faithfully bring back even the world as we perceived it. Memory is a palimpsest. It bears the marks of revisions and elisions.

2.2.6 A LIST OF THINGS THAT MAKE US REMEMBER

Research confirms the memory-aiding factors we've always known about. The following qualities help people remember.

SIMPLICITY

The less to remember, the better remembered. Nested organizational structures help simplify complex sets of information into better-remembered chunks.

CONCRETENESS

We remember concrete, sensory things. We tune into the sensory world.

Lawyers deal largely in abstractions, but you can make abstractions concrete, either through examples or through metaphor. "Defendant asserts laches and the statute of limitations as an affirmative defense." Or "Acme says Theresa sat on her hands and lost her chance to sue." Or "Acme says the statute of limitations blocks Theresa's path to the courthouse." Or something else with some of the texture of real life.

EMOTION

We remember things better if they come with emotion attached. Subtle emotions count, too; it's not all howling and wailing. Often you can add appropriate emotion with a simple choice of words, or a factual detail. You could say, "Janet suffered multiple serious injuries." But a broken arm carries more emotion than that. And a broken "arm" carries more than a broken "ulna." The word "child" carries emotion that "minor" does not. And "little boy" carries more than "child," though "little boy" wouldn't fit all contexts.

Emotion includes surprise and amusement. Surprises stick in our heads. So do things that make us smile. Again, these effects can work subtly. The actress Joan Crawford apparently dressed up every time she left the house. When asked why, she said, "If you want to see the girl next door, go next door." If the line sticks in your head, that's because it delivers a tiny buzz of surprise and humor — emotion.

STORIES

Nothing sticks like a story. Stories package a lot of information efficiently. Stories connect bits of information together, so that one leads to the next. Stories suggest causation, intent, and motivation. And stories usually spark emotion to one degree or another. Stories are the original mnemonic device. We all know hundreds of stories, maybe thousands, many of which we learned in childhood and haven't thought of in years but could recite instantly on demand.

One example: I read Paul Fussell's book *Wartime* just once, over 20 years ago. Fussell relates an urban legend from post-World War II Germany. I've never read or heard that story anywhere else. I've thought about the legend perhaps five times over the years. Until now, though, I repeated the story only once in 20 years, and I never went back to read it again. I recently dug out the book and discovered that I remembered the little story almost exactly. Here's Fussell's recitation:

One narrative popular in Germany just after the war when food was extremely scarce could have been written by Poe himself. It was said that a blind Wehrmacht veteran, tapping along the street with his white cane, encountered a healthy and amiable girl and asked her to help him by delivering a letter to a certain address. As she set off she looked back and saw the blind man stepping out briskly, his cane now abandoned. She was so suspicious that she took the letter not to the address indicated but to the nearest police station. The police went to the address and found a shoe shop run by a couple. All seemed perfectly ordinary until the police stumbled upon a concealed cellar full of fresh meat, suggesting a black-market butcher shop. But closely inspected, [] the meat turned out to be human flesh. Until now the police had overlooked the letter which the blind man had given the girl. When they opened it they found a piece of paper on which was written a single, chilling sentence: 'This is the last one I shall be sending you today.'"

That story has everything: simplicity, sensory detail, emotion (surprise, disgust, horror, relief), an intuitive progression, intent and causation. Few stories, especially true stories, can match that, but most contain those elements in greater or lesser degree. Stories stick.

CONTEXT, COHERENCE, RELATING NEW TO OLD

Where information can't reasonably be fitted into a story, we can still embed it in a context. We struggle to remember isolated bits of information. It helps to have information packaged into a larger, tightly related whole. Each part reminds you of connected parts.

The context helps especially when it allows us to relate new or unfamiliar information to what we already know. From birth to death, learning works best when we can move from one stepping stone to a neighboring one. Jump to far-off stones, and often enough you'll fall. Thrust into a mess of unfamiliar words and concepts, we lose the track. The information doesn't find a hook in our brains. We need someone to show us how the new vocabulary and concepts relate to something we already know. Hence the power of metaphor, simile, analogy.

Similarly, we remember information better when we get it in a coherent, organized form. The more intuitive the organization, the better. We forget random grocery lists.

IMAGERY

We rely heavily on vision. We're built for seeing: Our brains have a big visual cortex. An image can encapsulate a great deal of text and make it stick in memory. Lawyers underuse both actual pictures and word pictures.

REPETITION WITH VARIATION

When we want to memorize something, we repeat it to ourselves. Repetition often works best when the thing you want to remember changes slightly among repetitions. Putting some space between repetitions helps, too. And so does employing multiple senses — for example, varying metaphors that by turns invoke different senses.

Repetition requires a light touch, though, and some variation to keep it from going stale. Telling the same story or making the same point over and over again bores and annoys people.

NUMBERING

Numbering helps us see, digest, and remember things. Simply knowing there are five points, and having a number pinned to each one, helps you remember all five.

POETRY

The music of language helps you remember. Rhyme, rhythm, alliteration, imagery, a satisfying turn of phrase — anything that makes a nice line helps you remember. It's usually just a sentence that sticks with us in this way, but occasionally it can be a larger passage. Ravel's *Bolero* builds a memorable crescendo over 15 minutes. If you've heard it, you probably remember it. Those who haven't read *A Tale of Two Cities* know the first two clauses: "It was the best of times, it was the worst of times." But if you've read the book, it's the effect of the whole paragraph that stays with you, its parallel clauses building to a surprising, dribbled-out anticlimax:

> It was the best of times, it was the worst of times, it was the age of wisdom, it was the age of foolishness, it was the epoch of belief, it was the epoch of incredulity, it was the season of Light, it was the season of Darkness, it was the spring of hope, it was the winter of despair, we had everything before us, we had nothing before us, we were all going direct to Heaven, we were all going direct the other way — in short, the period was so far like the present period, that some of its noisiest authorities insisted on its being received, for good or for evil, in the superlative degree of comparison only.

Music can work garishly or elegantly. Anyone who followed the OJ Simpson murder trial remembers "If the glove doesn't fit, you must acquit." That was 20 years ago, but crude as it is, you remember the line. But you also remember Thomas Paine's "These are the times that try men's souls" or, less grandly, "ghoulies and ghosties and long-leggedy beasties and things that go bump in the night."

Poetry, in the loose sense I'm using it here, goes beyond the music of the language. It includes a clever juxtaposition, a nice reappropriation of an old phrase — whatever makes for a nice line. Stanley Fish collects some of his favorite lines in *How to Write a Sentence*. He takes one from the villain in *The Magnificent Seven*, defending his banditry of peasant-farmers: "If God didn't want them sheared, he would not have made them sheep." There's music in the line — count the syllables in the paired phrases, mark the stresses — and the music plays a vital role in the effect of the sentence. But the surprising and funny content, the sheared sheep and God's will, also carries much of the power. Talk about a thing dully, and we forget. Make it snap, and we remember.

As a side benefit, good writing can make things sound more believable, too. Anything that sounds like a maxim sounds more believable. The bandit's quip about the sheep convinces you for half a second. "A fault confessed is half redressed" sounds right. But "Confessing a fault makes up for half the injury" sounds like special pleading by a wrongdoer.[2] Beyond maxims, nice writing has this effect more generally. You can think of this as a sort of linguistic halo effect: You like the sentence, or the style and tone, or the author's persona, so you want to believe what it says. If you've had the experience of taking favorite authors to your heart, and years later coming to disagree with what they say, you can look back and see how your fondness for the mere writing nudged you to embrace the ideas. Good writing sticks, and persuades.

THE FIRST, THE LAST

Finally, it's at least commonplace to say we remember best what we hear first and what we hear last. As a matter of convention in legal writing, though, last place usually signifies least importance. So for briefs, first place carries the greatest force.

~

FIGURE OUT what you most want judges or jurors to remember, and find ways to enhance their memory of those things. As with anything, the factors listed here require care and judgment. Don't model a brief on nursery rhymes or Aesop's fables.

2.3 IMMEDIATE RESPONSES, CONSCIOUS REASONING, ULTIMATE JUDGMENTS

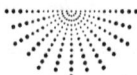

The following discussion moves on from mere perception and memory to evaluation of the thing or situation you have perceived, the formation of judgments about it, and deciding on a course of action.

2.3.1 WE FORM JUDGMENTS IN A SNAP.

In section one, I talked about the importance of the unconscious self. I want to expand here on some of that discussion. The unconscious doesn't care about abstract truth. It tries to grasp reality well enough and fast enough to keep you alive. But the unconscious lacks humility. It constantly offers guidance in matters for which it has no expertise.

What attitude should we take, then, toward the unconscious? It's complicated. Our unconscious mind remains an extraordinary, deep, magical force. Intellectuals probably undervalue their "gut." Others probably overvalue it. Just about all of us, though, ignore how the unconscious works, fail to harness its power effectively, and fail to work around its systematic errors. There's probably no great way to do so, but we should cultivate self-awareness and do what we can.

INTUITION VOLUNTEERS ANSWERS AUTOMATICALLY AND CONFIDENTLY.

The unconscious, or intuition, has an answer to nearly everything. The answer won't necessarily be any good, though. Four related aspects of intuitive judgment deserve separate notice.

First, intuitive judgment works preemptively. It doesn't wait on an explicit question before feeding you judgments. As the flux of experience pours in through your senses, your unconscious evaluates it automatically and sends you feedback. This feedback doesn't cover every possible question — "Does this car salesman have a normal esophagus?" — but it covers the things likely to matter to you. Read the introduction to a brief, and you form intuitive judgments about the merit of the argument as a whole, the ability of the writer, the rightness or wrongness about what happened in the case, and so on. You may revise or discard those judgments as you go on, but they arise in advance of any conscious question.

Second, intuitive judgment works confidently despite great ignorance. As Kahneman puts it, "What you see is all there is." Show people a picture of someone they've never seen before, and ask if the person in the picture is smart or dumb, nice or mean, good or bad. The viewers should say, "I have no idea." But usually they do have an answer, courtesy of their overconfident unconscious, even if they have the sense to keep their mouths shut. We form snap judgments based on virtually no information, and we feel stupidly confident. Skimming the headlines, you see that a Muslim guy shot someone on the street. Whatever your politics, your unconscious will whisper (or maybe shout) "terrorism." Some of us will pause to question that assumption, but the intuitive judgment still flashes into mind. Intuitive judgment uses assumptions to fill gaps in our information. Give someone a couple scraps of information, and they'll make a story out of it.

We might broaden the point here to say, "What *comes to mind* is all there is." You have a trove of knowledge, attitudes, and so on lodged in your brain. You form judgments based only on the information active in your mind at the moment. When you see a headline about a Muslim guy shooting someone, your judgment depends on what happens to be activated in your mind then. If you've just been reading about attacks on Muslim-Americans by fearful bigots, then you're more likely to question whether the shooter acted in self-defense. If you've just been reading about terror attacks by Muslims, you'll likely assume this new shooting was terrorism, too.

"What comes to mind is all there is" brings us back to one of the primary jobs of an advocate: to bring to mind the considerations that move the audience toward your position. Any two people in conversation start with different sets of things in mind. Communication and persuasion only happen when their minds converge on more or less the same set of thoughts and feelings.

Third, intuition substitutes easy questions for hard ones. How is Ford stock going to perform over the next five years? That's a hard question. How much do I like Ford management and Ford cars? That's an easy question, but it tells you little about whether Ford stock is going to rise or fall. Ask yourself the first question, and your intuition will probably answer the second one instead.

Improving decision-making requires us to recognize hard questions when they arise, and to question the intuitive answer that presents itself. That's not easy, though. Sometimes we do recognize hard questions. But others never even arise as questions, because intuition has interpreted and responded as the problem was coming in.

Fourth, everyone's intuition differs. You have yours, I have mine, and each is unique in its information, virtues, and vices. We can't easily guess how someone else will respond to an event or a piece of information — but we still have to guess (with the aid of whatever investigation we can perform).

WE "DECIDE" ONLY OCCASIONALLY, AND ECONOMIZE EVEN THEN.

When we talk about making a decision, we usually mean an explicit, conscious process in which we consider alternatives or puzzle out a mystery — usually resolving some doubt or uncertainty. Most of our thoughts, judgments, conclusions, beliefs don't flow from that sort of process. Gary Klein says that early in his study of decision-making, he asked a veteran firefighter how he made decisions at the scene of a fire. The veteran said he had never made a decision, that fire commanders never make decisions.[1] Nor do the rest of us, mostly (in the sense the commander meant it). The vast bulk of what we think just comes to us.

When we do engage in conscious decision-making, we economize. Generally, we consider alternatives serially, and stop at the first one that seems satisfactory. Unless forced into it, we don't pursue elaborate rational choice strategies. If left to ourselves, even our slow, laborious thinking tends toward simplicity and frugality.

2.3.2 WE THINK LARGELY IN STORIES.

We discussed stories earlier, as an aid to memory. Here we discuss other aspects of stories.

We are creatures of stories. I use "story" loosely here, to refer roughly to any narrative that states or suggests relations between events. Stories come short or long, simple or complex, dry or rich. *"They met; he swooned; she died; then him."* That counts as a story for purposes of this discussion.

Nature wired our brains for stories, just as for finding agency and causation. (Stories reduce largely to agents and causes.) Children in all cultures recognize and respond to stories that follow a goal-focused protagonist encountering a conflict and resolving it. Religions teach largely through stories. Stories organize our lives. Lose your memory of those stories (through Alzheimer's disease, for example), and you lose your identity.

STORIES ORGANIZE INFORMATION AND CARRY POWERFUL IMPLICATIONS.

Stories accomplish a variety of major cognitive feats. They:

- organize information and relate the pieces to each other
- help us remember the information, as one piece brings the next to mind
- evoke unstated facts
- indicate unstated causality and intention, and
- elicit, organize, and direct emotion.

Stories do much of this implicitly. Consider the following passage attributed to Hemingway: *"For sale: baby shoes, never worn."* You'll remember the line because of what was implicit, not what was explicit. But take a dry, unemotional example:

"Workmen installed solar panels on the roof in May. The electric bill for the next month (June) came to $120 — a savings of $30 compared to last June."

An assumption of causality enters your mind instantly, unbidden: *The solar panels caused the reduction in the electricity bill.* Maybe you challenge the assumption, but you can't stop it entering your head. Maybe this June was cooler than last. Maybe the Joneses took a vacation this June but not last. Maybe they replaced old appliances with energy-efficient ones. We don't have near enough information to justify confidence in the solar panels' effect. But chances are, even after I've pointed that out, you *still* feel confidence in the causation hypothesis. All that, from a one-sentence narrative that doesn't say a word (explicitly) about causation. The story "just" selects which of the innumerable details of reality to pick out, and then puts them together. Stories carry tremendous power to suggest causation.

As we gather facts, we start building a story. We revise the story as we go along. If facts come to us erratically or randomly, we have trouble figuring out what to make of them. If they come to us in a way that lines up with some story template in our head, then we form the story more easily. The smoother, more coherent, more naturally a story seems to us as we build it out, the more we'll hold to it — or the more it will hold us.

A fact carries different meanings depending on which story it gets slotted into, and the choice of story in turn can depend on nothing more than the sequence in which the listener hears the facts. Selection and sequence determine which of 10 (or 100) stories you tell. At some level, this seems too obvious to bother saying, but we make choices about selection and sequence far too thoughtlessly, noticing neither the decisions nor their impact.

Suppose jurors first learn from the defense lawyer's opening statement that the cops did not find John's fingerprint on the bloody knife. The prosecutor didn't mention that, and this new fact jars against the story a juror created out of the prosecutor's facts. A juror may conclude the prosecutor lied, and reject the story they heard from the prosecutor. But if the prosecutor includes the no-fingerprint fact in the right sequence with other facts, the absence of a fingerprint may provide *stronger* proof of guilt.

We need to think about — and research, where we can — what story templates likely exist in the minds of judge and clerk and juror. You want to lay out the cookie crumbs so the listener will follow them to your conclusion. Choose the right crumbs and sequence them to mesh with the story templates in their heads, and you'll lead them to your conclusion. Choose the wrong crumbs, or the wrong sequence, and you'll lead them to your opponent's conclusion. Choice and sequencing of facts shape the stories that listeners create in their own minds. That in turn shapes the listener's sense of reality.[2]

STORIES STRUCTURE EMOTIONAL RESPONSES.

Stories have power to direct and shape emotion. Stories do this in multiple ways, but consider just one. The point of view from which a story is told — which character the mental video camera follows around — guides the reader's imagination, empathy, and emotion. You focus on the character you see; you fill in unstated backstory and details about that character's situation; you join their team. That's partly why stories told entirely from the point of view of a rapist or serial killer disturb us. The story makes you feel just a little empathy for the criminal. You can't help that, and it creeps you out. For less revolting examples of this effect, consider the following pair of stories.

Version 1

The coyote left her pup in the den and went in search of food. The pup snuffled as the mother walked off. For hours, the mother moved through the woods, stopping to listen and sniff the wind. At last, she caught the scent of a deer. She stalked the deer and caught sight of three in a clearing. The coyote approached softly, synchronizing her movements with the deer's. Finally, the coyote attacked. She raced toward the smallest one and bit into its neck. The deer jumped, but the coyote held firm, bit deeper, and cut into the throat. After a brief struggle, the deer lay dying. The pup would eat today.

Version 2

The deer slept in a clearing. They were two does and a little spotted fawn. The three rose before the sun and started their daily trek through woods and clearings, looking for flowers, weeds, and fruit. The fawn scampered around the adults and occasionally succeeded in getting his mother to play with him. At the third clearing, the fawn ran around again, then stopped to eat some clover. Then a flash of color to the side, a terrible low noise, and a searing pain in his neck. The does snorted in alarm. The fawn struggled, but his throat was ripped open, he couldn't breathe, and a huge weight pulled him down. As he lay dying, a grey beast paced around him.

Individual responses vary, but for most of us, each version will draw empathy to its own protagonist. Of course we can make the effort to think about other points of view and see where those other views take our emotions. But to do that, we have to swim upstream against our natural responses. Given only one version, we rarely make the effort. Stories shape our emotions, often profoundly, often irreversibly.

In a legal context, however, a second effect may overpower the general structuring of empathy — that is, the story's effect of focusing scrutiny on the main actor. Consider these stories:[3]

Version A

Susan was driving on the interstate when her car started to stall. There was hardly any traffic. She pulled mostly off the road, but not completely. Her driver's side wheels rested on the painted line at the side of the road. Susan got out of the car and opened the hood. After finding nothing wrong, she decided to try starting the car again. She stood up from under the hood, and she poked her head out to the driver's side, to see if the road was clear. As she did that, a motor home was passing, and its side-view mirror smashed Susan's face. The mirror threw Susan several feet backward and broke her jaw, several teeth, her cheekbone, and other bones in her face. Susan was in her 20's. She had been pretty. The accident disfigured her and distorted her speech.

Here, you follow Susan. You identify and sympathize with her, but you also evaluate her. You can only evaluate what you see, and since all you see are Susan's actions, that's what you scrutinize. Most of us will fault her for not pulling all the way off the road, and for sticking her face out into traffic. She probably could have gotten off the road, and even if she couldn't, she didn't have to stick her head out. We feel terrible for her, but she seems responsible. Now consider a different version:

Version B

Karen was driving a motor home down the interstate, going about 60 miles per hour. About a quarter-mile ahead, she could see a car pulled off the road. The engine hood was up. Karen was in the right-hand lane of a four-lane, divided highway. There was no traffic. The left-hand lane was clear. Karen stayed in the right-hand lane. Within that lane, Karen didn't move to the left. She didn't slow down. She got closer. At least 100 yards away, she could see the car wasn't fully off the road. She couldn't tell if there was a person looking under the hood or not. Karen stayed on a path to skim past the car. As she passed, a girl looked out from behind the hood. Karen's side-view mirror smashed the girl's face and threw her backward. The impact broke the girl's jaw, several teeth, her cheekbone, and other bones in her face. The girl was in her 20's. She had been pretty. The accident disfigured her and distorted her speech.

In this version, you still see the two points on which to criticize Susan, but you focus on the motor home driver. We may still hold Susan partly responsible, but most of us will put the bulk of the blame on Karen. In part, this is because we have information about Karen that we didn't have before. But we also scrutinize and evaluate Karen more because we focus on her.

The same thing happens in briefs and trials. In reading a brief or sitting through a trial, we judge people, and we can only judge the person we look at. What you see is all there is. The spotlight focuses moral scrutiny along with attention.

The importance of stories may seem obvious for narrating events, but what about all the other stuff we talk about? Arguments may include references to events, but they don't take the structure of a story. They consist of observations, qualifications, implications, and so on, most of which are not events. Nonetheless, as a rule of thumb, you want to put into story form anything that reasonably can be put into story form. Stories can apply to a broader range of material than you might expect. Behind every law, there's a story. In generic form, the story of a law (in a lawsuit) goes like this: "*We had a problem. We created this law to fix the problem. Now here we are with these guys flouting it and making trouble again.*" A story of this type might only take three sentences, but it can give the law impact it would not otherwise exert.

IMAGINING A THING MAKES IT REAL.

When we actually imagine a thing, it feels more real or true. Conjure an idea in your head, imagine it vividly, and it will then seem more likely than it did 10 minutes earlier. Watch a movie in which a serial killer hides in some poor couple's attic, and you'll feel a little buzz of apprehension next time you go up to your attic. Listen to a vivid conspiracy theory about a real-life politician involved with CIA agents in a cocaine deal, who orders the murder of various witnesses and political enemies. The story may make you feel more negative toward that politician the rest of your life, even if you consciously discount the story. Conjure an image of a trespasser skulking around your house, and you'll feel an urge to go check the locks. Merely imagining a thing gives it some seeming reality in your head. The more easily and fully we imagine it, the more real it feels.

WE SPOT NARRATIVE INCONGRUITIES EASILY.

When someone tells a story or otherwise elicits imagination, we spot narrative incongruities easily, better than we spot other errors. Where we have enough background information, we easily spot things that don't fit. Overhear a man's voice say "I think I'm pregnant," and your ears perk up automatically. The brain detects and responds to that sort of abnormality within two-tenths of a second.[4]

Spotting incongruities differs from spotting errors, though. An error may still fit in with our expectations and thus pass unnoticed. Many people won't stir when asked how many animals of each kind Moses took into the ark. As Kahneman explains, the question puts you in mind of the Bible, and Moses fits into the set of expectations that arise from the reference. So even if you grew up with Bible stories, you may not notice that the question should have been about Noah, not Moses.

TOO MANY FACTS CAN HURT IMAGINATION AND PLAUSIBILITY.

More detail can sometimes hurt the plausibility of a story. A sketch may carry more force than a detailed picture. Readers will fill in the gaps of a story with assumptions. But if you give them every detail, that can get in the way of their imaginative engagement. Worse, if some detail in the writing jars against the reader's expectations, it can spur skepticism. Finding the sweet spot between too much and too little detail requires fine judgment.

2.3.3 WE NAVIGATE LIFE LARGELY BY MEANS OF SNAP JUDGMENTS, BUT VERY IMPERFECTLY.

The natural substantive tendencies of our snap-judgment apparatus require careful attention, because snap judgments play an enormous role in our lives.

WE BELIEVE WHAT COMES TO MIND EASILY.

Our sense of truth depends on how easily an idea comes to mind. First, the more easily we can understand or produce support for an idea, the more true it feels. Second, the more narrative or emotional plausibility an idea has, the more true it feels.

In our minds, cognitive ease indicates truth. I make a statement. You search your mind for confirmation of what I said. If confirming information comes to mind quickly and easily, you believe what I said. If you have a hard time finding confirmation, you feel skeptical. This makes a certain amount of sense as a criterion of truth, but it relies on arbitrary chance. Cognitive ease depends on what thoughts and feelings happen to be readily available at any given moment. That in turn depends on what billboards we drove past as we came into work, what we heard on the radio, what's been in the news, what we were talking about with a friend last night, and a million other contingencies.

Cognitive ease can also directly oppose evidentiary weight.

For example, ask one group of people to each write a list of three times they acted generously. Ask another group to each write a list of 10 times they did so. The second group will have a harder time. They'll have to search their memories longer. Most will strain to come up with 10 times, though they surely could if they had access to all the memories stored in their unconscious. After the groups have made their lists, ask them each to rate how generous they are. The second group has produced more evidence of generosity than the first group. The first group, however, found it easy, and the second group found it hard. So the people in the first group will give higher self-ratings of generosity than the folks in the second group. Cognitive ease signals truth; difficulty signals falsehood. It's wrong, but that's how it is.

As a corollary effect, since we're lazy, cognitive ease makes us feel good. And positive feeling opens us up, reduces skepticism, makes us more willing to believe.

Narrative or emotional plausibility also reads as truth to us. We can see plausibility as a kind of cognitive ease — the ease of imagining or picturing a thing. For example, consider "the Linda problem" devised by Kahneman and his research partner, Amos Tversky:

> Linda is thirty-one years old, single, outspoken, and very bright. She majored in philosophy. As a student, she was deeply concerned with issues of discrimination and social justice, and also participated in antinuclear demonstrations.
> Which alternative is more probable?
> Linda is a bank teller.
> Linda is a bank teller and is active in the feminist movement.

Even though I've warned you that this is a "problem" and have suggested that your intuition will lead you astray, most readers will still say the second option is more probable. That's obviously wrong. (It's *always* more probable that a person meets condition X than that the person meets both condition X *and* condition Y.) Yet even if you catch the problem, it still *feels* like the second option is more probable, and it's still hard to actively veto that feeling.

Similarly, given a few shreds of information, we automatically construct the most plausible story we can with those shreds; and that story will feel true. Someone tells you that a guy drove home from a bar at night, and on the way ran into a light pole. You hear a story about a drunk driver. You fill in that assumption without even noticing you did so. Think about the story a week later, and you'll remember the richer version you imagined, forgetting that you filled in the details.[5]

FAMILIARITY FEELS LIKE TRUTH.

Familiarity makes things seem truer. Even for ideas you disagree with, the more you've heard it, the more serious it seems you should take it. The more voices express anti-Muslim bigotry, the more people will adopt it as true and proper, and the more seriously the rest of us will take it even if we oppose it. The "mere exposure effect" helps to explain both the ubiquity of Coke ads and the power of climates of opinion. An opponent makes some frivolous argument, but by the end of the brief it seems almost serious, through the cheap magic of mere exposure and repetition. Familiarity breeds the feeling of truth.

INTUITION DOESN'T GET STATISTICS.

We don't naturally thrill much to numbers, statistics, or math, and we have no inborn ear for them — what they mean, how to use them, how they inform judgment and decision making. Knowledge of these recent human inventions may inform effortful thought, but it does not inform intuitive judgment. Even scientists who routinely work with statistics have shabby intuition about them. Our intuitive blindness to numerical reasoning plays out in several ways.

First, particulars dominate generalities. The details of a single instance out of millions can hijack our perception of a general class. A handful of violent attacks in the United States over 15 years, involving a handful of Muslims, have colored public perception of millions of American Muslims, and 1-1/2 billion Muslims worldwide. Statistics don't cure the misperception. Statistics don't get under our skin and shape how we see the world. Particulars do that.

Intuition does care about generalities; it just gets its generalities in the dumbest way possible — by extrapolating directly from whatever particulars grab attention. In a study of the relative impacts of anecdotes and statistics, Richard Nisbett and Eugene Borgida noted, "Subjects' unwillingness to deduce the particular from the general was matched only by their willingness to infer the general from the particular."[6] You don't get far fighting anti-Muslim bigotry (or anything else) with statistics and generalities. You fight stories with stories.

Second, we don't really believe in randomness, and we ignore reversion to the mean. Most things in life (performance on the golf course, performance on a math test, how many jellybeans fit into a particular jar, how well a company or a stock performs this year, etc.) involve constant variation within some range. The variation arises for reasons we can't discern, predict, or control and that don't last. We might as well call it luck, or chance. Most outliers revert to the mean as time goes on, and that should form our starting expectation. But it doesn't. If the company had an unusually good year, that must mean its CEO is brilliant. If the pole vaulter performed exceptionally well, he must have had a breakthrough in training. Of course, there must be a cause for the exceptional performance, but it may be an essentially meaningless complex of things that we can't divine and can't rely on — chance.

Third, we just don't get numbers. If we don't do the annoying work of thinking hard, we fall into absurd errors. For starters, we tend to focus on absolute numbers rather than percentages or, relatedly, to ignore the denominator when chances appear as fractions. An alarmingly high percentage of people will opt for an 8 in 100 chance of a good thing, over a 1 in 10 chance.

Similarly, we handle ranges of variation poorly and erratically.

Depending on the circumstances, the average will dominate the range in our thinking so that we irrationally discount the amount of variation. In other circumstances, the extremes will dominate the average. We move from one error to the other, jumping over the numerically rational approach. In handling the extremes, sometimes we erroneously compress them, and other times we erroneously exaggerate them. We only arrive at whatever meaning can be taken from a series of numbers if we endure hard, conscious thought.

Along the same lines, we mistake the unlikely for the magical. You think about your brother, and as you're thinking about him, he calls you. Even if you think psychic nonsense is nonsense, you'll get a little thrill of the eerie. In the time you took to read the last sentence, an indefinitely large number of things happened in the world. In that mass of events, in just those couple seconds, hundreds of thousands of bizarre coincidences occurred around the world. An industrious peddler, given a list of just a single day's bizarre coincidences, could make a compelling demonstration of true magic at work in the world. We fall for that sort of thing, because the intuitive mind does not believe in coincidence.

Fourth, we misjudge small risks. Some we disregard entirely because they don't attract our attention with picturesque images or anecdotes, or emotionally loaded words. Apart from the elderly, or parents of small children, we mostly disregard the risk of choking to death on our food. We mostly disregard the risk of asphyxiation from a wood stove or gas furnace. These risks matter, though, and they merit some level of concern greater than zero.

On the other hand, we dramatically overestimate small risks that come to mind with emotion attached. People exist who say they won't use seatbelts in their cars, for fear of getting stuck if their car goes into a lake. We get worked up over tiny increases in our risk of cancer, far out of proportion to the amount of increased risk, even as we ignore graver increases of the risk of osteoporosis or other less charged maladies.

In these cases, we do seem to respond irrationally. These cases differ from loss aversion, the endowment effect, and desperate gambles (discussed below), where we have a non-linear scale of values. Here, we just seize on emotionally loaded details and make judgments we would not endorse on reflection.

Finally, quantities don't matter much to emotion. We respond about as strongly to the murder of one little girl as to the murder of 100 little girls. If you show people a picture of a seabird soaked by an oil spill and ask for donations on behalf of 2,000 dead birds, people will give about the same amount as if you ask on behalf of 200,000 birds. The more people or events involved in a tragedy, the harder it is to focus on narrative details in a way that comports with the numbers. As Stalin supposedly said, the death of one man is a tragedy, but the death of a million is a statistic. Emotion comes from particulars, not numbers.

In addressing judges, clerks, or jurors, we should take special care with how we think and talk about numbers and statistics. You can't assume easy or accurate comprehension. Consider using carefully designed visuals. We understand visual representations of numbers more easily than mere talk about them. Most importantly, remember that stories and specifics dominate. To reason well, we do need accurate, carefully presented numbers. But we must support them with details that carry force.

WE EXTRAPOLATE FROM LIKES AND DISLIKES.

Suppose you meet a guy and instantly like him because he charms you with friendliness and self-effacing humor. You'll also be inclined to think he's responsible, morally decent, and hard-working. It would pain you a little to think of him negatively in any respect, because you like him. For all you know, he may be a con man who steals from old ladies. But because you like him, you won't wait for the evidence. This is the halo effect. The effect works in reverse, too. If you meet the guy and he strikes you as smug, rude, and condescending, you'll assume he falls short in other ways, too. You'll *want* to think badly of him generally.

The halo effect holds an important implication for legal argument: Make yourself decent and likable. If you come off as unlikable, judges and jurors and clerks will look for ways to reject your case. They'll be more ready to distrust your characterizations of facts and authorities, to look for objections, to interpret your statements in a negative light, to grant the other side more credence.

No one tries to be unlikable, but plenty achieve it anyhow. Be reasonable, fair, decent, and grown-up. Don't whine. Don't insult. Avoid snark and snidery. Keep a lid on anger, mostly. Deal with opposing parties and arguments respectfully. Keep perspective. Take account of your judge's pet peeves. Show consideration for the judge's and jury's time. And so on.

The halo effect is such an old, obvious insight that the more sophisticated of us want to reject it. That's a mistake. Mere stupid likability carries enormous power. Willy Loman was wrong about a lot, and he made a mess of his life, but he was right about the usefulness of being well-liked.

FAST JUDGMENTS AREN'T NECESSARILY BAD JUDGMENTS.

If you chronicle the ways in which human thought goes wrong, it's easy to take a pessimistic view of intuition. That can lead us to over-value laborious conscious thought. But we probably developed these mechanisms of fast thinking because they pay off, on average. Slow thinking carries a heavy price in time, energy, and opportunity costs as scarce mental space gets used up. More importantly maybe, slow thinking carries its own flaws.

Gerd Gigerenzer argues convincingly (to me, anyway) that many fast-but-flawed decision-making processes perform as well or better than slow, costly processes. This holds true in a range of areas from catching a baseball to creating an investment portfolio. A reflexive, unthinking bias in favor of slow, laborious mental processes would probably hurt as much as help.

How much it makes sense to trust in fast thinking over slow thinking depends on the circumstances.

EXPERT INTUITION RARELY OR NEVER APPLIES IN LAW.

We develop expert intuition with tasks we perform many, many times and for which we get fast, unambiguous feedback that clearly shows whether we performed well or badly. Thus, for example, most every experienced driver of cars has expert intuition for braking at a stop sign or slowing to make a turn.

Most, or at least many, things in life do not lend themselves to the development of expert intuition, because they do not take place in a "high-validity" environment. Most things we care about involve too much complexity, too much delay in feedback, too many confounding factors. In those situations, we can't know precisely what we did right and precisely what we did wrong. We can't become effortlessly expert in such matters.

A legal practice does not furnish a high-validity environment in which expert intuition can develop. That doesn't mean a thoughtful veteran has nothing over this year's law school graduates. We develop knowledge over time, and our intuition does get better. But probably not as much as we think. Most of us don't get hundreds or thousands of iterations of exactly the same thing. Most situations present far too much complexity to say exactly what drove the result.

The lack of expert intuition in law suggests two points. First, we should consider jury-testing for trial and judge-testing for motions and other disputes. Focus groups provide insights into jurors. For insights into judges, usually we can only get feedback from other lawyers — though where the stakes justify it, we can spend the money on a focus group of retired judges.

Second, without cultivating an unhealthy distrust of our intuition, we should devise explicit, institutionalized ways to mitigate its foibles.

~

WE'RE STUCK with the quirks of intuitive judgment. God or

nature has cooked them into our brains. Only a fool would try to exploit them where an opponent gets to point out errors, and a professional skeptic reads with a squinty eye. But these points do imply a few useful suggestions. *First*, make everything as easy as possible to understand and confirm. In general, the more sophisticated and impressive an argument sounds, the harder it will be to understand, and the more feebly it will punch. Obvious simplicities beat sophisticated subtleties. (Maybe this sounds obvious, but not one lawyer in ten follows this rule.) *Second*, prime the reader with particulars. An argument puts concrete words, details, specifics, examples, hypotheticals, metaphors, and so on in front of the reader. Select them to trigger other supporting thoughts and feelings. *Third*, enlist the reader's imagination. Conjure a scene that shows the bad consequences you're warning of. Do the same with the good consequences you say will follow a decision in your favor. But take care to make it plausible, without adding so much detail that it gets in the way of the reader's imagination. *Finally*, learn as much as possible about the expectations your audience brings, and find a way to work with them, not against them.

2.3.4 WE BELIEVE WHAT WE FEEL INCLINED TO BELIEVE — EVEN AFTER HARD, CONSCIOUS REASONING — BUT IT'S COMPLICATED.

We believe what we feel inclined to believe. This old scrap of cynical wisdom is the most clichéd and most profound of all the ideas in this book. Everyone knows this, but some think the point applies only to stupid people, or only in moments of weakness, or only to decisions that don't matter. That gets it badly wrong. All of us, however smart, in matters profound and trivial, believe what we feel inclined to believe — sort of.

What we feel inclined to believe depends on many factors. It can change in minor ways over short periods, and in major ways over long periods. Furthermore, as we go through life we form contradictory beliefs and store them up. Which of them become active at any given time may determine what we feel inclined to believe right then, right there.

COMING TO BELIEVE SOMETHING AND FINDING JUSTIFICATION FOR THE BELIEF ARE TWO DIFFERENT THINGS, AND USUALLY OCCUR IN THAT ORDER.

We don't usually come to believe things because we see all the evidence and realize that it compels the belief. Typically, we believe because something other than cosmic rationality draws us to the belief. Usually, the belief fits in with our existing worldview, our existing beliefs, so it makes sense to us. Beyond that, something about the belief just feels right. And that's usually enough to believe it. To adopt a belief, we don't need — and almost never have — what we would deem, on searching critical review, evidence sufficient to justify the belief.

Having been drawn to a belief, though, we often search out evidence to support it. Or maybe we won't, depending. The search for justification may strengthen our confidence in the belief, but usually we'll have slanted the search. Usually we'll have over-looked or dismissed evidence that undercuts the belief. Those with exceptional diligence and integrity may abandon beliefs they're drawn to, when the effort to verify the belief repeatedly fails. But we don't have many of these heroes of intellectual integrity. To pick a merely rhetorical number from thin air: Maybe one out of a thou-sand people have this degree of intellectual integrity. And even these heroes only have time to inspect a handful of the thousands of beliefs they form. Most of us, most of the time, believe what we feel inclined to believe.

We come to most of our beliefs, in whatever realm, through a process very different from rigorous, rational evaluation of adequate evidence. In our everyday lives, at home, in our profes-sions, in our families, everywhere, we come to hold beliefs for reasons other than the compelling weight of the evidence. Bob thinks he got transferred to another department because his boss didn't like him. The evidence? His boss seems cold to him and doesn't talk to him much. That evidence doesn't impress you, but Bob feels certain. We're all Bobs. We feel pulled to ideas that fit our sense of things.

As we've discussed, stories exert special power over us. A plausible story convinces us even when it shouldn't, often more powerfully than adequate evidence would. We're plausible-story creatures, not critical-analysis-of-evidence creatures.

To be sure, we do sometimes revise beliefs when later experience forces us away from them. Sometimes that later experience consists of critical scrutiny. On learning more about the accident involving the driver who looked down to pick up his cigarette from under his seat, you might decide he didn't cause the wreck after all. More often, though, our changes in belief come about just because we get pulled, we don't know quite how, to some other belief. Over the years, our beliefs change. Usually, these changes seem to come about on their own. We didn't make them happen; something else did. We can look back and make up stories about how they happened, but we didn't just scoop up a bunch of evidence, sift it critically, and accept a conclusion thus forced upon us.

Sometimes we hold stubbornly to a belief even after we've seen strong, contrary evidence. Costly, compelling evidence shows you're a lousy stock picker, but you keep picking stocks. Dozens of projects like yours have gone dramatically over budget and over time, but you still risk heavy losses based on an optimistic budget. And so on.

Before getting too moralistic about such things, though, let's acknowledge that it's hard even to say what evidence would suffice to justify or compel a belief. An extreme case helps drive the point home. Consider Daniel Dunglas Home, the first psychic.[7]

I present a long discussion here of what will strike you as an odd, marginal topic. And so it is. But the weird topic throws into relief difficulties and uncertainties of rational inquiry that we don't see against an ordinary background.

Daniel Dunglas Home is probably one of the greatest magicians who ever lived, though he presented himself as a spiritualist, not a magician. In the second half of the 19th Century, DD Home

performed hundreds of séances, mostly in England, but also inter-
nationally. He performed séances for Emperor Napoleon III and
for the Tsar of Russia. He claimed that the effects produced in his
séances were caused by ghosts. Home never took payment directly
for a séance, though he accepted lodging and support from
patrons. He suffered from tuberculosis, and he failed in various
attempts to support himself in other ways. Home's tubercular body
was slight and weak.

Home produced effects that astounded his audiences. He
produced these effects for intelligent, critical, skeptical audiences
including scientists. He conducted séances in the parlors of his
patrons — not on stages or other places he could freely rig. He
conducted them in what Victorians considered good lighting, as
well as in darker light. He invited skeptics to examine the room
and the objects in it for trick devices. No one ever caught Home
cheating — setting aside a handful of claims made only years after
Home died. Sober, sane, intelligent, educated witnesses, skeptics as
well as believers, scientists as well as laity, wrote that they saw
large, heavy tables move across the floor with nobody touching
them and no sign of mechanical trickery. They saw and heard
accordions play music, though the instruments sat across the room
with no one near them. They saw heavy tables and pianos levitate
inches or even feet up in the air. They heard loud, unaccountable
rappings from all over the long tables. They saw heavy tables
shake violently, like a ship in a storm. They saw and felt "spirit
hands" emerge from tables and touch them. They saw and heard
bells ring, though the bells sat on the carpet, well away from any
person and with no sign of string, wire, or any other trick device.
The participants saw Home himself levitate, with several inches of
open air under his feet. Then they saw him levitate to the ceilings
of rooms — ceilings in parlor rooms in which Home probably
could not have rigged an overhead apparatus, and which his audiences could inspect. Home produced these effects for prominent
skeptics who hated him, feuded with him, and wanted nothing
more than to expose him as a fraud. (The poet Robert Browning

was one of these enemies.) But none of them ever caught him cheating.

Scientists and professional magicians speculated about how Home produced his effects. Maybe he played a little harmonica to simulate the accordion playing, and people got confused about where the sound was coming from. A chemist speculated that the accordion effect had something to do with a "monster locket attached to Mr. Home's watch-chain," but the value of this insight has been lost to history, because the chemist neglected to explain what a "monster locket" is. Others speculated that Home hypnotized his audiences and made them think they saw and heard things they didn't actually see and hear. Experts in hypnosis discredited this theory. Maybe Home had confederates slip into the room unnoticed and use their own hands as "spirit hands." Or maybe the spirit hands were just Home's feet, or even his actual hands, or fake hands at the end of sticks. (But you'd think someone, sometime would have caught out these tricks just by grabbing a spirit hand and holding on to it.) Maybe Home's levitations just consisted of climbing up onto furniture in a dark room, or playing tricks with shadows. Or maybe the audiences, however intelligent and educated, exaggerated what they saw. But no one ever proved any of these explanations, and none seem sufficient to account for Home's long record of success.

Most remarkably, though, Home twice conducted séances in controlled conditions in a sort of laboratory created by the scientist William Crookes. Crookes had done pioneering work with spectroscopy and vacuum tubes and had discovered the element thallium. Crookes recruited two other witnesses, an amateur astronomer and a Serjeant-at-Law and former Member of Parliament, to observe. Crookes also had a laboratory assistant present.

Crookes rigged up two experiments. First, he put an accordion inside a metal cage under a table. Crookes bought the accordion himself, to make sure no one rigged it. Home held the accordion from the top of the cage with one hand, the keys downward. With the four observers watching, the accordion played a few notes, Home's hand only holding it by the end (the end with no keys).

Crookes' assistant crouched under the table to watch, and he said the accordion was expanding and contracting, as if being played. It played a simple tune. Home took the accordion out of the cage, put it in the hand of one of the witnesses, and took his own hand off it. The accordion continued playing. Home put it back in the cage, and the accordion floated there. Neither Crookes nor the other witnesses could explain what they saw.

Crookes set up another experiment. He placed a three-foot wooden board with one end supported by the edge of a table and the rest of the board hanging over empty air. The far end of the board hung from a spring balance that could measure the downward pressure on that end of the board. The idea was that if you sat at the table, you couldn't physically do anything to make the far end of the board move downward. Crookes confirmed this by climbing up on the table and standing on the edge of the board there. With his whole weight on it, he could only put two pounds of downward pressure on the far end of the board. Slight, unmuscular Home sat at the table and put his fingers near the board. The board started moving and eventually exerted three pounds of downward pressure on the far end of the board, half again as much as Crookes had done with his whole weight. Then Home put a little bell and a matchbox on the table between his fingers and the near edge of the board, so he couldn't touch the board. Again the far end of the board moved downward. Crookes later replicated the experiment by putting a bowl of water on the near end of the board, above the fulcrum, and allowing Home only to put his fingers in the water at the surface. Then Crookes rigged a device to make a physical mark that registered how much the far end of the board moved — to avoid relying only on observation and memory. Again Home succeeded.

Crookes could find no natural explanation of Home's effects; nor could anybody else. Some scientist-skeptics responded by trashing Crookes' reputation. Crookes, they said, was an unobservant, gullible fool, and so were the other three witnesses. Probably, one wrote, a passing train caused a rumble that forced the far end of the board downward. These suggestions hint at desperation. As some observers noted, if the word of Crookes and his fellow observers couldn't be trusted on the simple, observable facts, then how could the word of any scientist, on the facts of any experiment, be trusted? For that matter, how could anyone's word, on anything, be trusted? How indeed.

Later, though, in connection with lesser mediums who got exposed as frauds, Crookes did reveal himself as either an embarrassingly complete dupe or a willing confederate — at least where the frauds were pretty young women he was rumored to be bedding. For example, a young woman named Florence Cooke said she could allow the spirit of one Katie King to materialize in Florence's own body. Florence proved her claim by donning a nightgown and saying she was now Katie King. Florence would then, through her gowned self, allow Katie to have tea with the séance guests. A stupider feat can hardly be imagined. Yet Crookes at least professed to believe that Katie really had taken up lodgings in Florence's body. Crookes vouched for other pretty young mediums, too.

We reject the idea that DD Home possessed paranormal powers — at least I reject it — but the story should make us uneasy all the same. We can't say that *nothing* could convince us that "paranormal" phenomena exist. That would make us irrational. And Home's record does constitute substantial evidence for the paranormal. We can speculate about the natural causes, but we can only speculate. Crookes' experiments need not convince us. Scientists have repeatedly proven themselves easy dupes, even with crude, juvenile magic tricks. As a class, scientists do seem gullible when dealing with magicians. Crookes himself was either a dupe or was willing to misrepresent his own beliefs in order to get into bed with young women. And other magicians claiming no paranormal powers have died with their secrets and left their colleagues baffled. Even so, we can't fully dismiss Crookes' experiments with Home. The experiments do seem well-designed. They produced objective, observable effects. And it wasn't just Crookes vouching for the experiments. Three other observers vouched for them, too. Maybe Home or Crookes just found three other liars.

Who knows. Still, even apart from the Crookes experiments, Home's entire record remains significant.

The problem of DD Home illustrates in an extreme way the problems that apply less visibly in mundane settings: We can't easily decide what counts as meaningful evidence. We can't easily decide how to evaluate the stuff that does count. We can't easily decide how much evidence suffices to justify a given belief. When we knuckle down to examine evidence critically, our eyes fool us, our minds play tricks on us, we make mistakes and exaggerate.

Objective evidence requires interpretation, and it usually allows a range of interpretations. For example, the English epidemiologist Bradford Hill proposed an influential set of criteria for evaluating evidence — in particular, the mix of weak and uncertain evidence that relates to medical or public health matters. These criteria amount largely to common sense, and formalizing them serves as much to honor uncertainty as to beat it back. The criteria do little to avoid debate when applied to particular matters.

On any given issue, within the range of reasonable interpretations of whatever we count as evidence, we're apt to move to whatever corner we feel inclined toward, for reasons we couldn't fully specify. Whatever you think of Daniel Dunglas Home, your belief does not spring solely from the evidence we can itemize and label. Your belief arises from that evidence, thrown into a mixer with a bunch of other aspects of your preexisting worldview, the separate pieces of which you could not catalog and fully justify.

These points are as banal and trite as they are profound, but they bear emphasis because we so easily slide into thinking that people form beliefs through critical analysis of evidence. We fall for this illusion because we see our conscious, critical thought. We hear our voices jabbering away in our heads as we think things over. We don't see the rest of the iceberg shaping our beliefs.

The problems of critical analysis apply in law, obviously. Plaintiff lawyer, defense lawyer, judge, clerk, or juror — we each have a bent; we each lean this way or that. We vary in what we make of a pile of evidence. A lawyer errs grossly — but charmingly, quaintly, comically — in thinking that by laying out facts and law in a rational argument, we must surely bring a judge or clerk or juror to our view.

THINGS CONSTRAIN WHAT WE FEEL INCLINED TO BELIEVE.

We all believe a host of unpleasant things that we wish weren't so. We can't feel inclined to believe just any pretty thought.

The outside world constrains what we feel inclined to believe. You don't incline toward the belief that you can make yourself invisible, or that pigs fly or life is but a dream or tiny green men live in your head. Unless you drop acid or develop a mental illness, you will never feel inclined to believe these things. Experience is given to us. We mold the raw flux of sensation into the forms we perceive — but we mold it only within limits. We can't mold experience into just any form we choose, and we don't feel inclined to do so. If your beliefs didn't match the world reasonably well, you'd walk into traffic and die in a puddle of blood.

But the objective world doesn't constrain belief too tightly. We can and do indulge all sorts of errors that stop short of killing us but lead us into misfortune. Misled and mistaken, we elect fools and charlatans to run the country. Misunderstanding how people work, we mishandle our bosses, our employees, our neighbors, our spouses, our kids. Under erroneous beliefs about other nations, we bumble into wars, mismanage occupied territories, and spawn decades of instability throughout entire regions. The objective world constrains human belief tightly enough that we have not yet gone extinct (give us time though), yet not so tightly as to prevent us making a mess of things.

As I've mentioned, the culture and society we live in also constrain what we feel inclined to believe. If you grew up in a Christian community, you will never feel inclined to believe in the reality of Kartikeya, son of Shiva and Parvati, as the god of war commanding an army of male gods.

As I've also mentioned, our physical brains, and our brain chemistry, constrain what we're inclined to believe. These include relatively stable things like neural circuits, and more variable things, like the cocktail of chemicals sloshing around in the body and brain at any moment. The cocktail varies for each of us over time, with different personal norms and ranges of variation. Some people are moody, some happy, some glum, some impulsive.

Our personal experience, aside from things common to the culture, also constrains what we feel inclined to believe. We've each had experiences that strongly pull us toward this or that belief. If you experienced what you interpreted as a miracle, you'll likely believe in miracles, probably for the rest of your life. If Uri Geller tricked you into thinking he bent your house key with only the powers of his marvelous mind, you might, like Clint Eastwood, embarrass your friends by endorsing Geller on his website. If a cop once assaulted you for no good reason, you'll probably take a dim view of cops. So it is with more or less everything.

Circumstances and social psychology also influence what we feel inclined to believe. This influence goes beyond the particulars of moment-to-moment experience. Social psychologists are cataloging an array of situations that systematically nudge us in one direction or another. For example, if you're in a position of power, you'll exaggerate how powerful you are and tend to believe the potential upsides for a course of action will come true, and the downsides won't. Thus, politicians are at greater risk of sending Weiner pictures to young interns, and so on.

Finally, our worldviews constrain what we can feel inclined to believe. At each moment, we possess a mass of existing thoughts and feelings — values, ideological commitments, beliefs, attitudes, convictions, and so on. Call this a worldview. It's not especially coherent or consistent, but it holds you in its grip. No one veers wildly from one set of values, beliefs, and attitudes to another. From where you are today, you can't just pick and choose what you'll feel and believe tomorrow. Today you're a hardcore libertarian. You can't choose to be a communist tomorrow. You can't even choose to *desire* to be a communist. You don't control your thoughts and feelings as much as they control you. Your worldview changes as you bump through life, but it has mass and inertia. The older you are, the larger and more developed your worldview has grown, the more inertia it has built up, the more neural connections have built up to write your beliefs into the physical substance of your brain. Damascene conversions don't happen very often.

Everyone's worldview includes a desire to hold true beliefs, so we can navigate the world without stepping into holes. But that desire sits alongside others, including the desire to feel good, to hold comforting beliefs, to avoid the discomfort of doubt, to avoid the challenge to our identities that comes from questioning important beliefs, to fit in with our families and friends and communities, and so on. Life presents more complexity than any piece of fiction. Just as a novel allows multiple reasonable interpretations, so do most things in life. The world rarely limits us to a single possible belief. Of the live options, we necessarily end up with one chosen by us (or for us) according to a vast network of factors. We would reject many of these factors as irrelevant and irrational if they presented themselves to us consciously, but they don't.

Our possible beliefs stay tethered to reality, but the tether is long.

Every judge, every clerk, every juror will believe according to an impenetrable mass of forces other than the explicit evidence and arguments. The same holds for you.

IGNORANCE EXPANDS OUR RANGE OF POTENTIAL BELIEFS.

Even if a complete, perfect understanding of the facts would narrow you down to only one of the answers you can believe at the moment, you never have a complete, perfect understanding of the facts. On most things, you know practically nothing. That expands the range of things you can believe.

We never investigate and analyze things thoroughly — at least not concerning anything worth bothering to investigate in the first place. First, what would it even mean to "thoroughly" investigate and analyze the facts? There's always more to know. The foremost expert on the effects of increasing the minimum wage surely hasn't read everything potentially relevant to the issue. There's much too much to read. And beyond mere reading, you'd need to conduct experiments, original historical research, interviews, and so on. Second, we don't have time to perform even a limited investigation of everything we form a judgment about. You go to work, you come home, you make dinner, and if you don't have kids, you've got a couple free hours a day before you go to bed. Two hundred hours' work won't buy you expertise on any complex subject, but where will you find even a mere 200 hours to investigate the science on climate change? How will you come up with another 200 to look into police violence, 200 more to research racial disparities in housing, or the Syrian civil war, or the advantages of breastfeeding, or the costs of heating your house with natural gas? We hold beliefs on a multitude of things for which our investigation would rationally justify only saying, "I have no idea." But what're we gonna do? We have to make decisions, which requires forming at least tentative conclusions, which tend to harden into lasting beliefs.

That applies in law, too, of course. You, your opponent, the judge, and the jurors may all have some relevant experience and expertise, but probably less than any of you think. Unwarranted confidence in unspecified beliefs creates a minefield to navigate in every brief and every trial.

WE BELIEVE WHICHEVER POSSIBLE ANSWER APPEALS MOST TO THE FEELINGS AND THOUGHTS WORKING MOST STRONGLY WITHIN US AT THE TIME.

Of the beliefs possible for us at a given time, we usually accept the one that fits most consistently with the beliefs and feelings active within us at the time. If we already have a belief that covers the question, we tend to go on believing it. Overturning an existing belief takes work, and the more deeply entrenched the belief, the more work to overturn it. If we face a new question, we go with the answer that appeals to the assortment of feelings and thoughts working most strongly in us at the time.

For example, I'm not a climate scientist, and I don't follow the science at all seriously. But I have the following preexisting beliefs: I believe science does a decent job, over time, of honing in on the truth. I believe a broad consensus among scientists in a range of related disciplines, over decades, provides a strong indication of truth. I believe certain news outlets generally provide reasonably accurate reports. I believe that when a variety of those outlets report similar information over years, the reports likely get it right. I've seen many news reports suggesting that for decades a broad consensus has prevailed among scientists on the issue of climate change. I believe that on important practical matters, public policy should follow a strong consensus among scientists. So my existing beliefs create for me a new belief in climate change and the urgency of government action to mitigate the problem. I didn't choose to believe this. I just do. In a sense, the world and my pre-existing beliefs chose the belief for me. New information could change this belief, but my climate-change belief sits atop a mass of related, supportive beliefs, so change would require something big.

Existing beliefs don't compel every new answer, though. When existing beliefs don't force a particular answer to a new question, we feel inclined to believe whatever possible belief most appeals to us. We value truth and accuracy, so we give some attention to facts. That leaves various possible answers. We feel drawn to one of the possibilities more than to others, so we accept it. Often, we're drawn to what feels nice to believe. It may feel nice because it comforts us, because it makes us feel smart or sophisticated, because it gives a sense of identity, because it makes us fit in with the people around us, because it supports our sense of being enti-tled to keep the money we've made, because it makes us feel noble, or whatever. The belief-motivating thing need not be positive, though. Sometimes we're angry or depressed, and we pick the answer that confirms the world is out to get us, or that people suck, or that our parents have never respected us and they damn well never will regardless of how hard we try or how much we accom-plish so screw them.

Again, none of this means we choose *solely* based on emotion, or *wholly* irrationally. We apply reason to the piles of information in front of us, under time constraints, with limited energy and patience and insight. We sift the piles with credibility judgments and apply preexisting beliefs and attitudes. Reason and knowledge narrow the field, but not all the way down to a single option. That's why reasonable people disagree on damn near everything worth talking about.

For example, consider defensive attribution. You present a medical malpractice case to a focus group. A female patient went to her doctor with a breast lump to see if it was cancer. The doctor ran tests, the radiologist said the tumor was malignant, but the doctor misread the radiologist's report and told the patient she was all clear. The resulting delay in diagnosis turned what should have been excision of a small part of one breast into a double mastectomy. The focus group hears all this. The men blame the doctor for malpractice. The women blame the plaintiff. The women say they would have gotten a second opinion. You say well, actually, the patient did get a second opinion, and that doctor just read the first doctor's report and repeated it. The women dig in. They would have gotten a third opinion. You say well, actually, the patient did that, too, and the same thing happened. Still the women blame the patient. It seems we need to believe we live in a safe world, a just world. The women in the focus group need to believe they're safe from breast cancer. So they come up with a story that confirms they're safe — because your client acted irresponsibly whereas they would act diligently. We all tend toward beliefs in this fashion.

WE ACTIVELY BIAS OUR OWN BELIEFS. ALL OUR REASONING IS MOTIVATED.

Actually, it's worse than I've said. We actively bias our own thinking. The bias begins with perception and memory, and when we give thought to our biased perceptions and remembered "facts," we bias our reasoning about them, to support what we feel inclined to believe.

Call it confirmation bias and motivated reasoning. You've

noticed other people engage in this corrupt process, but you do it, too. If you like something, you downplay its disadvantages. If you dislike it, you pooh-pooh its advantages. Remarkably, if you've already committed to an idea, hearing strong arguments against it can actually deepen your commitment to the idea. The emotional tail wags the rational dog. Or, in Jonathan Haidt's metaphor, emotion is an untrained elephant, and the rational mind is a rider. The rider mostly just goes along for the ride, but comes up with reasons to justify what the elephant is doing. If you've ever made a big decision that turned out badly, you can probably look back and see how these forces skewed your decision-making. Your wife warned you, and you made a show of listening, but you damn well wanted to change jobs, so you reasoned away all the predictable problems that later led you to grief.

Confirmation bias and motivated reasoning go a long way toward explaining the persistence of irrational beliefs. When a skeptic exposes the trickery behind mind-reading or psychic communication with the dead, the fraud's audience does not throw flowers to the skeptic, in gratitude at having the scales lifted from their eyes. The audience boos the skeptic for challenging the beliefs that provided comfort.

Smart people enjoy no exemption from these biases. Consider Project Alpha. In the 1970s and 80s, some scientists took claims of "paranormal" powers seriously. The chairman of McDonnell Douglas endowed a research group at Washington University in St. Louis to study psychics. (I said psychics, not physics.) The magician James Randi sent two magicians to pose as psychics for the study, to test the integrity of the research. Randi wanted to see if the scientists would validate the tricksters as having genuine psychic powers. Out of fairness, Randi sent the scientists a letter warning them of common ruses and advising specific protocols to avoid falling for them. Furthermore, Randi told the scientists that these two "psychics" were fake. The scientists failed to check the backgrounds of the two fakes, failed to implement the protocols Randi suggested, and got duped. The whole affair ended in disgrace for the research program.[8] This example is exotic; the phenomenon is not. The scientists weren't stupid. They had the bad luck to be caught out in a particularly clear and public way. But they fell into the same sort of hole we all fall into, repeatedly, all our lives. Judges do it. I do it. You do it. If you think you don't, you're just a special kind of dupe.

You can see these biases at work in every political disagreement you've ever heard. We perceive what we expect to perceive, we remember the data points that fit our existing views, and we look for ways to use the biased facts to support our existing beliefs.

The biases play out in our work as well as in our political quarrels. Thomas Kuhn showed that scientists become wedded to a broad theory and tend to overlook anomalies. Scientific revolutions happen when a new generation with less personal investment focuses on the anomalies and creates a new theory with greater explanatory power. Scientists operate with as much disciplined rationality as we can ask of human beings — with institutions, rules, and cultural norms all geared toward creating as much rational rigor as possible. But scientists still have their elephants and riders.[9]

We can reason with more or less diligence, more or less integrity, but even at our best, we still reason with human brains. We needn't despair about that, but it should prompt caution, and even a little paranoia. We should attend to the broad range of things that influence beliefs.

WE BELIEVE AND FEEL MANY CONTRADICTORY THINGS, BUT THEY DON'T ALL GUIDE US AT THE SAME TIME.

For someone who needs to persuade, the good news is that we believe and feel many contradictory things, and only some of them float near the surface at any given time. So if you're trying to persuade someone who holds hostile beliefs, your listener probably also holds more compatible feelings and thoughts, too. If you can bring those to the surface, you might get somewhere. If you can draw attention away from things that call forth hostile feelings or thoughts, so much the better.

We're not individuals in the way we sometimes think we are. We don't possess a single, coherent, integrated self — a single, consistent set of feelings and beliefs. Our brains contain a multitude of circuits that pull in different directions. Our subjective experience bears that out: We feel conflicted, torn, ambivalent, unsure. We waver, vacillate, war with ourselves. The Apostle Paul agonized, "For that which I do, I allow not: for what I would, that do I not, but what I hate, that do I." Walt Whitman felt less tortured about it: "Do I contradict myself? Very well then I contradict myself, (I am large, I contain multitudes.)" You want the ice cream, but you don't want the ice cream. You think people are good; you think people just ain't no good. You want to be with your friends; you want to be alone. You want to tell the son of a bitch exactly what you think of him; you want to be the better person. We have stable, recurring thoughts and feelings that contradict each other. On many things, what we believe depends on the time of day, or what news story we just heard, or what the guy we like to disagree with just said. So you sometimes say "I think I believe" such and such or "I think I think" such and such. If we could list everything we think and feel, we'd find an incoherent mess.

We carry most of our beliefs and attitudes in nascent, unripe form. You have some set of feelings and beliefs about the United Nations, about paraplegics, about lies, about authority, about corporations, about insurance, about pomegranates and latex masks and toe fungus and Proust and a million other things. You don't walk around with all those beliefs and feelings in mind all the time. They come to mind when something calls them up from the deep. You may never have thought about how you feel about putting a price tag on human wellbeing for purposes of cost/benefit analysis. But when asked about it, you'll have an answer.

So you should think carefully and creatively about what helpful feelings and thoughts might reside somewhere in the judge's or clerk's or juror's minds. A judge may have obvious beliefs and feelings that cut against you — a pro-defense or pro-plaintiff bias, say, or a cheerful optimism that reputable companies or federal prose-cutors don't misbehave. But your dispute may contain facts that would draw out other, more helpful beliefs and feelings. Your judge may not be moved by your client's injuries, but your oppo-nent might have disregarded authority or failed to live up to a promise in some way that would move the judge to anger and disgust. Then again, your situation may hold nothing at all that helps. Life is hard. Sometimes you strike out. But don't despair until you've thought creatively and comprehensively.

The point here is not to dig for dark impulses that lie buried in the fetid id. Don't go mining for the decision-maker's inner bigot. That will probably lose you the immediate issue, brand you as sleazy, and harm your career. The point is to search for legitimate values and beliefs — those that you, the judge or juror, and moral norms in society at large would consciously endorse, but which may not arise if you don't purposely draw them out.

WE BELIEVE WHAT WE'RE TOLD, IF IT DOESN'T CONFLICT WITH OUR PREEXISTING THOUGHTS OR FEELINGS.

Among our various conflicting tendencies, we have a tendency to believe what we're told. This tendency does not sweep all before it, but neither does it limp along ineffectually. Our confirmation bias does not just apply to ideas that draw us. Given a wholly new idea, we'll test it by looking for confirmation. Then, foolishly, we'll stop. A rational truth-seeker would also look to falsify the idea, because you can easily find confirming evidence for many falsehoods. "Bob is a decent guy." Well, he loves dogs, so sure, I guess. But does Bob also beat his wife? Unless you're already committed to an opposing view, or have been put into a distrusting state of mind, intuition usually doesn't think to look for falsifying evidence. Intuition thus buys all sorts of nonsense.

For legal argument, our innate gullibility implies that you shouldn't take too much for granted. You should not assume too easily that the judge or jury will see through the other side's merit-less arguments. Even *obviously* bad arguments can win when no one exposes them explicitly. (But you should not, of course, rely on gullibility to carry the day for your side.)

2.3.5 WE SOMETIMES INFER OUR BELIEFS FROM OUR BEHAVIOR.

Much of the time, we act in accordance with our thoughts and feel-ings, but sometimes the direction of causation reverses, so that we think and feel in accordance with our actions. That is, we interpret our actions in order to decide what we think and how we feel — who we are. Recall Gazzaniga's split-brain patients and the Inter-preter. Much of the time, even with the halves of our brains connected, we don't know ourselves directly, and we make up stories about ourselves to interpret our own behavior. Get someone to donate $5 to the policemen's charity, if only to get a decal for their car to ward off speeding tickets, and they may start thinking of themselves as supporters of the police, and become habitual contributors. The Catholic guy who keeps dating Jewish women may recognize the pattern and decide he has a thing for Jewish women.

This suggests the need to take care in adopting legal positions. Lose too often in front of a given judge, and you risk becoming, for this judge, "the lawyer who takes losing positions" or just "the loser." Worse, you may start thinking that yourself. Win often enough in front of a judge, and you may become the winner. Of course you can't play it safe all the time. At times, you should make new arguments, bold arguments, risky arguments. Every lawyer suffers losses. If you never fall short, you're not aiming very high. Few judges will form a lasting negative impression from a single loss. But every loss poses some risk of long-term damage; so take only calculated risks.

2.3.6 WE STICK TO OLD, PRE-WRITTEN ANSWERS, RIGHT OR WRONG.

If we think we've figured a thing out before, we rarely think it over again. Instead, we just plug in the answer we think we already know. We don't go back to first principles and reason our way up to the present question. We make a pot of coffee the same way we always do. We line up a billiard shot without investigating geometric theorems. We solve for X in an algebra problem without investigating the foundations of the algorithm we learned in high school. These things feel familiar and comfortable, so we do them mechanically, mindlessly. Whatever mistakes we made in the past, we'll tend to make again, unless the mistake made itself felt sharply.

Unlike with coffee or billiards, though, a mistake in answering a question in a legal dispute does not announce itself clearly and force a correction. Screw up the coffee, and you'll soon know it. That's rarely true for the decisions judges and jurors make. That makes knee-jerk views all the more powerful in legal disputes. The invisibility of error makes our pre-written answers all the stronger, all the more dangerous. The norms of decision-making in legal disputes nudge the decision-makers to check themselves, but it's just a nudge, not a controlling drive. A judge can just have a law clerk plug some cites into an opinion, or draft some fig-leaf language to dress up specious reasoning, or just rule summarily without explanation. Jurors never have to explain themselves. We avoid mental effort in law as much or more than in other domains of life. If a judge or juror has already figured a thing out in the past, it's going to take some doing to move them off their pre-written answer.

2.3.7 WE LEARN WHEN WE FEEL MOTIVATED TO LEARN — USUALLY TO SOLVE PROBLEMS.

Motivation matters to almost all mental work — how much we pay attention, and to what; how and what we see and remember; how we understand or misunderstand; what we learn. Put a lecture on cellular dynamics and the folding of proteins in front of students who live for tennis, and they won't learn it. Put it in front of students who want to become doctors, and they might learn.

You create motivation best by giving someone a problem they care about. Then you offer information that helps solve it. Mystery stories often work this way: We see the twisted corpse and wonder how it happened. We pay attention to what comes next because we want to answer the question. The more important the initial problem — the more it relates to the decision-maker's interests or feelings — the more it motivates.

2.3.8 WE MORALIZE INTUITIVELY.

Most legal disputes raise moral concerns. A contract dispute, the correct application of a regulatory scheme, or similar issues don't scream with moral urgency like a rape case, but even quieter issues bear on moral questions of liberty, honesty, authority, and the like. Even the interstitial decisions judges make in lawsuits — on discovery, confidentiality, admissibility, and so on — raise their own subtle moral concerns.

Morality sits at the heart of our individual concerns, and at the center of society's. Nearly alone among the species in the world, and completely alone among the higher animals, humans maintain societies with hundreds of millions of members. That feat requires balancing individual self-interest with group interests, and at times subordinating self-interest entirely. That is, civilization rests on morality.

We routinely keep self-interest in check, to maintain an orderly, stable society. Given a clear chance to steal from a blind lady we've never seen before and will never see again, we don't do it. At least an astonishingly large number of us don't. Bad as we are (and we're plenty bad), most of the time all but a handful of us subordinate self-interest to group cohesion, order, and stability — routinely, automatically, unquestioningly.

We do this not because we reason our way to a conclusion that we should act pro-socially. We don't calculate our ultimate self-interest by assessing the value we draw from society, the risk of other people behaving as we do, the ultimate outcome years or generations down the road, and how that might impact us or our kids if and when the chickens come home to roost. These imponderables have nothing to do with our decision right here, right now. We don't have the time, energy, brainpower, or information to make calculations like that as we go through daily life. If morality relied on that sort of thing, we'd have no morality and no society.

Moral *feelings* glue us together. Moral feelings keep large societies from being pulled apart by individuals acting in their own self-interest. Our inner sense of right and wrong, our feelings of guilt or shame or righteousness, our concern about reputation, our willingness to enforce moral codes and punish the guilty — these things all work to keep cheats, liars, free-riders, and gold-brickers in check. These feelings prevent bad actors from growing into a horde that clambers over everything built up by long group effort, looting it, and selling it for scrap. Morality keeps us from killing strangers to take their stuff, keeps testosterone-filled men from raping women, keeps us from needing a cop for every civilian, and a super-cop for every cop. Moral feelings don't work perfectly, of course. Self-interest, aggression, cruelty, and chaos still plague us. But millennia after emerging from the wilderness, here we are with many largely decent, stable societies despite the basket-case ones.

WE MAKE MORAL JUDGMENTS INTUITIVELY AND AUTOMATICALLY, AND THEN WE RATIONALIZE THEM.

Reflecting a more general theme we've already discussed, moral reasoning can serve an important role in deciding what to do with our judgments, but it does not produce those judgments or even inform them much in the first instance. Reasoning, without moral emotions, does not produce a moral sensibility. Psychopaths possess reason, but they lack shame, guilt, compassion, empathy, etc. Psychopaths respond to incentives and may act intelligently in pursuing their goals. But reason does not compensate for a lack of moral emotions.

Moral reasoning doesn't need to be very good in order to rationalize judgments. We can satisfy ourselves with virtually any nonsense to justify our judgment. Most of the time, as long as we can think of words to push out of our mouths, we feel satisfied with whatever justification we come up with.

Usually though, we don't feel any need for justification in the first place. The event happens, a moral judgment flashes into mind, and we run with it.

Jonathan Haidt illustrates these points with some test scenarios. Haidt presented test subjects with the following scenario and asked for their moral judgments:

> Julie and Mark, who are sister and brother, are traveling together in France. They are both on summer vacation from college. One night they are staying alone in a cabin near the beach. They decide that it would be interesting and fun if they tried making love. At the very least it would be a new experience for each of them. Julie is already taking birth control pills, but Mark uses a condom too, just to be safe. They both enjoy it, but they decide not to do it again. They keep that night as a special secret between them, which makes them feel even closer to each other. So what do you think about this? Was it wrong for them to have sex?[10]

You, me, and everyone we know find this repellant and immoral. We might or might not want to criminalize it, but we feel it to be wrong.

If asked to justify our intuitive judgment, however, most of us middle-class, 21st Century Americans can't. Our culture doesn't have an explicit moral ideology that comports with our moral intuitions. The best that most of us can say by way of moral reasoning about the Mark-and-Julie problem is "It just feels wrong." Try to say more than that, and we embarrass ourselves with nonsense. Haidt says that when he forced his test subjects to articulate reasons for their judgments, they mostly insisted that the sex would cause physical or emotional harm, despite the pill+condom birth control and the lasting sense of good that the fictional Julie and Mark took from the event. That is, test subjects just fought the hypothetical.

But recognizing the feebleness of our justifying reasons does not weaken the moral judgment itself. However we embarrass ourselves with sputtering failures to justify our judgment, the judgments mostly stick.

The other defects in our general thinking also carry over to moral reasoning. So, for example, we tend to confabulate — to misremember, to rearrange the facts, to make things up — to rationalize our knee-jerk reactions. Haidt gives us a perplexing little story, we form a judgment, and then we change the facts to fit the judgment. We may do that without even noticing we've done it. Democrats will have noticed that much moral condemnation of President Obama fit this model. Republicans will have noticed the same as to George W. Bush. Everyone passing judgment on you or your client — including judges, clerks, and jurors — possesses this same tendency to retrofit reality to fit a moral judgment.

We fool ourselves with our own confabulations. Why didn't you empty the dishwasher? Or take the package to be shipped? Or get the letter drafted? Why did you pull up to the school and yell for your 14-year old, though she has told you *never* to do that? You feel a little guilty, defensive. When called out for your sins, chances are you'll quickly take some bits of reality and almost unconsciously rearrange them into a reasonable-sounding but not-quite-true story that mitigates your shame.

None of this means we should give up on moral reasoning. Moral reflection can help us sort through conflicting feelings and judgments. Through conscious moral reasoning, we can veto feelings we deem wrong. We can to some limited extent influence our feelings themselves. Moral reasoning also helps decide what actions to take based on our feelings. Reasoning helps especially with formal decisions about public policy. We can and should make those decisions consciously, slowly, through effortful reasoning. But feelings still drive our moral sensibility.

WE POSSESS (OR ARE POSSESSED BY) AN INNATE MORAL SENSE WITH CULTURAL SETTINGS.

We have fair evidence to suggest that a sense of morality, like language, comes to us innately as a more or less universal system with dials that get set by the particularities of culture and individual experience. For example, Asian cultures tend to value group interests more than the individualistic culture of America does. These varying emphases inform varying moral sensibilities. Within the broad outlines of any given culture's moral style, you can identify sub-groups. And of course even within the most narrowly drawn sub-groups, you find differences between individuals.

Moral psychologists have tried to identify general concerns that get expressed in varying ways in different moral sensibilities. It's hard to say that any particular typology identifies essential, fundamental moral feelings innate to all human beings. Even so, these typologies can help understand ourselves. They can help figure out what feelings exist in the decision-maker we're trying to appeal to.

For his part, Jonathan Haidt distills six fundamental concerns. Different cultures and individuals dial the various concerns up or down, and operationalize them differently. But most everyone cares in some way about each of these concerns:

CARE: We wouldn't survive as a species if we didn't care about — and care for — our kin. We wouldn't survive in large groups if we didn't care about a much broader circle than that.

FAIRNESS: Almost everything necessary for human life depends on group activities. But every individual has an incentive to cheat. If we didn't care about fairness and cheating, society would collapse and in time grass would cover all.

LOYALTY: Groups wouldn't cohere, and we couldn't cooperate to stave off the wolves, if we didn't reward loyalty to the group and punish betrayal.

AUTHORITY: A stable society, even among apes and

dolphins, requires some measure of hierarchy and authority. So we all see obedience to authority as carrying some moral force, though we disagree about the details.

SANCTITY: This refers to our basic sense that some things possess intrinsic value and demand respect — the human body, for instance.

LIBERTY: To one degree or another, everyone wants to be able to do their own thing, free of constraints.

These generic moral concerns stand in tension with each other. They get assigned different weights, different priorities, different balances.

Societies and individuals also differ in how they conceive of each concern and put it into practice. Does the sanctity of the human body *preclude* using cadavers in medical training, or does it *require* such use? What about fetal tissue? Within a single church congregation, different individuals answer such questions differently. We learn or develop the specifics of our moral sensibilities through experience and the climates of opinion we breathe in.

Differences in moral sensibilities run deep. We can't yet be sure, but it seems that some moral differences get set at the genetic level. For example, some people seem innately more attuned to threats, and some to opportunities. These differences influence the weight we assign to concerns like fairness/cheating or loyalty/betrayal.

Some differences in sensibility reflect more contingent matters. If you perceive no meaningful threat to social order, the concerns of loyalty and authority will feel less urgent. That doesn't mean loyalty and authority don't matter to you. It just means that in the world you inhabit, those matters don't demand much attention or concern.

Whatever the particulars of your moral sensibility, though, you didn't choose them, and they control you, more or less. In the moment at least, you don't have much more control over your intuitive moral judgments than you do over whether, when someone says "rabbit," you recognize it as a word and know what it means. Occasionally, fearful moralists worry that learning about other cultures and coming to appreciate and respect them will create a corrosive moral relativism that will corrupt the youth and render them incapable of moral judgment. You might as well worry that learning Spanish will render you incapable of understanding English. It doesn't work that way. Moral judgments will continue popping into your mind unbidden, and you don't get to choose the content of those judgments much more than you get to choose what "rabbit" means.

However, moral change does happen slowly over time, and your conscious choices influence your experience and thus the development of your particular moral sensibility. You can decide to live among porn stars or preachers. Whichever you choose, over time you'll pick up some of their sensibility, though you'll probably never go native. The influences of today don't eclipse entirely the influences of yesterday. And since the moral sensibility you have today will guide any choice you make today, your sensibility evolves gradually, from one stepping stone to the next. Great leaps in moral change rarely happen. On rare occasions, major life events can provoke big, sudden changes. If you take the subway home after work and get swept up in a horror-movie scenario of hijacking, torture, and murder, that may work an immediate revolution in your moral sensibility. Campaigns of fear-mongering, perhaps combined with misery, can deform moral sensibilities over a short time — as in Weimar Germany or 1994 Rwanda.

These points suggest two implications for legal argument. First, judges, clerks, and jurors each are held in the grip of a moral sensibility they did not, in any very meaningful sense, choose. And their sensibilities won't change quickly. So far as you and your case are concerned, their moral sensibilities stand as immovable facts. You find some existing moral feelings within their minds that you can appeal to, or you lose. Of course, legal decision-making is supposed to be about more than *personal* moral judgment. It's supposed to be about the moral and practical judgments embodied in law. But personal moral feelings always, at minimum, sit in the background commenting on the action and pushing the ultimate decision this way or that. Most of the time, they'll push hard.

Second, even if the decision-makers have moral sensibilities greatly at odds with yours, you can still understand them, appreciate them, and appeal to them. For all our differences, no one has radically idiosyncratic moral sensibilities. We recognize the components of others' moral matrices, however malproportioned the components may seem. We can imagine the view from others' eyes at least a little. We can see how to present the issues so they make sense and carry force within someone else's worldview. Anyone trying to live decently in society should make a point of understanding and appreciating the worldviews of other people. Anyone trying to persuade *must* do so.

2.4 WE THINK AND FEEL THE WAY OUR LANGUAGE TELLS US TO — TO A FAIR EXTENT

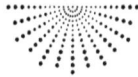

The language we use influences both the thoughts and feelings we invoke in the head of a listener (obviously) and also the thoughts and feelings in our own heads.

Language doesn't completely control our thoughts, of course. In some domains, we think in non-linguistic ways. When you play Tetris, you picture arrangements of blocks as they fall toward the bottom of the screen. That doesn't involve what most of us would call language. Even when we think consciously with words, we have some pre-linguistic sense of what we mean. We can distinguish between what we meant and what we said. We recognize when it came out wrong, when we said something we didn't mean to say. We recognize when we're grasping for, and failing at, a way to say what we vaguely, sort-of have in mind.

Even with those caveats, though, we do a great deal of conscious thinking in language, and the particular words matter. For most things, we have a choice among ways of talking. The way you talk sets your listeners down a cognitive pathway. Find five different ways to make the same general point, and you've probably found five subtly but meaningfully different sets of responses from your listener.

2.4.1 WORDS IMPLY A LOGIC THAT MAY OR MAY NOT FIT THE SITUATION.

Most words exist in networks of related concepts. When you say "above," you invoke a set of spatial relationships — *below, beside, around, higher, lower*, etc. You may also invoke a metaphor of hierarchies of value. When you say "flubbed," you raise the conceptual frame for competence and mistakes. When you say "transaction," you imply a buyer, a seller, something of value, and a commercial rather than personal context. These related ideas hover in the air, even if no one speaks them out loud. They create an atmosphere and influence everyone in the room.

Usually, we have multiple conceptual frames we could use in a given situation. Each potential frame functions a little differently, contributes slightly different meanings, with different advantages and disadvantages. Speak of a "contract," and we start thinking in terms of parties, counterparties, agreements, exchange, obligations, and law. "Contract" gets us thinking of commercial relationships. Maybe instead of "contract" you could have spoken of a "promise" or of someone "giving his word." Those alternatives raise thoughts of personal, moral obligation. Maybe you could speak instead of commitment and sacrifice, or communal bonds, or something else. One of these frames will probably work better for the particular thoughts and feelings you want to evoke. One of these frames will imply a logic, a mode of analysis, a broad conceptual context, a way of thinking that best fits what you're trying to say.

We often adopt conceptual frames that don't fit well, or that work against us. We accept the first way of speaking about a thing that pops into our heads. That way of speaking seems natural and inevitable. It's not. Worse, we may unthinkingly adopt an opponent's way of speaking, which slants the playing field in their favor.

An inapt conceptual frame can misdirect your thinking. It can cause you to mis-analyze situations. If you'll indulge a tedious example, consider this:

Bill rents a car from RentCo in his name. He names himself as the sole driver. Alice rides in the car as a passenger. Bill negligently crashes the car, causing Alice catastrophic injuries. Bill is underinsured, and Alice appears to be largely on her own, with no source of coverage for her injuries.

However, RentCo has an insurance policy with Acme. That policy gives Alice underinsured motorist coverage, for up to $1 million.

Alice eventually learns of the Acme policy, but Acme straight-up lies to her, saying no coverage exists that would benefit Alice.

Later, a lawyer refers Alice to you, to consider a potential bad-faith claim against Acme. The referring lawyer points out, however, that Alice is a third party to the contract and in your state, third-party claimants can't sue for bad faith.

Alice is indeed a third party to the contract. The law does indeed forbid third-party claims for insurance bad faith. A lot of lawyers would see instantly that Alice has no bad faith claim because she's a third party.

But "third-party" is the wrong phrase to use in analyzing the case. While Alice is a third party to the contract, she is also an insured. As an insured, Alice is a first-party insured for UIM coverage. Acme owed coverage to her directly. Alice would be bringing a first-party-insured claim for bad faith, not a third-party claim. The phrase "third party" seems correct and applicable (because it really does have limited application), but that phrase distorts the analysis. If you don't think about this natural-seeming language, if you don't think about alternative words and concepts, the phrase may well lead to error.

Frequently, though, you can't say that one conceptual frame clearly works and another clearly does not. Sometimes you simply have alternative frames that carry subtly different meanings but both seem reasonable. Is the testifying expert "explaining her basis" for saying the company complied with industry standards, or is she "vouching for the company's witnesses"? Did the school "prohibit t-shirts with statements printed on them" or "institute a dress code"? Did the automaker "deceive emissions-testing systems" or "boost performance in highway conditions." Is the Presidential candidate proposing "tax relief," "tax reduction," or "revenue cuts"? Depending on the circumstances, it may be that none of the alternatives clearly get it wrong. But each suggests a different logic, different considerations, different values. Those differences elicit different responses from the listener.

You can't consider an alternative if you never see it. We miss alternative ways of talking, and our thinking suffers for that. After someone offers an alternative description, it may instantly seem obvious, but you didn't see it before, and you might never have seen it on your own, because you didn't spend the time and energy to think up alternative ways of talking, or to mull it over with a friend or colleague.

Sometimes a framing so thoroughly infects our thinking that even when someone proposes an alternative, we can't see it. It seems nonsensical. If we'd heard that framing when we first encountered the issue, it might have seemed obvious, but the frame we've been using has taken over our heads. Every day, lawyers reject reasonable arguments because they've bought into a frame so long they can't see past it. In movies, lawyers possess great powers of sophistry — framing and reframing, describing and redescribing, conceptualizing and reconceptualizing so fluidly as to open a chasm of indeterminacy and relativism. That's Hollywood fantasy. In fact, most of us don't seem much better at reconceptualizing things than the average high school kid.

This is not to say, of course, that you can call anything by any name you please, that any frame will do. We do not, in fact, stand above a chasm of indeterminacy and relativism. When an insurance company falsely denies the existence of coverage, having company witnesses repeatedly say they provided excellent customer service won't get the company very far. Reality does present different faces to different people, but reality does not wear an infinitely malleable play-doh mask.

2.4.2 MORE GENERALLY, LANGUAGE RAISES ASSOCIATIONS THAT HELP OR HURT YOUR POSITION.

The logical relationships invoked by the framing of an issue count as a particular sort of priming. More general priming effects matter, too. Every word you use primes the reader to recognize or feel other, related things.

In any communication, you're trying to control the thoughts that arise in the listener's head. That's what communication means, and it's a tricky business. You accomplish it in part by focusing the listener's attention as narrowly as possible on your point.

To the extent you can, you want to prime only thoughts and feelings that relate tightly to your point. You want to keep everything else out of mind. If you use words that prime unrelated thoughts, you risk going off the rails. A guy talks about tax policy, but he keeps referring to Nazis and slavery. That brings a lot of extraneous thoughts and feelings to mind (only one of which is that the speaker is a hysteric). The same effect occurs in more subtle ways, too.

Think of all the words you might use to talk about a concept or issue as being laid out in a word cloud. The words most tightly related to the concept lie in the center of the cloud. The more you use words at the margins — the words most loosely related to your topic — the more you risk unrelated thoughts or feelings popping up. If you're lucky, they'll just cause a little distraction. If you're not lucky, they'll change the light in which the reader sees your argument. Extraneous associations may cause the reader to misunderstand your point and raise unnecessary objections. You've lost control of the reader's attention and endangered the communication.

Consider especially the emotional resonance of your language. For most things, we have logically equivalent language that exerts very different emotional force. If you want to support legislation to help the unemployed, don't call them the unemployed. Talk about people who've lost their jobs. "The unemployed" conjures an abstract category or a nameless mass. "People who've lost their jobs" puts you in mind of individuals who have suffered a blow that could hit any of us.

The more sophisticated a piece of language sounds, the less emotional impact it usually exerts. Doctors, police officers, and the like use technical language in part to numb emotion, to get distance so their jobs won't make life too depressing. Judges use language in a similar way, to signal that they haven't been improperly influenced. But you're not a cop, and you're not a judge. You have a different job, with different needs. You don't want to overdo the emotional intensity of an argument, lest you harm your credibility, but you don't want to create artificial distance, either.

Tending to the way you're priming the reader's mind requires imagination, empathy, and guesswork. All communication consists of guessing what this word or gesture will do in someone else's mind. That leaves vast room for misfires, and you will inevitably make plenty of them. But you still have to work thoughtfully, despite the tragic lack of guarantees.

Unless you're writing a haiku, you can't limit yourself to words that exist only in your main conceptual frames. Nor can you obsess about every damned word. You'd never get anything done. But for all that, you should take some time to think about both the risks and the opportunities. You can't be impossibly thoughtful, but you can be reasonably thoughtful.

~

THE IMPACT of subtle associations may raise the distressing thought that we flit from one position to another based on arbitrary trivialities, but that overstates the problem. No one is going to change settled, fundamental beliefs or attitudes because of a subtle cue in their environment, or a brief-writer's word choice. Using the word "gourmet" to talk up McDonalds will only make people snicker.

Even so, subtleties can matter — especially in close cases. A small shift in emotional resonance, a difference in implied logic and analysis, a mere distraction — these won't always affect outcomes. They may change an outcome only in rare cases. But you never really know if your case is one of the rare ones. And even if this case is not one of those, you still want to form working habits that routinely maximize your chances.

2.5 SOME SUBSTANTIVE CONTENT
OR LEANINGS

Thus far we've discussed cognitive processes more than the substantive content of thoughts and feelings. We now shift focus more toward substantive content.

2.5.1 WE LOOK FOR AGENTS, INTENTION, AND CAUSATION — AND OFTEN FIND THEM WRONGLY.

The brain looks for agents, intentions, and causality, and often enough makes them up. The discovery of Gazzaniga's "Interpreter," and other research besides, confirms this. Our brains abhor chance, randomness, the unexplained, vacuums of intention and causality. We watch a bland animation of a square and a triangle moving about on a two-dimensional background. Even here we see the shapes as agents engaging in intentional action within a social relationship. We see the shapes as chasing or blocking each other. Similarly, you show a baby a wooden block moving up an incline. Then another block comes along either behind or in front of the first block, lending momentum to go further up the incline, or standing in the way. The baby seems to interpret the second block as intentionally helping or obstructing. (So do adults.) Given a choice of which to play with, the baby reaches out for the helper-blocks and declines to play with the bully-blocks. So we find agency and intention even with mere shapes and blocks. Of course we do so much more with actual human events. We do so automatically, involuntarily, and often irresistibly.

Just as we see agency and intention easily, so we see patterns and causation easily. We see random collections of things (rock arrangements, basketball shots, news events and stock prices) as non-random. Random distributions include groupings, but we can't believe that, so we see a grouping of good basketball shots as evidence of "hot hands." We see causality in the day's news events and the movements of the stock market — a complex aggregation of indefinitely many events and decisions. We may change the causal story randomly, though, without ever noticing the fickleness of our stories. At noon, a finance journalist writes that "Early morning comments by the Fed chairman sparked increased confidence and a rise in the markets." In the evening, after the market has fallen, the same journalist may change the story to "Early morning comments by the Fed chairman worried investors and sparked a decline in the markets." We can find plausible, contradictory stories in the same pile of facts.

More generally, whenever someone isolates two events that occurred in sequence, we look for a connection. We look for a way to see the first as causing the second, and we believe the connection too easily. Thus, this little joke from Mark Twain (as channeled by Hal Holbrook): "I joined the Confederacy. Served for two weeks. Deserted. And the Confederacy fell."

We err on the side of false positives. We find agency, intention, and causality like we find faces. Just as we're wired to see human faces so easily that we see them in clouds, cliffs, and pancakes, so we see actors intentionally causing things to happen.

Obviously, this does not mean we see only illusions. To the contrary, our brains look for agency, intention, and causation because they're often real, it helps to see them, and they can be hard to spot. It must have taken early humans a great leap of insight to recognize that sex sometimes leads to pregnancy. That connection lies hidden in months of life events. How could you know the pregnancy came from the sex, rather than from sleeping uncovered under the full moon, or from eating root paste, or from the shaman's dance, or the ten thousand other things that happened in the months before the belly swelled? The signal comes shielded in enormous clouds of noise. Nor can it have been easy to identify plants as poisonous or helpful, when their effects played out hours or days after ingestion, with much else happening at the same time. Similarly, since people dissemble and deceive, we often have trouble distinguishing good will from bad. Our hair-trigger for seeing agency, intention, and causation helps us ferret these things out when they're hidden.

Presumably, false positives hurt us less on average than false negatives. Few people ever came to grief from being scared by a rubber snake or a Halloween mask or an assumption that someone put the arsenic in your tea deliberately. A guy believes the dowsing rod showed where to dig the well (ignoring all the false positives and the unknown false negatives). But so what? The dowsing rod is mostly harmless nonsense. Failing to spot a real snake, though, or a real person hiding in the woods, or a truly malicious neighbor — that could kill you.

False positives do sometimes cause problems, though. At the low end, when a group of friends puts their hands together on a wooden pointer over a Ouija board, they feel a powerful illusion of ghostly agency. As the pointer moves over the board, they feel that some agent is moving the pointer. The hands of three or four friends looking at the board converge on a path to a letter, and then another, until words get spelled out. There is no ghost guiding the pointer, but brains expect agency, so they damn well find it. (We can dismiss the idea of the ghost, because if you blindfold the friends, the pointer spells out gibberish.) So people believe in ghosts. Some of these people spend money they can't afford, seeking to contact the dead.

The brain finds false intention and causation in more harmful ways, too. A huge industry of stock market analysts and stock pickers still exists, despite decades of research that shows the industry to be based mainly on a delusion. Professional stock pickers as a group perform no better than chance. Virtually none outperform the market consistently. As a group, the pros achieve results consistent with a random distribution around the baseline of the overall market. And yet professional stock pickers and their clients believe all the pickers' hard work causes their picks to beat the market (sometimes) — while mere bad luck often makes them lag the market. In these and many other ways, the human penchant for false assumptions about intention and causality causes us to lose money, to lose opportunities, to lose friends, to lose motions, to lose cases.

For lawyers, our inclination to see agents, intention, and causation acts in ways both helpful and harmful. If you're representing a defendant (civil or criminal), you've obviously got an uphill climb if you need to argue innocent coincidence — whether on an issue of intent or an issue of causation. In those cases, the civil plaintiff or the criminal prosecutor have an advantage. But for the same reasons, the civil plaintiff or a criminal prosecutor may hold the short end of the stick, where the plaintiff or the complaining witness confront a charge of contributory negligence or other fault.

2.5.2 WE PUT TOO MUCH STOCK IN A SIMPLISTIC VIEW OF PERSONAL CHARACTER.

We tend to see a person's actions — especially if it's a person other than our own precious self — as driven primarily by enduring traits of character, rather than by temporary circumstances. We tend to see a person's decisions as being driven by factors internal to the person, rather than by external forces. This might not fairly count as an error, except that we also see human character as simpler, more coherent, more consistent and predictable across circumstances, than it really is. If a guy steals your laptop, you tend to think he does so because he's a thief, and you figure he'll probably always be a thief, even if he learns to control his thieving impulses. If you hear he stole somebody else's laptop, too, your view will harden. We don't have a lot of patience for explanations about how hard up the thief was and how, in different circumstances, he's really a decent, honorable guy. We believe in character above circumstances, and we confidently make predictions from character.

Of course we are far more complicated than this intuitive view of human nature allows. We are capable of far more variety of behavior than we tend to think. Even subtle changes of circumstance can elicit significant changes in conduct. When we judge character and make predictions of future behavior, we tend to judge too simply and too confidently.

Here, too, the implications for lawyers are obvious: Judges and jurors will tend to see a party's actions — whether good or bad — as reflecting the essential character of that person. If your client did a good thing, so much the better. If he or she did a bad thing, so much the worse.

2.5.3 WE DIVIDE THE WORLD INTO US AND THEM, AND RESERVE GOOD FEELING AND THINKING FOR THE FORMER.

We're tribal creatures, and tribal affiliations exert profound influence on our feeling and thinking. We care about people who are part of Us, but we'll let Them starve to death as we turn away. We'll make exquisitely nuanced distinctions when thinking about our own kind, but lecture in crude eugenicist terms about population groups not our own kind.

Obviously, we inherit many of our tribal affiliations. A guy hates Irish Catholics or German Protestants or Blacks or Whites or lawyers or red-heads or Democrats or motorcycle riders or conservatives or fat people or skinny people or cat people or whoever because the family and communities he was born into shaped him to hate those people. But those affiliations can change over time.

We have lots of tribal affiliations, and particular aspects of identity can fade in or out of view, their order of importance switching around, depending on circumstances. The lefty peacenik and the NRA zealot despise each other, until it turns out they both love fly-fishing. Suddenly they're friends, and can occasionally hazard a conversation about guns, without yelling insults at each other.

Through the magic of abstract thought and imagination we can feel a common identity with people we've never met. We do so based on any characteristic that carries meaning for us — other Americans, other Baptists, other parents of a child with Down Syndrome, other Springsteen fans.

Broadly speaking, we classify or reclassify people as part of Us when we see ourselves as standing in a cooperative relationship with them, working together for some common goal. And we banish people into Them when we see ourselves as competing with them for some scarce thing. This is why when times get hard, people get mean. Brute, objective reality forces us into competition over water rights or jobs or restaurant reservations. Then we get nasty.

For the most part, we reclassify people as Us or Them (and grow nice or nasty) without conscious thought or even awareness. Our attitudes change without our knowing it. Indeed, when we become aware of our attitudes, they may surprise us. A guy used to feel sympathy for the homeless, but he realizes with a little jolt that he doesn't anymore. He can't point to any obvious thing that changed his attitudes, so what accounts for the change? Who knows.

In classifying people as Them, our subjective understanding of the situation — not its objective reality — governs us. The complex, debatable, maybe inscrutable reality doesn't govern whether I favor or hate our NAFTA counterparties and want to trade freely with them. All that matters is whether I *think* we're in a zero-sum economic trade competition with other countries.

Propaganda and public relations campaigns and social media campaigns and all the various forms of influence — these things affect who we see as Us and who we see as Them. Famously, the

Rwandan genocide of 1994 came after a massive propaganda campaign against the Tutsi minority — despite a history of the Hutu and Tutsi living together peacefully. Less extreme media campaigns against this or that group frequently form a part of ordinary life.

Our classifications of Us and Them often gain a phony objectivity from physical, sensory tokens. Divisions marked by skin color or language or accent or clothing, etc. come to feel in some way solid, real, objective. That's an illusion, but a powerful one. So powerful, in fact, that in our cruelest moments we force physical tokens onto those we despise, to bestow an even stupider false objectivity onto the us/them division — for example, yellow stars for Jews who might otherwise look like any other German. The star proves they're objectively different.

Some physical characteristics have intrinsic power to make us classify people as Them — sickness, death, and its signs (smelliness, ugliness, dirtiness, deformity). For obvious reasons, ancient brain circuitry wants us to avoid sickness, and it pulls us to shun the sick, to turn away, cross the street, quarantine them on their island of lepers. Those impulses sometimes make sense, but they operate crudely and generally. Here again, to "objectivize" hatred we may force these characteristics onto groups we despise — forbidding Jews or Blacks or Okies or undocumented immigrants or the out-of-work-and-poor from toilets or bathing facilities or motel rooms, etc. We can force filth and stink upon them, force them to be artificially filthy, bestial, "objectively" alien. We can thus justify despising them. We force a group to shit beside the railroad tracks, then hold our noses and sneer: "Think any of us folks 'd live like that? Course not."

It's not all bad news, though. Because we have so many cross-cutting identities and such capacity for shared experience and feeling, we always retain the ability to extend our hands across the barbed wire fence. Even seemingly trivial experiences can create a meaningful buzz of shared identity. You've been standing in line for an over-priced coffee drink for five minutes. You catch the eye of the guy next to you and give a tiny, rueful raise of the eyebrow. He replies with a silent grin and shake of the head. As you leave the parking lot, you recognize each other and each make a special effort of courtesy. Bestially cruel though we sometimes are, the better angels of our nature hover nearby.

For lawyers, our inborn Us/Them tribalism raises the importance of presenting yourself and your client in a way that allows judges, law clerks, and jurors to relate to you and your client. This may require a light touch, since people are pretty good at spotting phonies, and coming off as a phony will only make you a particularly noxious Them. But in every case, the thoughtful lawyer will spend at least a few minutes thinking about how to get both lawyer and client into the Us category, in a way that's true and genuine.

2.5.4 WE RESPOND MORE TO THE BAD THAN TO THE GOOD.

Nature has designed our brains to respond more intensely to bad things than to good things. Losses matter more than gains. We avoid pain before seeking pleasure. We'll pay more and fight harder to avoid losing what we already have than to get something new. That goes for an army's fighting spirit in war, responses to proposals for new taxes, and digging in for a long slog in litigation.

This tendency to first protect what we have affects the value we put on things. The moment something becomes ours, we find it more valuable. Before it's yours, it's just an old chair. When it becomes yours, it turns into an heirloom. This is the "endowment effect." Ask a guy to put a dollar value on someone else's losing an arm, then ask him later to put a value on the loss of his own arm. The two numbers will differ, because the same thing is more valuable if it's yours than if it's someone else's. This helps explain why people have trouble selling their used stuff. Until you dissociate the old kitchen table from yourself, until it becomes a nuisance taking up space in your garage, your sense of a fair price is less likely to meet up with a would-be buyer's sense of a fair price.

Our aversion to loss contains a wrinkle, though. The bigger a potential loss becomes, the less sensitive we get to additional, marginal losses, and the more prone to desperate gambles. Faced with a high likelihood of losing 85% of the business, the owner makes a desperate gamble to save it all, practically guaranteeing the loss of even the 15% he could cash out and use for the next venture.

It's easy, but wrong, to regard these effects as irrational. Values aren't rational or irrational. Values can be common or bizarre, expected or shocking, sound or perverse, good or bad, but not rational or irrational. It makes no more sense to call the endowment effect irrational than to call it irrational to love your mom, or to sacrifice your life for your country.

The bad-over-good principle plays out more generally. It's a gloomy fact of life that anything negative draws our attention more, provokes more of a response, and has more impact, than corresponding positive things. As Paul Rozin remarks, one cockroach will ruin a bowl of cherries, but a cherry will do nothing for a bowl of cockroaches.[1] Destruction works faster and more effectively than construction. Relationships succeed as much or more by avoiding bad things as by cultivating good things. In a 2001 article, Roy Baumeister and colleagues surveyed a wide range of studies concerning the effects of bad things and good things. The authors put their conclusion in the title: "Bad is Stronger than Good." Here's the abstract:

> The greater power of bad events over good ones is found in everyday events, major life events (e.g., trauma), close relationship outcomes, social network patterns, interpersonal interactions, and learning processes. Bad emotions, bad parents, and bad feedback have more impact than good ones, and bad information is processed more thoroughly than good. The self is more motivated to avoid bad self-definitions than to pursue good ones. Bad impressions and bad stereotypes are quicker to form and more resistant to disconfirmation than good ones. ... Hardly any exceptions (indicating greater power of good) can be found. Taken together, these findings suggest that bad is stronger than

good, as a general principle across a broad range of psychological phenomena.

As politicians know, inspire a little fear, and you can move a nation to all manner of cruelty and self-destruction. Hope is nice, but weak compared to fear.

Sometimes mere imagination can turn potential gains into potential losses. Imagine a potential payoff long enough that you can taste it, and if you don't get it, you may feel it as a loss of something that was already yours. Participants in an auction get sucked into bidding wars, to avoid losing what they've come to feel is theirs, and they end up paying far more than they would have said it was worth a moment before the bidding started. Test drive the car, start getting comfortable in it, and your willingness to pay starts drifting upward. We can be haunted by the specter of losing even things we never had.

In one way, the bad does taint the good irrationally. You sell two identical sets of dishware, except that one of the sets adds two extra pieces, both of them broken. You could buy the set with some broken pieces, throw away the broken ones, and be left with the same thing as the other set. But buyers will pay less for the set that includes broken pieces. The broken pieces spray a stink on the good pieces. This applies generally. Make three good arguments, and then add a dumb throwaway argument. Now the first three look weaker. This is the smelly version of the halo effect.

In a corollary to the bad-over-good principle, we treat zero risk or zero cost as a special thing. Reducing a harm to zero thrills us. We might pay $1,000 to decrease the risk of some bad thing from 20% to 10%. But we might pay three times that to reduce the same risk by the same amount, if we're moving it from 10% to 0. Our values don't scale up or down in a linear way. Just as we show decreasing sensitivity to losses above a high threshold, so we show increasing sensitivity to cost or risk reductions as they approach zero. Certainty, complete safety, full guarantee, free — these all feel especially good and command a premium.

The bad-over-good principle holds obvious implications for

legal work. First, of course, no dumb arguments. Besides that, you generally want to paint the other side as threatening a loss of something we already have. The other side threatens to take away a little bit of justice or safety or efficiency or whatever that we've gone to a lot of trouble to secure. All else equal, you probably want to focus more on the other side's bad behavior than on your side's good behavior.

2.5.5 THE MORAL SENSIBILITIES OF LIBERALS AND CONSERVATIVES DIFFER IN PREDICTABLE WAYS.

The labels "liberal" and "conservative" don't do justice to the wonderful individuality of you or me, of course, but they serve a useful purpose all the same. Haidt concludes that Americans do have two dominant styles of moral sensibility. Liberals tend to place great weight on care and fairness, while placing little weight on loyalty, authority, sanctity, and liberty. Conservatives tend to place roughly equal weight on all six concerns. We should take account of these differences in deciding how to shape a case.

The psycho-linguist George Lakoff describes generic moral worldviews of liberals and conservatives:

> The progressive view [] is that democracy depends on citizens caring about each other and taking responsibility both for themselves and for others. This yields a view of government with a moral mission: to protect and empower all citizens equally. The mechanism for accomplishing this mission is through what we call the Public, a system of public resources necessary for a decent private life and a robust private enterprise: roads and bridges, education, health care, communication systems, court systems, basic research, police and military, a fair judicial system, clean water and air, safe food, parks, and much more.
>
> Conservatives hold the opposite view: that democracy exists to provide citizens with the maximum *liberty* to pursue their self-interest with little or no commitment to the interests of others. Under this view, there should be as little of the Public as possible.

Instead, as much as possible should be relegated to what we call the Private. The Private is comprised of individuals (private life), businesses owned by them (private enterprise), and institutions set up by groups of individuals (private clubs and associations). The Private is, for conservatives, a moral ideal, sacrosanct, where no government can tread, whether to help or hinder, regulate, or even monitor. No one should have to pay for anyone else. Private interests should rule, even if that means that corporate interests, the most powerful of private interests, govern our lives through a laissez-faire free market. Citizens are free to sink or swim on their own.[2]

Other researchers have offered other descriptions of basic moral worldviews that predominate in America now. Anyone hoping to persuade other people should take a look at the literature on these issues.

Unless you're arguing to a judge and law clerk you know well, a lawyer making an argument needs to look for facts and issues that make the case compelling to the range of moral and ideological sensibilities. Obviously some cases will have more potential for universal appeal; some will have less. But whatever potential the case does have, you probably won't find it without making a special effort to look.

2.5.6 WE ENJOY ALTRUISTIC PUNISHMENT.

Whatever our moral sensibilities, we take pleasure in altruistic punishment. When someone breaks the rules in a way that threatens to harm others, we enjoy punishing the rule-breaker. In experiments, people pay money for the privilege of punishing someone who cheated a third person. The pleasure centers in the brain light up. We cheer when the bad guy gets his comeuppance. Plaintiffs will sometimes give up a good settlement offer, as the price for a trial that will punish the wrongdoer with public exposure. Judges and law clerks will sometimes work extra hard to dismantle offensively dishonest arguments. Jurors may dig in and fight for a verdict that reflects their anger at the offending party. That should not only encourage us to behave ourselves in litigation; it should inform the stories we tell in briefs and in trials.

2.5.7 WE FEEL THAT OTHER PEOPLE SEE THINGS AS WE DO.

Our own view of things seems so natural and clear. Other people, or most of them at least, must see things more or less the same way. Intellectually, you know that's false. But despite this abstract insight lodged in one circuit of your brain, most of your brain goes on believing that everyone else sees things the way you do. As you go about your daily life, focusing on this or that other thing, with no thought in mind about cognitive science, this feeling of false consensus takes hold of you.

Many a lawyer, and the clients, have been brought to grief by the false consensus effect. You write a brief or present a case at trial, confident that the judge or jury can't get it wrong. Then they do, and your world gets turned upside down. You're mystified, betrayed, and heartbroken. The ship is rudderless and has slipped its moorings. The world is chaos. There's no understanding or predicting anything. Well, maybe; more likely though, you just didn't do enough work to identify the likely range of views you'd encounter from the judge or jury.

2.5.8 WE NEED TO FEEL THE WORLD IS SAFE, JUST, UNDERSTANDABLE.

Of the deep, enduring mental tendencies that shape our responses and judgments to particular questions, one of the most important for lawyers is our need to feel that the world is safe, just, and understandable.

Ironically, stupidly, tragically, this tendency can contribute to making the world less safe, less just, less understandable. The tendency nudges jurors to blame the cancer victim for the doctor's missed diagnosis. If this doctor could miss the cancer, then maybe my doctor could, too. Maybe the danger applies generally, to all of us. I don't want to believe that, so instead it was the plaintiff's fault for not getting a second (or third, or fourth) opinion. I would know better, so I'm safe, and the same goes for everyone close to me. So no accountability for the negligent doctor. And the world becomes a little more safe for negligent doctors and a little less safe for the rest of us.

Obviously, no one reasons this way consciously. We just respond this way, instantly, unthinkingly. If the need to feel safe presented itself to our conscious selves and elaborated its argument in detail, we'd reject it. But it doesn't happen that way. We just see a thing and respond to it, the response shaped without our awareness.

Any lawyer raising the specter of injury from negligence (or worse) should avoid scaring us with the thought that the world is less safe than we thought it was. Exactly how to do this depends on the particulars of the situation. In general, though, the lawyer should present facts that first show a comforting norm, with rules that people routinely follow and that keep us all safe. Only then should the lawyer present the facts that show a departure from the normally followed rules. Then, expressly or by implication, the lawyer should evoke the insight that if we give this person a pass for transgressing the normal rules, the norms will decay over time and we'll lose the safety we've created over time through hard work.

2.5.9 WE BLAME DEPARTURES FROM THE NORM.

Along similar lines, we over-invest in what's normal, and when things go wrong, we tend to look for — and blame — departures from the norm. Often enough, this makes sense, but the tendency also operates when it makes no sense. A guy goes home from work the same way every day. Today, though, he changes his route, and he gets rear-ended. It sort of feels like it's his fault, doesn't it? We're not powerless against the knee-jerk tendency to mindlessly blame the departure from the norm, but a lawyer should take account of that tendency.

2.5.10 WE SEE RACE, GENDER, AND CLASS.

The big demographic categories — race, gender, and socioeconomic class — are fraught with complexity and anguished controversy. A serious discussion of them lies well outside the scope of this book. We can safely say, though, that these things matter. At the level of large groups, differences in these categories are associated with differences in experience, thought, and feeling. And we tend to think and feel differently about others, depending in part on these demographic categories. If you're a decent person, you don't like this fact about how you think and feel, and in your better moments at least, you try to counteract it. But in 21st Century America, race and gender do still matter to all of us, even nice people like you and me.

To some extent, a person's race or gender or class influences how that person thinks and feels about things. In some domains at least, males and females do tend to think and feel differently. For example, women tend to pay closer attention than men to relationships and the feelings of others. To the extent that people of different races — still in 21st Century America — tend to have characteristically different personal backgrounds, those differences presumably affect how we each tend to see things. Black people tend to put less trust than white people, for example, in the police. Obviously, these are only tendencies, not universally applicable iron laws. And the categories — especially race and gender — get complicated at the boundaries.

For a lawyer, it makes no difference whether these differences in thought and feeling arise from inculturation and personal history or from intrinsic nature. Wherever they come from, if they're here, they matter. Again, this book attempts no serious discussion of these factors, but the thoughtful lawyer will investigate their impact on legal disputes. These factors matter most obviously in jury selection, but they may work in subtler ways in case selection, case development, depositions, and so on. We needn't focus unduly on race, gender, and so on, and we need not give up the ideal of a world in which they no longer interfere with fairness, but until we attain that ideal, it would be unwise for a lawyer to ignore these factors.

2.6 WE CAN IMPROVE DECISION-MAKING A LITTLE

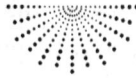

The human mind achieves stupendous things in many realms, and reliably screws up in others. As for fixing the screw-ups, we have cause for only modest optimism.

2.6.1 HARD THINKING HELPS, BUT LESS THAN WE'D LIKE.

To make good, careful thinking work effectively, we need to embed it in habits and in explicit policies and processes. A generic commitment to careful thinking doesn't help much.

A general commitment to careful thinking quickly runs up against several limitations. *First*, hard thinking is hard, and we don't like to do it. It takes effort and usually feels unpleasant. It requires challenging answers we feel sure of, and that annoys us. We like the feel of certainty, of having resolved a problem. We don't want to jump back into confusion. Further, thinking hard takes time, and we're always short on time. Indeed, disciplined thinking comes so unnaturally to us that we have a name for one of its main varieties — "the scientific method" — and we speak of it as having been "invented" long after civilization got under way.

Careful thinking is hard enough that we often substitute a mere schoolboy rhetoric of rigor, which we smear over rotten arguments. The rhetoric of rigorous thinking usually sounds formal, uses specialized words unnecessarily, insists on the speaker's objectivity, and ostentatiously avoids emotion. That sort of rhetoric can make us feel sophisticated and can impress children, but it does not improve our thinking.

Second, a general commitment to careful thinking is pitched at too high a level to do much practical good. Think carefully how? By doing what? We almost always think we're thinking carefully. No one sets out to think sloppily. Sloppy thinkers (which includes you and me) think they're thinking carefully.

Third, along the same lines, we underestimate how much effortful thinking we need in order to check our intuitive judgments, because those judgments usually feel solid. Our intuitions convince us. Often, we think checking them may serve as an intellectual virtue but isn't really necessary. Your grade school math teacher taught you how to check the product you got from multiplying two numbers. But do you regularly check your work that way? Me neither. Worse, lawyers and judges, and maybe jurors, feel especially confident in their intuitions, because the more powerful we feel, the more confident we feel.

Finally, careful thinking requires conditions that often don't exist. We get motivated to think rigorously when three conditions obtain: (1) we know before forming any opinion that our audience will hold us accountable for it, (2) we don't know what the audience thinks, and (3) we think the audience understands the issue well, can evaluate our opinion critically, and cares about accuracy.

Obviously we should commit to careful thinking. Deliberate stupidity won't help. But to get the most out of our capacity for careful thought, we need something more.

2.6.2 WE NEED GOOD ROUTINES FOR GOOD REASONING.

Habits and policies help by pushing the decision to think carefully down into the unconscious or into routine office procedures, where — once established — following the habit or policy becomes easy and automatic. Habits and policies can ensure we pay attention to things we naturally neglect. They can raise automatic dissent to force a second, more effortful look.

Together with deliberate practice, well-designed habits and routines provide the closest thing a smooth-skinned bipedal ape can get to a golden key to success and happiness. Thoughtful consideration designs the prospective habit, and deliberate practice creates the habit.

We create office procedures more easily than personal habits, but we can make useful headway even with the latter. Follow a routine long enough, and you begin following the steps automatically.

Routines and habits seem uninspired, but they serve as a tolerable substitute for genius. We grew up with the idea of genius as some sort of inspired spontaneity, suggesting that we should just let our minds alone and see what they come up with. But fishing for inspiration does only part of the work of thinking, and habits can help even with that part.

Here are some general suggestions that mostly work both as stages in an office workflow and as personal habits.

First, systematize and formalize as much as you usefully can. Create written rules, procedures, checklists, workflows. Identify the things you think about or the steps you would ideally perform in this sort of project. Most complex things can't be fully reduced to rote procedures, but the more you can systematize and record a procedure, the less you have to rely on serendipity. The less you'll forget important things. The more well-formed your ideas will be early on.

Second, isolate the different parts of the process you're trying to formalize — the various constituent tasks — and go through them one at a time. If working in a group, do this together. This approach both ensures thoroughness and creates efficiency.

Third, employ an adversarial process before finally deciding on a course of action. Have someone play devil's advocate. If you're working solo and can't get anyone to help with this, at least simulate an adversarial process in your own head. Make it a formal thing you spend real time and energy on. A serious devil's-advocate effort will help scour your thinking for errors or unaddressed problems. It will help you identify competing values and emotional responses that the issues may implicate. It will help identify alternative frames, to see things from all angles. Lawyers usually play devil's advocate at least casually, but turn this into a serious effort.

Fourth, conduct a pre-mortem. Gary Klein and his colleagues invented this exercise. Before beginning a project, pretend you've been transported into the future and you just learned that the project failed. Write an explanation of why it failed. This will force you out of the comforting perspective from behind your own eyeballs.

Fifth, consider whether the circumstances for expert intuition apply in your situation. If you're a lawyer, they probably don't. Facing up to that unpleasant fact can give you a useful check against over-confidence.

Sixth, act things out, when possible. Pretend. Use role-playing. Adopt roles and talk out loud. Imagine yourself into the shoes of other people potentially involved in whatever you're thinking over. The out-loud role-playing enlists useful parts of your mental apparatus that lie dormant when you just sit in your armchair stroking your chin. Don't worry about looking dumb or feeling awkward. If you treat this as a natural, normal part of thinking things over, other people quickly acclimate to it.

Finally, write a list of the ways your characteristic mental errors may trip you up in the particular project at hand. Each of us has a unique set of mistakes we tend to make. Figure out what yours are, and write them down. Ask other people about it. If they're comfortable enough to be candid, they'll have insights that you don't have. Having identified these problems, you'll much more easily spot those problems in any given project.

Other routines may help, too. No mental habit or routine serves as a magic bean that eliminates error, but in a world bereft of magic beans, and beset with biases, our best hope for good thinking lies in nudging ourselves and improving incrementally.

2.7 FURTHER READING, ETC.

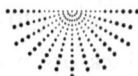

We have a large lay-audience literature on cognitive processes, judgment, and reasoning. I suggest starting with the following, in addition to the books I've already recommended. These materials will lead you to others.

BOOKS

- Daniel Kahneman, *Thinking, Fast and Slow* (2011).
- Roy Baumeister and Brad Bushman's *Social Psychology and Human Nature*, 3d (2013).
- Matthew D. Lieberman, *Social: Why Our Brains are Wired to Connect* (2013).
- David Berreby, *Us & Them: The Science of Identity* (2005).
- Gary Klein, *Streetlights and Shadows: Searching for the Keys to Adaptive Decision-Making* (2009).
- Gerd Gigerenzer, *Rationality for Mortals: How People Cope with Uncertainty* (2010).
- Dietrich Dorner, *The Logic of Failure: Recognizing and*

Avoiding Error in Complex Situations, translated by Rita and Robert Kimber (1996).

- Rüdiger Pohl, ed., *Cognitive Illusions: A Handbook on Fallacies and Biases in Thinking, Judgment and Memory* (2004).
- Richard Thaler and Cass Sunstein, *Nudge: Improving Decisions about Health, Wealth, and Happiness* (2009).
- Jonathan Haidt, *The Righteous Mind: Why Good People are Divided by Politics and Religion* (2012).
- George Lakoff and Mark Johnson, *Metaphors We Live By* (1980).
- Douglas Hofstadter and Emmanuel Sander, *Surfaces and Essences: Analogy as the Fuel and Fire of Thinking* (2013).
- Dan Ariely, *Predictably Irrational: The Hidden Forces That Shape Our Decisions* (2010).
- Philip Tetlock, *Superforecasting: The Art and Science of Prediction* (2015).
- Richard Nisbett, *Mindware: Tools for Smart Thinking* (2015).
- Chip and Dan Heath, *Made to Stick: Why Some Ideas Survive and Others Die* (2007).
- Albert Jonsen and Stephen Toulmin, *The Abuse of Casuistry: A History of Moral Reasoning* (1988).
- David Hackett Fischer, *Albion's Seed: Four British Folkways in America* (1989).
- Richard Nisbett and Dov Cohen, *Culture of Honor: The Psychology of Violence in the South* (1996).
- Lisa Feldman Barrett, *How Emotions are Made* (2017).
- Anders Ericsson & Robert Pool, *Peak: Secrets from the New Science of Expertise* (2017).
- Martin Seligman, *Learned Optimism* (1991).

OTHER MATERIALS

- National Geographic TV series *Brain Games*. This series

provides entertaining demonstrations of many of the
psychological principles discussed above.

- NPR's *RadioLab* podcast.
- NPR's *Invisibilia* podcast.
- NPR's *Hidden Brain* podcast.
- BBC's *All in the Mind* podcast.
- American Psychological Association podcast, *Speaking of Psychology.*
- Derren Brown BBC TV shows and specials. Brown is a British entertainer who specializes in the mentalism form of magic. Some of his productions consist of mere fakery that can be entertaining but is of no interest here. However, a number of Derren Brown's shows provide striking demonstrations of various psychological principles discussed above. Brown's productions may be useful, provided you watch skeptically. As of 2020, it appears that all Brown's BBC productions are available on YouTube.

PART III
COMMUNICATION AND PERSUASION

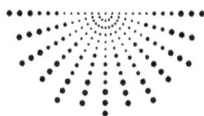

Communication and persuasion have a lot to do with the points we've already discussed. The following discussion tries to build on the preceding discussion with minimal repetition.

Persuasion appeals to, and works through, the whole person. In brief, persuasion occurs when you (a) communicate effectively — itself a high bar to clear — (b) attract listeners to your idea and (c) overcome whatever resistance they feel. The shorter the distance you need the audience to move, the easier to get them to do it. And the more that listeners trust you, the more willing they'll be to move your way.

Most of the time, we process persuasive appeals thoughtlessly — when we see TV commercials, drive past billboards, dismiss the kids' demand for a puppy, and so on. We respond to those appeals based on feelings and intuitions that we don't give much thought to. Under the right circumstances, however, we process persuasive appeals thoughtfully. Even then, though, feelings and intuition still drive the process.

3.1 WE COMMUNICATE BY EVOKING THOUGHTS AND FEELINGS IN SOMEONE ELSE'S HEAD — ALWAYS IMPERFECTLY

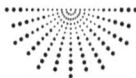

W e use a variety of metaphors to talk about communication. Most commonly, we speak of communication as "conveying" ideas or information from one person to another, like pouring water into a jug. We sometimes speak of communication as encoding a message, which the audience then decodes. Both these ways of speaking serve useful purposes.

Here, though, it helps more to think of communication as evoking (or provoking) responses in the listener's or reader's head. You want to get some fact or idea or feeling into the other person's mind. But you can't just write it on a slip of paper and shove it in their ear.

We have no device for simply, cleanly prompting someone else's brain to generate an exact set of thoughts and feelings. Instead, we have sticks to poke someone's brain, to make it generate the activity we want the listener to have. Everything we use to communicate — words, grimaces, tears, grunts, pheromones, scary masks, arm-waving, hoots of derision, a tilt of the head, a wry smile, an artillery shot across the bow, etc. — they all work by provoking the other person's brain to generate mental activity. In trial, we have lots of sticks to poke with. In brief-writing, the sticks consist mostly of bare, disembodied language, and a graph or picture here or there.

But poking brains — even with a precise, subtle stick like a carefully crafted sentence — communicates crudely. Any given word, say *"foot"* or *"truth"* or *"symmetry"* for example, does slightly different things in each of our heads. We each associate different things with the word, understand it differently, respond emotionally to it in different ways, and so on. All communication is crude. All communication is approximate.

The following points elaborate on these general comments.

3.1.1 COMMUNICATION EVOKES INTELLECTUAL, EMOTIONAL, AND PHYSIOLOGICAL RESPONSES.

The response-evocation metaphor should remind you that the other person responds as a whole person — an emotional as well as intellectual being, a body, not a spirit. Even a dry sentence in a brief evokes more than just antiseptic intellectual understanding. *"The Court has held that 'one legitimate purpose of the use of other acts evidence is intent.'"* If you know anything about the law of evidence, the sentence probably does evoke the idea of "other acts" evidence to show intent. But the sentence also draws related ideas and emotions up from your unconscious. They might include a preemptive aversion to what's probably going to be a sketchy argument for admitting irrelevant, prejudicial information. The sentence might remind you of occasions on which a judge wrongly excluded plainly admissible evidence. The sentence might bore or annoy you. The sentence might make your shoulders tighten or your stomach turn.

All language carries some private meaning for the reader — much of it emotional. It helps to recognize the mystery of communication and to approach it with some muted, everyday awe and apprehension.

3.1.2 THE AUDIENCE IS EVERYTHING (SORT OF).

All of this emphasizes the old truism that you have to know your audience. The better you know your audience, the better you can predict what thoughts and feelings you'll evoke. Most of the time, you can communicate with a long-term partner better than with a stranger. You come closer to speaking the same language. The same principle works with everyone else. The more you know about your audience, the more landmines you can avoid, the closer you can get to the bullseye.

3.1.3 COMMUNICATION ALWAYS FAILS, A LITTLE OR A LOT.

However much you know your audience, communication always fails to some degree — sometimes trivially, sometimes tragically. That it always falls short of perfection shouldn't surprise us; the wondrous thing is that it works at all. We make noises, put squiggles on paper, wrinkle our faces, gesticulate, and somehow that gets other people to have thoughts in their heads that are roughly similar, apparently, to the thoughts we want them to have. This is high magic, but we do it every day, so we get complacent. Communication is crazy complicated, and it always goes wrong to one degree or another.

For starters, you mostly want your listener or reader to have some collection of the thoughts and feelings in your own head. But you don't even know your own intention completely. You think you do, but you don't. For example, you text your daughter, saying you'll be home from work a little late. That domestic banality may entail a range of related thoughts and feelings you're only half-aware of. At some level, you want your daughter to know you're working late because of an obligation you can't reasonably avoid. And you want her to know you're done being mad at her for speaking rudely to you the night before. You want to warn her against going out tonight. And in some small way you mean that you love her. You want her to feel attended to, cared for. But you don't spend an hour of introspection before writing the text. You just write, "Working late tonight. I'll be home a little late," without a full, conscious knowledge of everything you vaguely want to convey.

Of course not every communication carries the complexity of this nine-word text message. But every communication carries some unspoken complexity. The full weight of our speech almost always goes beyond what we've consciously considered.

If you don't even know your own mind fully — and you don't — you can't possibly know how to make the other person's mind perfectly replicate the thoughts and feelings you want to evoke.

Often, you know enough about the other person's mind (and your own) for practical purposes, but not even always for that. "What's the electoral college?" the guy asks, 10 minutes into your rant. Before you started complaining about the antiquated counter-majoritarian institution, it hadn't even occurred to you that the guy had never heard of the electoral college.

Nor can you ever really know to what extent you've succeeded or failed in communicating. In response to your text about working late, your daughter texts you back: "OK." She certainly under-stood that you'll be home late (unless she replied without bothering to read your text). But you don't know — and she probably couldn't tell you — what else she understood of the ill-defined thoughts and feelings you in some sense wanted to communicate. We don't see all our miscommunications. Sometimes we find out only weeks or years later that we misfired. Often, no doubt, we never find out. When we're lucky, we find out in time to take another stab at it, before trouble takes hold irreparably.

The mystery of communication leads to problems that range from the inconsequential to the heartbreaking. Milan Kundera elaborates this point in his novel *The Unbearable Lightness of Being*. In a section called "Words Misunderstood," Kundera discusses the misunderstandings between Sabina and Franz, which would ulti-mately doom their relationship.

But let us return to the bowler hat.

First, it was a vague reminder of a forgotten grandfather, the mayor of a small Bohemian town during the nineteenth century.

Second, it was a memento of her father. After the funeral her brother appropriated all their parents' property, and she, refusing out of sovereign contempt to fight for her rights, announced sarcastically that she was taking the bowler hat as her sole inheritance.

Third, it was a prop for her love games with Tomas.

. . .

The bowler hat was a motif in the musical composition that was Sabina's life. It returned again and again, each time with a different meaning, and all the meanings flowed through the bowler hat like water through a riverbed. I might call it Heraclitus' ("You can't step twice into the same river") riverbed: the bowler hat was a bed through which each time Sabina saw another river flow, another semantic river: each time the same object would give rise to a new meaning, though all former meanings would resonate (like an echo, like a parade of echoes) together with the new one. Each new experience would resound, each time enriching the harmony. The reason why Tomas and Sabina were touched by the sight of the bowler hat in a Zurich hotel and made love almost in tears was that its black presence was not merely a reminder of their love games but also a memento of Sabina's father and of her grandfather, who lived in a century without airplanes and cars.

Now, perhaps, we are in a better position to understand the abyss separating Sabina and Franz: he listened eagerly to the story of her life and she was equally eager to hear the story of his, but although they had a clear understanding of the logical meaning of the words they exchanged, they failed to hear the semantic susurrus of the river flowing through them.

And so when she put on the bowler hat in his presence, Franz felt uncomfortable, as if someone had spoken to him in a language he did not know. It was neither obscene nor sentimental, merely an incomprehensible gesture. What made him feel uncomfortable was its very lack of meaning.

. . .

If I were to make a record of all Sabina and Franz's conversations, I could compile a long lexicon of their misunderstandings.[1]

Slight degrees of miscommunication can spark a married couple to argue for hours, cause a lawyer to lose a motion, or cause a space shuttle to launch despite flaws that will kill the crew.

Failures of communication occur with terrifying ease. A friend of mine lost a case after the jury deliberated for half an hour. He spoke to a few jurors afterward and realized they had missed the most basic, undisputed fact of the case — that his client had paid his mortgage on time, every time. If you give it a minute, you can probably think of similarly shocking misunderstandings in your own past. If you're not paranoid, you're not paying attention.

This, incidentally, furnishes one reason we should listen and read generously. When something sounds ridiculous or vile, we should look for a misunderstanding before accepting that the speaker meant the ridiculous or vile thing we first heard. To do otherwise reflects a childish but uncharming faith in the transparency of language and meaning — and it makes life worse than it needs to be.

Lawyers (like everyone else) lose sight of the difficulty of mere communication, and we thereby harm our efforts. We may obsess over the nuances of appealing to jurors, and spend enormous time and money figuring out how to get through on a personal, emotional level — all while forgetting the simplest, oldest techniques for making sure the bare information gets through. The attention to those subtler things is right, but only after first seeing to the fundamentals of mere communication.

3.2 WRITING AND READING MAKE THE PROBLEMS WORSE

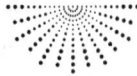

The difficulties of communication get worse when you move from talking to writing. Writing, unlike talking, is a recent invention. Reading and writing don't come naturally to anyone. Moreover, in writing you lose a host of cues we give each other in person. You don't see the nodding, the querulous furrow, the snide grin, the impatient stare, and so on. That makes it harder to communicate and understand.

3.2.1 WRITING AND READING ARE UNNATURAL.

We possess an innate ability for talking, but we do not read or write naturally. That's an acquired skill. We invented writing only about 5,000 years ago, thousands of years after we started living in sedentary agricultural societies. From those early beginnings, it still took thousands of years for modern alphabets to emerge. Through most of that history, literacy remained a specialized skill limited to small numbers of people. Only in the last few hundred years has literacy expanded, in some countries, to a majority of the public. Even now a large minority of Americans can't read beyond a grade school level. Statistics on this are uncertain, but moderate proficiency — the ability, say, to read a New York Times article — probably remains limited to fewer than half Americans.

Even for expert readers, the lack of context and nonverbal cues makes reading hard. Even for those of us who read for a living, we use language mostly in direct conversation or simulated conversations through TV, radio, YouTube, and the like. Reading remains a little rarefied even for us.

Writing is even harder than reading. In spontaneous speech, we're in the moment; we speak from within a single train of thought. That gives coherence to oral speech. In writing, though, a single page or paragraph may be written over several times. We move sentences and paragraphs around. We forget what we were first thinking when we wrote a given passage.

When you write, a hidden knowledge gap makes you confuse the reader. You understand your point because you have a mountain of contextual information beyond what you put on the page. You don't know how much of that context the reader has in mind. In face-to-face conversation, the listener will look confused or ask a question, and you'll clarify. In writing, we assume too much shared understanding. Our own knowledge starts feeling familiar and obvious. So we don't mention the context, and we confuse the reader.

Psychologists and linguists have identified other principles concerning how we read. I'll briefly address only what strike me as the most important points.

3.2.2 MERELY PARSING THE DAMNED SENTENCE TAKES WORK.

We have to hold a sentence in working memory until we close the subject/main verb/object loop. We have a tiny working memory. Short sentences help us. With them, we quickly close the loop, clear our working memory and start over with the next sentence. You can make a long sentence easy on memory, too, so long as the reader can parse clauses in sequence, without suspending words in memory too long. *"I went to the airport, then to the hospital, then to the morgue."* You parse "I went" instantly, and then you just have a sequence of three prepositional phrases. You could add another 10 items to the series, and you'd still parse it easily enough. Modifiers work the same way. *The first Congress wisely created the venerable tradition of laziness, which has served the country well by limiting how much the federal government tries to interfere in our lives."* Here again the modifiers don't overburden working memory, because the longer modifying phrases occur at the end, after you've closed the subject/main verb/object loop (*Congress created the tradition*). You can easily parse the long "which has served" phrase separately.

The limitations on working memory also argue against long noun phrases. We frequently need to talk about things we don't have short names for. You want to talk about "the tendency of courts interpreting ERISA to disregard the imperative for insurers to cooperate with claimants." That long phrase identifies a single thing, but if you use that phrase as the subject of a sentence, you'll overtax the reader's working memory. Long noun phrases abound in legal writing. They slow us down and make us miserable.

The limitations on working memory also support the principle, *light before heavy.* When you must use a long phrase that burdens the memory, put it at the end of the sentence, after the reader has parsed everything else. Steven Pinker cites the prayer to deliver us from "ghoulies and ghosties and long-leggedy beasties and things that go bump in the night." "Things that go bump in the night" requires more processing, so it comes last. Even if you had no sense of rhythm, you wouldn't write "long-leggedy beasties and ghoulies and things that go bump in the night and ghosties."

3.2.3 UNFAMILIAR THINGS GET IN THE WAY.

Anything unfamiliar slows the reader down. Words the reader doesn't often hear make the reader search memory to pull them up from the unconscious. That takes time, and the reader might retrieve the wrong memory and grow confused. Words wholly unfamiliar to the reader pose a greater problem. At best, the reader has to figure out the meaning from the context, which takes time and effort. If that doesn't work, the reader either has to stop to fetch a dictionary or just make do without the meaning of the word.

How much risk of this (or any) sort you can tolerate depends on the situation. When you write a book largely for the fun of saying what you want to say, then you can tolerate throwing up a little obstacle here and there for a subset of readers. In a magazine essay, your readers might enjoy a little esoterica here or there. When you write a brief to win a motion, it makes no sense to allow obstacles for the judge and law clerk.

3.2.4 DIFFERENT PEOPLE READ DIFFERENTLY.

Even lawyers and judges vary significantly in how they read, depending on personal characteristics and on the situation. We may skim or skip around. We may read at leisure or in a rush. We may assume we already know everything important in a brief, or we may look to it for education. Attend closely, when you can, to the sort of reader you've got and the particulars of the situation.

3.2.5 EXPECTATIONS SHAPE WHAT WE READ.

We read with expectations about what the text is going to say. Those expectations come from standard syntax, from our instinct to find agents and actions, from word associations, and from the content we've already read. If the text says, "The cat in the hat sat on …," you probably expect the next words to be "the mat." Where the text violates expectations, it may either make the reading harder or make us misread the text. If the misreading creates confusion, we might go back to figure out what's going on. But often enough we don't bother.

Ambiguities work the same way. If readers see the ambiguity, they have to consider the possible meanings and figure it out. More often, readers won't spot ambiguities until they become confused and realize they misread something — at which point they may go back to untangle it, or they may just shrug, miss your point, and plow on.

Since the reader forms expectations based on syntax, a writer should have a good handle on standard syntax and stick to it unless there's a good reason not to. The default English sentence goes like this: *Subject* [then] *action verb as the main verb* [then, optionally] *objects*. Thus, "I ate" or "Jesus wept." Or "I ate lunch" or "Jesus wept tears." Our brains look for agents performing actions, and native English speakers digest language more easily when the syntax follows the archetypal structure. Thus, "Congress enacted the law" not "The law is in effect." The latter version does not show an action; it describes a state of being. "The law was enacted" gives us an action, but it leaves out the agent. Even "The law was enacted by Congress" botches the job. That sentence gives us an agent performing an action, but it screws up the sequence. The agent comes last, not first. The agent (Congress) gets cast not as the subject, but as a modifier to the main verb. That makes the reader's job harder. The difference adds just a fraction of a second of extra processing time. But pile hundreds of sentences like that into a brief or opening statement, and you'll wear down your audience by imperceptible degrees. They'll find your brief or statement burdensome, probably without knowing quite why. They'll have less mental energy for thinking carefully and exercising self-discipline. Bad syntax hurts your chances of winning.

Sometimes you should violate expectations. Violations can surprise, can draw attention to something important, can make the reader smile. "The cat in the hat sat on the *mate*" is funnier than the cat that sat on the mat (unless the reader misses the change). But anything that may create confusion or difficulty for the reader demands special care. Any purposeful violation of expectations must call enough attention to itself that the reader won't miss it.

The English language accommodates a variety of sentence forms. We sometimes have good reason to use them. We do sometimes want statements of identity or states of being. *"Reading is hard"* or *"The argument seems frivolous."* As for complexity, English lets you stick modifiers almost anywhere. You can rearrange the elements of the sentence, putting both the main verb and its complements before the subject. *"Through the mist strode a giant."* You can use all this flexibility to nice effect, occasionally. But the default structure remains *Subject (agent) — main verb (action) — object (goal or recipient of the action)*. Native English speakers have that primordial sentence structure baked into our heads. Use it as your default sentence pattern.

That sounds simple enough, but it's not. Intellectuals like complexity. We lawyers are a sort of second-rate intellectual, and we share the bias. We naively think we show sophistication by departing from simple syntax. Unlearning that way of speaking takes work.

3.2.6 COMPREHENSION DEPENDS ON CONTEXT.

Reader comprehension depends largely on context to signal the meaning and significance of each statement within the whole. Without knowing the overall point of a paragraph, say, a reader has more trouble understanding the individual sentences within the paragraph. The reader needs to know where you're going, to understand what you're saying.

The need for context explains the need for thesis statements and topic sentences. As your high school composition teacher said, the piece as a whole should have an introductory statement that says clearly what you mean to prove (in the case of argument) or talk about (in non-argumentative pieces). Each main section should have its own mini-thesis statement. And each paragraph gets a topic sentence. These elements help the reader make sense of what comes next. For example, consider the following passage from a semi-famous study of reader comprehension:

> The procedure is actually quite simple. First you arrange things into different groups depending on their makeup. Of course, one pile may be sufficient depending on how much there is to do. If

you have to go somewhere else due to lack of facilities that is the next step, otherwise you are pretty well set. It is important not to overdo any particular endeavor. That is, it is better to do too few things at once than too many. In the short run this may not seem important, but complications from doing too many can easily arise. A mistake can be expensive as well. The manipulation of the appropriate mechanisms should be self-explanatory, and we need not dwell on it here. At first the whole procedure will seem complicated. Soon, however, it will become just another facet of life. It is difficult to foresee any end to the necessity for this task in the immediate future, but then one never can tell.

The researchers made the passage artificially abstract, but even so, it makes a lot more sense if you first read this: "The following paragraph says how to wash clothes."[1] Hearing the context at the outset helps the reader understand.

The need for context explains another principle: *Topic, then comment; given, then new.* Understanding comes easier when you start from what's familiar or easily understood and then add on something new. *"Even in his lifetime, Daniel Boone frequently got confused with Davey Crockett. Boone resented being confused with Crockett, because he regarded Crockett as a violent racist. Daniel Boone was born in 1734 and became a famous frontiersman and one of America's early folk heroes."* It slows you down to get thrown right into little-known detail about Boone first, with no context, and then to have a bland introduction to the topic afterward. We build comprehension the way we build scaffolding. We establish what we know and put that in place. Then we add something new and firm it up. Then another layer on top of that. Putting the new or controversial before the old or agreed-upon is like trying to hang the top layer of scaffolding first and then filling in beneath it. Maybe you can pull it off, but it's a bad idea all the same.

3.2.7 READERS NEED COHERENCE MARKERS.

Readers need coherence, and they need clear markers to signal how the parts relate to each other. The parts of a passage must relate closely to one another and to the declared point of the passage. This holds true for the whole text, a section of it, or a paragraph. At each level, the parts must unfold intuitively. Irrelevancies and erratic jumps cause trouble. Each part should flow organically out of the preceding part, or otherwise clearly mark its role in the discussion. Often, explicit connectors help show how the new sentence (or paragraph, or section) relates: *thus, so, third, for example, again, although, afterward, in short, further, but, even so,* and so on. With or without an explicit connector, the relationship of each new piece must make itself clear.

3.2.8 LEGAL WRITING AND READING ARE THE WORST.

In some respects, the legal setting makes written communication harder than other kinds of writing. Your audience doesn't feel especially receptive. The judge (or maybe just a law clerk), reads your brief for work, not for pleasure. They may resent having to read your stupid brief in the first place. They may just be looking for a quick way to dispose of the issue. They may do no more than to skim the brief. (Sometimes they won't even do that, but in those cases it doesn't matter how well you wrote the brief.) If you doubt any of this, go get a random set of briefs from someone else's case. Try to read them. You'll soon decide you've got better things to do. So do the judge and clerk. To make it worse, when they do read the briefs, they often don't read even a single brief in one sitting, let alone a whole set of briefs. And frequently they don't make decisions until days later. So you get their attention in disjointed pieces. You have to hope they remember what they read earlier in the morning, or a couple days ago.

Despite these drawbacks, however, in legal writing you often have the advantage of knowing your audience, at least a little. At the trial level, you generally have a single judge and law clerk as your primary audience. You can learn a lot about the judge. In many appellate courts, you can only guess which three judges from a larger group you're writing to. Still, you enjoy an advantage over the general magazine writer who can only imagine what sort of person will start reading a story.

～

A FULL SET of brief-writing advice lies beyond the scope of this book, but the problems of reading and writing require focused attention.

3.3 PERSUASION WORKS BY ACCOMMODATING THE DECISION-MAKER'S EXISTING VALUES, ATTITUDES, AND BELIEFS

We've discussed this general point, but it requires a separate point heading in any discussion of persuasion: We feel drawn to things that express, support, or are at least consistent with, our existing thoughts and feelings. That includes simple factual elements of our worldview — our sense of how things work, what kinds of things happen, what types of people exist, and what they do. For example, Judge Jed Rakoff has commented that having served as a prosecutor, he used to think false convictions existed mainly in urban legend. When DNA exonerations started multiplying, they changed Rakoff's sense of the world, and of criminal law.[1] You want to know how the decision-maker sees the world, so you can fit your argument into that worldview.

The more you accommodate your position to the decision-maker's existing beliefs, values, attitudes, worldview, and so on, the more you'll succeed. That's obvious, but we forget it. Our own view seems so compelling. If only we present our own view clearly and simply, we *have* to win. Wrong. A trial won't change a juror's existing beliefs, except minimally. A brief won't change a judge's beliefs. If you can't appeal to thoughts and feelings that already reside in the decision-makers' minds, you lose.

3.4 WHEN YOU CAN GET IT, THOUGHTFUL CONSIDERATION MITIGATES IRRELEVANCIES, BUT IRRELEVANCIES ALWAYS MATTER

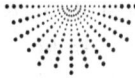

We want legal disputes settled by sound reasoning that accounts for all relevant, legitimate factors and that excludes everything else. But humans aren't built for that sort of thing. What to do about all the irrelevant but human stuff that influences decisions?

We should start by acknowledging reality. All sorts of irrelevancies affect our decisions. It is true, of course, that the more thought we give a question, the better our judgment and the less difference irrelevant influences make. Even in a legal setting, though, that's less comforting than it sounds. Thoughtful consideration happens only when you have ability, motivation, time, self-control, and freedom from distraction. We often don't have all those ingredients at the same time, even with disputes resolved by a judge, at relative leisure, after briefing. And even under optimal conditions, irrelevant factors still carry some impact, even if it's limited.

Whether in trial or in brief-writing, we should make a point of identifying illegitimate irrelevancies and finding some way around them. Your opponent may bring them up, or they may arise on their own. If your client has a commercial breach of contract case but gained local notoriety for eating his neighbor's cat, you'll want to counteract the influence of that pungent, but probably irrelevant, fact. (If you're on the other side, you'll want to look for a reasonable argument that the cat-eating does somehow bear fairly on the issue. If you can't find any reasonable hook for it, you'll need to work on your self-control.)

You should also try to get any *legitimate* irrelevancies pulling in your favor. Legitimate irrelevancies include things that will come into play whether you like it or not. In a brief, for example, your prose will be good, bad, or indifferent, but whatever it is, it will exert some effect on the judge and clerk. Whether you organize your argument well or badly will matter. Whether you use well or ill-chosen examples will matter. In heaven, it would make no difference whether you're a good or bad lawyer, or whether you write a good or bad brief. On Earth, the quality of advocacy does matter. There's no way out of it. Legal argument implicates a host of inescapable, and therefore legitimate, irrelevancies. Do what you can to get them pulling your way.

But of course you should scrupulously avoid illegitimate irrelevancies — a gratuitous play for sympathy or outrage based on some clearly irrelevant fact, for instance. We will disagree about what facts count as wholly irrelevant, what factors have no legitimate bearing, but wherever you draw the line in good faith, nothing on the other side comes in. Apart from your own sense of shame, you face the risk of being called out by your opponent or by the judge, and suffering harm to your reputation.

3.5 TRUST CONFERS POWER, SO WE GIVE IT WARILY

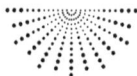

Trust plays a central role in our lives. Social life, cooperative effort, institutions, complex economies and civilizations — virtually everything in our lives — requires trust. You can't put money in a bank if you don't trust the competence and integrity of that bank, the larger banking system, and the thousands of nameless people who will become directly or indirectly involved in handling your money. You can't drop your kids off at school if you don't trust the people there to treat your child with care and decency. You can't get married if you don't trust your betrothed to love and honor you, and to faithfully unclog the kitchen sink and take the kids to soccer practice.

3.5.1 TRUST CONFERS POWER.

Trusting someone gives them enormous power over us. Trust well placed gives us love and friendship, fair value for the money we spend on a car, economic growth, skyscrapers that don't tip over, good medical care, and a million other things that make life better. Trust misplaced gives us broken families, Bernie Madoff, and a million other causes of misery.

This applies in litigation, too. Usually, neither a juror nor even a judge or law clerk can check the accuracy of every statement of fact or law. They certainly don't want to. Decision-makers need to be able to trust the accuracy and fairness of what you say. You need them to be able to trust you. Even if they spent the time to check everything that can be confirmed, some nuances come down to interpretive differences that can't be resolved by checking the record. In those instances, jurors, judges, and clerks want to be able to trust your competence, reasonableness, and integrity. It helps you if they can.

On the flip side of the coin, if a judge or juror does not trust you, your argument (and maybe your career) will suffer. I keenly remember when as a law clerk, I'd check selected citations in a brief and find that the brief seriously mischaracterized things. "Thanks, asshole," I would think. "Now I have to check every damned thing you say." I looked for other places where the author was lying or incompetent. I scrutinized the merits with extra rigor. I wanted to punish the lawyer whose sloppiness or lies made my work harder. I never drafted an opinion that betrayed any of this, but if you think it made no difference to my recommendation or the ultimate opinion, well … I'm sure you're right. Generally, though, we should assume an untrustworthy lawyer weakens the case.

Similarly, trust given and then betrayed provokes a special resentment or anger. A juror or judge may decide not to trust you in the first place. That's bad enough. But if you get them to trust you, and then you betray that trust — especially if you do so through a lack of integrity — you risk inciting greater, more lasting anger and contempt.

3.5.2 WE HAVE A HAIR-TRIGGER FOR UNTRUSTWORTHINESS, WHEN WE'RE WARY.

Questions of trust involve bewildering complexity. Because of the power of trust, we live amid an arms race between systems to figure out when to trust others, systems to get others to trust us, and systems to strategically reveal or conceal whether we trust them. Our brains have all three systems, and our success in life depends in part on how well they work. As a result of this arms race, we all have exquisitely subtle trust systems, but they often get it wrong.

When people are on heightened alert — like when they're buying a used car or resolving a legal dispute — they look for signs of untrustworthiness, and they err on the side of false positives. When we know people have reason to mislead us, we sense danger. Just as our brains err on the side of mistaking rubber hoses for snakes, rather than the other way round, so our brains err on the side of distrust.

This all means that lawyers should work hard to earn trust — honestly. Only a fool would try to win trust dishonestly. Few of us have the skill to pull off a convincing act in front of a jury scrutinizing us over days or weeks, or in front of a judge who serves as a professional skeptic who's seen all the tricks. And the lawyer on the other side is just waiting for a chance to expose you as a cheat.

3.5.3 TRUST BEGINS WITH GOODWILL.

Maybe the fundamental question of human life is "What will you do to me?" In the stone-age world, when a member of a tiny tribe encountered a stranger in the jungle, the two strangers typically either ran away from each other, or one killed the other. Strangers are dangerous. Modern societies have grown up on the back of expanding trust, so now we congregate in airports with thousands of strangers, and we rarely fear they'll kill us. But the fundamental question, the existential fear, remains: "What will you do to me?" We can't be safe, we can't live, if we can't answer that question with substantial accuracy. Will you help me, harm me, or leave me alone? Do you bear me good will or bad?[1]

These hard-shelled questions imply softer but equally urgent questions. Do you respect and value me? Are you paying attention to me? Do you care about me, my interests, my needs, wants, and desires? If not, you're dangerous to me in one way or another. Believing you poses a risk. I shut my ears to you.

In modern life, we don't react in extremes to everything that might make us doubt someone's concern for us — but we do so often enough. Your sister loves you and knows you love her. But she's always thought you see yourself as better than her. So when you disagree with her political comment on Facebook, she sees it as a personal attack and turns angrily away from you. In jury selection, you turn too quickly from one juror to another, without acknowledging the first juror's comment, and you can see that juror shut down and turn cold. You've lost him. At a hearing, answering a judge's question, your voice betrays a little impatience with a wrong-headed comment the judge made, and the judge grows hostile for the rest of the hearing. We don't encounter these reactions in every exchange, but in the time it's taken you to read this paragraph, some brother got a hurt, furious response from a sister; some lawyer felt that juror shut down; some lawyer saw that judge turn hostile.

Trust begins with my deciding that you respect me, that you see me as an equal, that you care about my interests, that you won't manipulate me. If I'm unsure, I eye you warily. But if I think you disrespect or disregard me, then to you I'm a brick wall. You can break your head against me, for all I care.

3.5.4 EMOTIONAL KINSHIP SERVES AS A MARKER OF GOODWILL.

Tribal affiliation, emotional kinship, makes us feel we can trust others. Emotional kinship can make us receptive both to noble truths and to poisonous nonsense alike.

The power of emotional kinship, like water, can be used to destroy or to sustain, but like water, there's no doing away with it. In a legal setting, cheap manipulation tends to backfire on the fool who tries it. Even so, an honest, decent, reasonable cultivation of connection on a human level plays a necessary role in creating trust. If you don't connect emotionally, you have no persuasive force to lend your message. And they may shut their ears to your message.

3.5.5 INTEGRITY AND COMPETENCE SERVE AS GENERAL MARKERS OF TRUSTWORTHINESS.

Emotional kinship can overwhelm other markers of trustworthiness, but it doesn't always do so. As a general matter, we also look to integrity and competence. Generally, we want to know whether the other person will deal with us honestly and fairly, and whether they have a firm grip on reality.

Discussions of trustworthiness so often focus on integrity that it's worth briefly emphasizing competence. A car mechanic can be thoroughly honest and decent, but if you think he doesn't know what he's doing, you won't trust him with your car. A perceived lack of integrity provokes anger and resentment that incompetence does not, but it would be cold comfort to know a judge or juror distrusts you only because you're incompetent.

The basic point is as simple as it is hard: Make yourself thoroughly competent on the issues, and speak with absolute honesty, fairness, and accuracy. The lawyer who shades the truth, who exaggerates, who misleads, who fudges the facts, who takes cheap shots, who incites dishonest emotion — that is, the lawyer who lies — deserves a good hard slap in the face, and often enough will get it. Here are some of the specific markers of competence and integrity.

REPUTATION

Obviously, if you have past experience with someone, you'll have a sense of their competence and integrity. That will color your perception of everything they say. If you know their reputation from others, that, too, will color how you see them.

Usually, jurors won't know you by reputation. With judges, though, every sentence in every brief, every comment at every hearing — everything you do, more or less — weighs on your future credibility and goodwill with this judge. A brief or a hearing never concerns only a single dispute. To one degree or another, each brief or hearing bears on your entire career.

CONCERN FOR ACCURACY, FAIRNESS, AND REASONABLENESS

We trust people who clearly care about accuracy, fairness, and reasonableness. Lawyers suffer from a counterproductive desire to turn away from the other side's points, to wish away drawbacks and objections. Lawyers feel pulled to the most aggressive version of our points. All of that is human and natural, but it undermines trust.

When people show no commitment to accuracy, fairness, or reasonableness, you can't rely on them to tell you the full truth, to interpret things fairly, to make reasonable requests. You have to parse their statements suspiciously. So you search out the inaccuracies, the self-serving spin, the exaggerated demands. Anything they're mixed up in smells rotten.

Fairness requires an advocate to look disinterestedly at the facts and law, tell you the full truth, and give a reasonable explanation of their position. They don't have to make the other side's argument; they can take a partisan's view, but they do have to fairly take account of all the important facts and law. If they don't, you can't trust them.

When a lawyer does demonstrate real concern for fairness, though, it can produce striking results. There's a story of David Boies at a hearing on a procedural dispute in New York state court. (Whether it really happened or not, I don't know.) The judge brushed off the dispute by telling the other lawyer, "Talk to Mr. Boies about this. He'll propose something reasonable." A reputation for fairness pays off.

KNOWLEDGE AND MASTERY

Competence shows itself through mastery of the issue and an absence of objective mistakes. Possible errors of strategy or tactics don't necessarily undermine competence, but objective errors do.

CONFIRMATION

The less you ask someone to take things on trust, the more they'll trust you when you need it. So in a brief, for instance, provide accurate citations for every statement of fact and law. At trial, show the evidence immediately. In some situations, it makes sense to relax that rule. You probably don't want to submit 50 exhibits in support of a motion in limine. Generally, though, the less you implicitly say "trust me," the more trust you'll garner for when it counts.

OPENNESS AND WILLINGNESS TO TRUST

We tend to trust those who trust us. We think well of people who think well of us. We give respect and generosity to those who give it to us. We give what we get, and so does most everyone else.

Speak and write in a way that indicates trust in the juror's or judge's intelligence, diligence, and fairness. That doesn't mean ignoring problems with a judge or juror. You have to keep your eyes open, but you can do so in a way that still signals trust. Even in writing, and especially in person, we give ourselves away. Our word choice, examples, imagery, tone, and body language reflect how we feel. Your decision-makers possess exquisitely tuned feelers. Even where we don't recognize subtle cues consciously, we do so unconsciously. Before writing a brief or speaking to a judge or jury, get yourself into a friendly, respectful, trusting frame of mind and maintain that. Often that's easy; sometimes it's hard; it's always important. You can't persuade someone if you let them know you don't like or respect them. And you probably will let them know.

We show trust in part by arguing openly and honestly. If you respect and trust someone, you don't hide the ball. You don't slant the facts. You don't sow confusion. You don't make deceptive arguments. You don't deploy inappropriate emotion. That sort of thing suggests contempt for the judge or jury, and you risk getting contempt in return.

CIRCUMSTANCES THAT DETER CHEATING

Even good people sometimes cheat. So everybody knows you can trust people more when the circumstances provide no incentive to cheat, or when they actively deter cheating.

To the extent you can show that the circumstances support honesty, you increase trust. In a legal dispute, both sides usually have an obvious incentive to cheat, and they also face obvious deterrents. These circumstances usually won't merit comment, but unusual departures might — where you take a position that runs against your own interests, where your opponent's incentives skew in favor of winning at any cost, and so on. (You'd want to present the facts and let the judge or jury draw the conclusion on their own. It likely won't help to say outright, "See, I don't even have an incentive to lie to you.")

EMOTIONAL MATURITY AND AUTHENTICITY

We don't trust people who get inappropriately emotional or unemotional. It's weird. It suggests something is off about this person.

Emotional maturity requires a sense of proportion. Exaggerated claims, extreme language or tone of voice, excessive passion or anger or enthusiasm — these things all suggest an advocate without a firm grip on reality, a quarreler prone to misstatements, an extremist or monomaniac. We trust the person who focuses on the issue at hand, without distracting preoccupations — like a need to show off or to cut the other guy down to size. A guy who can't keep his eye on the ball can't say what the ball looks like.

Emotional maturity doesn't come naturally to all lawyers. A lot of us got into this work because we like to fight. We get our backs up. We get worked up. Some of us have a taste, and a knack, for cutting language. It feels good to indulge. But neutral decision-makers don't enjoy the fighting. They suspect you're talking so loudly because you have so little to say. The satisfaction of letting loose comes at a high cost.

This does not mean we should avoid emotion entirely. Emotional authenticity generates trust, and that means expressing genuine emotion in a way that fits the circumstances. In a legal setting, that almost always means a subdued, understated manner, but not a completely flat affect. (More on this later.)

Striking the right tone, displaying emotional maturity and authenticity, is tricky business. Often, you can't do it alone. We need other people to tell us when we're going too far, or not far enough. But whatever difficulty we face in getting the tone right, we have to do it.

RESPECT FOR NORMS

We trust our own kind more than outsiders. This means lawyers should make reasonable efforts to fit in with the community the judge or jurors belong to. You can't put on a mask that doesn't fit you. But to the extent you can fit in without misrepresenting your-self, do so.

For brief-writing, this presents a special problem. Legal writing abounds with bad or pointless norms. Fitting in completely would mean adopting counterproductive practices. In those situations, just try to strike a good balance. The problem usually doesn't grow unmanageable, because most legal communities contain substantial variation and flexibility. Wander too far, though, and you'll find yourself outside the fence, eyed warily by insiders.

PHYSICAL PRESENTATION

Appearances matter. They matter to you and me, not just to those shallow people out there. Maybe that makes us all superficial or foolish, but it's baked into our brains, and however indignantly we scold the tide, it keeps rolling in.

A presentation that looks like it comes from a professional inspires a little trust. At trial, a lawyer who looks organized, well-prepared, deeply knowledgeable, confident — that lawyer inspires a little trust. In a brief, the appearances consist of document design, page layout, typography, headings, paragraphing, spelling and punctuation, and the like. The contents of a sloppy-looking brief may demonstrate genius, but the slop undermines the effect. Looks matter, so attend to them.

3.5.6 AN APPEARANCE OF HIGH COMPETENCE CAN BACKFIRE.

Everything is complicated. We can't trust incompetent people, but people who seem too competent can intimidate us, make us feel inferior, make us resent them, make us root for them to fail, make us look for (and make up) reasons to reject what they say. I know this sounds pathetic, but if you keep an eye on your own reactions, there's a good chance you, too, feel this sort of resentment for people whose high competence makes you question your own worth. We all have our insecurities, and they generate resentments, however ashamed we'd be to admit it.

What to do about this risk of resentment? The answer is not to make mistakes deliberately. Mistakes pose their own intrinsic danger, and if you make them intentionally, you'll probably come off as patronizing. There's a good chance you won't look charming: You'll look like you think you're better than me.

A better answer to the resentment problem is: (a) stop trying to impress people, (b) cultivate a sense of your own limits, and (c) do your best but don't try to hide your faults or limitations. We resent highly competent people mainly because we imagine they look down on us. But when someone shows actual, honest humility and shows they respect us, the urge to take them down a notch vanishes. We may even feel affection for them.

It's hard to know how much these dynamics affect this or that trial presentation, this or that brief, but caution suggests taking the problem seriously. Personality comes through at trial, and even in a lone brief. So in any presentation, it makes sense to consciously write from the persona of someone with a little humility and with the self-confidence to be open about limits, to the extent that relates to the discussion. Here as in many other areas, being a good lawyer dovetails with being a good person.

~

YOUR PRESENTATION in person or in writing will inspire trust or distrust. That will help you or hurt you. Work hard to make yourself thoroughly competent and to demonstrate integrity, maturity, and authenticity.

3.6 SOCIAL DYNAMICS PULL US THOUGHTLESSLY AND AUTOMATICALLY

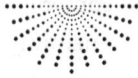

S ome situations elicit automatic responses. This happens constantly in social encounters, including the sort of simulated social encounter by which one person talks to another at a distance, through writing.

These social dynamics deserve attention, but lawyers shouldn't make too much of them. The larger the role played by thoughtful consideration, the smaller the role for these other factors. Still, judges and jurors remain human, and irrelevant social factors can matter.

3.6.1 WE CARE ABOUT OUR REPUTATION AND WANT OTHERS TO LIKE US.

Judges and jurors care about how others in the community regard them. Judges care about their reputation with other judges on their own court, with judges on higher courts, with practicing lawyers, politicians, and the public. Jurors care about how their family and friends will think about a verdict. Concern for the regard of others generally encourages thoughtful consideration. But we care more about some opinions than others.

3.6.2 WE WANT TO AGREE WITH PEOPLE WE LIKE.

We've discussed the halo effect. When we like someone, we want to agree with them. You may not be able to agree with them ultimately, but you try to. In argument as in almost every other part of life, therefore, it helps to make yourself likable.

3.6.3 WE RECIPROCATE.

Social creatures reciprocate as a matter of course. The pull of reciprocity runs deep. Knowing someone has done you a good turn can bias even your aesthetic sensibility in their favor, in ways that leave a signature in brain imaging studies.[1]

    Reciprocation has little room in a legal setting, but we shouldn't ignore it entirely. You can serve the interests of the decision-makers as well as possible. As a law clerk, I disliked lawyers who made my job unnecessarily hard — by sowing confusion with tendentious arguments, giving us hard-to-read briefs, supplying badly organized exhibits or appendices, and so on. I liked lawyers who kept their briefs trim, gave us accurate citations, characterized facts and law fairly, and so on. Those things make life easier for judge and clerk. Similarly, you can show respect for jurors by preparing well and moving efficiently, by not wasting their time with unimportant matters, and by making things as clear as possible.

3.6.4 WE WANT TO BE NORMAL.

We all want to be normal. We may judge normality by reference to a narrow community — Goths, evangelical preachers, judges, whatever — but within our community, we want to be normal. We like to say we don't care about that, but we're not fooling anyone. We never want to stand outside the palings of the community. It's dangerous out there.

    In briefs, align your position with widely shared views, and align your opponent's with departures from norms. If you have to argue against a common view, then look deeper. Try to align yourself with the underlying, widely-shared values.

3.6.5 WE LOOK TO AUTHORITY.

Authorities carry weight, whether in a legal setting or elsewhere. Lawyers tend to fixate on legal authorities, but authorities on fact and policy questions carry more weight on many issues.

3.6.6 WE AGREE MORE READILY WHEN WE'RE IN A GOOD MOOD.

We take a more generous, accepting attitude toward people when we're in a good mood. We analyze and criticize less enthusiastically. We agree more readily. Try to align the decision-maker's mood with the focus of attention. When you expect the jury to be in a bad mood, try to keep the focus on your opponent. Let your opponent take the harsh, critical stare. If you can manage it, put the judge and law clerk into a good mood when they read your brief.

Here again, there's only so much you can do about the decision-maker's mood. But if a jury comes in and sees your witness on the stand again three hours after they tired of her, you have not done your client any favor. If a judge or clerk opens your brief, reads two paragraphs, and sighs, "Oh, no. This is going to be painful," you've failed. If they think "To hell with this," before even opening your brief, because you've given them a thick stack of paper, you're in trouble. If, on the other hand, they instantly see you've given them a clear, easy-to-read brief that's no longer than it needs to be, they'll appreciate it. They won't bring you flowers, and they won't sing you love songs, but they're more likely to read to understand, not to find the nearest exit.

Less importantly but still worth a mention, humor and empathy can put us in a good mood and make us look more positively on a thing. Legal disputes allow little room for humor, and it often backfires, but the occasion does arise organically now and then. The other side makes an absurd argument. Sometimes you can demonstrate the absurdity in a dryly funny way, without coming off as mean. That can lighten the mood while discrediting the other side. Sometimes you can make a little flash of humor in passing, with your manner of speaking. But respect decorum, and ask around: If people say you're not funny, lay off the humor.

Empathy also requires delicate treatment but can do useful work. Judges and jurors resent cheap appeals to sentiment, but emotionally charged information often does bear on the issue. We can and should present information that evokes empathy, so long as we handle it appropriately. Don't wave the bloody shirt, but point to it.

Finally, personal conflict makes most people uncomfortable. Lawyers serve in part to put distance between disputing parties, to lift the cloud of animosity. When lawyers snipe at each other, judges and jurors groan. Your opponent behaves like an ass. I know; I feel your pain. But the judge and jurors probably won't. Even in the unusual case where judge or juror might share your anger, venting it yourself just lets the steam out of the kettle. Present the facts. Present them dryly. Let the judge or jurors boil with rage they can only vent through action.

3.7 A DECISION-MAKER'S FEELINGS TOWARD AN ADVOCATE — AND THE ADVOCATE'S FEELINGS TOWARD THE SUBJECT — MAKE A BIG DIFFERENCE

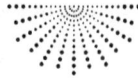

These two related points follow from what we've already discussed, but they need elaboration. The points seem simple, but they can all too easily lead into a maze of stomach-churning complexity, contradiction, and mystery.

As we've discussed, it's a lot easier to accept an advocate's position if you feel good about the advocate — if you like, respect, and trust the advocate; if you feel the advocate likes, respects, and trusts you. It is true of course that judges and jurors may decide in favor of a lawyer or party they don't like. It is true that we sometimes buy from a salesman we don't like. But in those instances the judge or juror or buyer has to swim upstream. This much is simple enough.

A less simple point: The advocate's feelings toward the subject under discussion will influence the decision-maker. We've talked about the significance of peripheral cues, heuristics, decision-making shortcuts that work automatically. The advocate's feelings toward the subject serve as one kind of peripheral cue. In most situations, an advocate knows more about the subject than the decision-maker. The decision-maker usually knows that. The decision-maker also knows that an advocate has an agenda and tries to make as strong a case as possible. Even if the advocate seems unusually honest and decent, the decision-maker still understands (and accepts) that any advocate, however honest, is trying to sell something. This means that any indication of the advocate's actual, unspoken feelings about the subject provide strong evidence of the truth. If you get the sense that, despite all his praise of this vacuum cleaner, the sales guy really doesn't think much of it, you won't buy it.

Sensing an advocate's actual feelings about the subject, however, gets tricky. The advocate can't just tell you how they feel — or at least their overt statements provide, at best, partial evidence. *"I really, really love this espresso machine."* Well, it's fine for a saleswoman to say so, but what really matters are all the soft, uncertain indicators of authenticity as she says it — tone of voice, facial expressions, posture, movement, hand gestures — along with other corroborating or non-corroborating information. These things communicate richly, but uncertainly. We vary tremendously in the manner and degree in which we express ourselves. And we vary tremendously in our sensitivity to these cues and how we interpret them.

To make it worse, we have shockingly limited conscious control over all the little ways in which we give ourselves away. As you focus on the words you're speaking, your eyebrows are doing something on their own, with no conscious control by you. So are your feet, and your hands, and the subtle creases at your cheeks, eyes, and brow. Try shifting your attention to those things, and they suddenly go off-kilter. Make a special effort to smile sincerely, and you look like a serial killer.

So all this means that one of the most important, powerful means of persuasion — expression of authentic feeling — works through one of the least reliable, least understood, least controllable modes of communication.

What to do with this knowledge? That's a conundrum. If you try too hard at any of this, you'll probably screw it up and make things worse. The guy who tries too hard to be liked just ends up annoying people and earning pity at best, contempt at worst. The woman who tries too hard to show that she really believes in her cause comes off as a phony.

It's almost impossible to avoid trying too hard, if you regard these things — the decision-maker's feelings toward you, or your feelings toward the subject — as tactical factors to work on in the moment of advocacy. Worry in the moment about whether the jurors like you, and you'll do something ham-handed to turn them off. Worry about whether you're expressive enough to let your real feelings show, and you'll make some clumsy gesture that looks like a dumb, theatrical attempt at manipulation.

Below, in discussing practical implications, I make some suggestions for how to act in light of the various principles discussed here. For now, I'll just restate the obvious: It's all very tricky.

3.8 WE ACTIVELY RESIST
CHANGING OUR BELIEFS

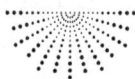

Persuasion involves two separate tasks: (1) attracting the audience to your message and (2) overcoming resistance. The things that create attraction may do nothing to overcome resistance, and vice versa. Attraction and resistance require separate attention.

Broadly, resistance wears three faces: (a) resistance to influence because it feels like a loss of autonomy ("reactance"), (b) resistance to change, regardless of the message (inertia), and (c) resistance to the message itself (skepticism).

3.8.1 WE DON'T LIKE BEING TOLD WHAT TO THINK OR DO.

We usually like being told we're right, but with that lone exception, we don't like being told what to think or do. Even if a message seems reasonable, something in us wants to push it away when speakers get pushy about it. This is "reactance" — a basic, gut-level aversion to anything that smacks of an effort to control you, to reduce your independence or autonomy. You can see it in toddlers who damn well don't want to have their faces cleaned, and

I've even read about husbands who don't like it when their wives say not to use so much syrup on the pancakes.

Reactance is not about the merits of the issue; so arguments don't overcome it. Tell a guy he can't say something, and he reflexively wants to say it. Maybe you gave him good reasons not to say it. Maybe he would never have said it on his own. But you said he can't say it, so now he wants to say it.

Generally, we have two broad ways of avoiding or reducing reactance. First, maximize the similarities between your message and what your audience already believes. The more you confirm what your audience already believes, the less you challenge their independence. Second, avoid pushy language.

More specifically, here are some of the main ways to avoid pushing your views onto someone else.

ACKNOWLEDGE POTENTIAL DISAGREEMENT.

Reactance can melt away almost magically, if you just acknowledge that the person you're talking with may disagree with you. That doesn't weaken your argument, but it implicitly acknowledges the other's intelligence and independence. You signal that you're not trying to force anything on them, but are just sharing your thoughts and hoping they'll hear you out.

Some lawyers seem to think that if you don't employ a little bluster, you signal a lack of power and confidence. It is true (though dumb) that we treat *confidence* as evidence of correctness. But confidence and bluster are two different things. You convey strength and confidence by acknowledging potential disagreement forthrightly. Bluster signals weakness. The guy who can't acknowledge disagreement looks like he has a glass chin: He's scared of critical scrutiny because it'll shatter his argument.

A note of caution, though: As with most of the advice in this book, nuance and balance matter. In acknowledging disagreement and modulating your language, you don't want to fall into the soft, syrupy manner of a second-rate social worker. Talking to people as if they're brittle neurasthenics who need cosseting will only insult them and provoke a different form of resistance. Similarly, acknowledging disagreement doesn't mean making the other side's argument for them. For purposes of avoiding reactance, you only need to acknowledge the bare potential for disagreement.

SPEAK AS A COLLEAGUE, NOT A SALESMAN.

The more you ask someone to do something for you, the more it feels like you're asking them to bow to your will. Sometimes you can't avoid a flat-out request. But look for a way to frame your argument as helping the decision-maker resolve some problem that circumstances (not you) have created.

Often you can say, in essence, "This case presents such and such issue. I've analyzed the facts and law carefully, and here's how I think the issue plays out." That sort of approach does not change the objective situation, but it does change the feeling of what you say. Where a tone of collaboration works in a reasonable, fair, non-smarmy way, use it.

AVOID COMMANDING LANGUAGE.

Why tell jurors or judges, "You must" do such and such? Or even "You should" do it? If the reasons you've given haven't already convinced them, your bald command isn't going to help. Language can threaten autonomy and provoke reactance in subtler ways, too. For example: "It cannot be argued that ..." or "It is indisputable that ...." This sort of language rarely adds anything, and it may undercut you. You've now challenged judge or juror to dispute your point. We're all contrarians when people tell us what we have to do or what we have to think. Just state the reasons in a way that *shows* the conclusion to be indisputable. If you've done that, you don't need to *say* it's indisputable.

In brief-writing, a simple "We ask" or "Bill Williams requests" or "Defendant asks the Court to ..." will usually serve the purpose. In live events such as a hearing or trial, stronger language may or may not fit the occasion. By the time you've reached closing argument, you may have earned permission to use much stronger language. In the moment, with eye contact and close attention to the folks you're talking to, you should have some sense of how strong an appeal you've earned, what language the judges or jurors will allow you.

IDENTIFY CHOICES.

The more you can frame an issue as presenting choices, the less you'll come off as insisting the judge or jury must do things your way. This doesn't require saying all the options are equally good. You still argue just as you otherwise would, but you lay out the possible rulings, the pros and cons for each, and say which you prefer.

Many issues lend themselves to this framing — damages amounts, apportionment of liability, discovery disputes, admissibility of evidence, limitation of expert testimony, confidentiality provisions, and so on. In opposing a motion to seal documents, one might write: "Acme gives the Court two choices: (a) scour the documents for information that might be both secret and sensitive, and order redactions accordingly, or (b) find that Acme has not carried their burden, and allow the presumption of public access to take effect." That passage doesn't play coy. It openly shows what side the author is on, but it still identifies a plausible choice. This approach won't work for everything. If you're opposing a summary judgment motion, it won't lessen reactance to say, "Judge, you can follow the law and deny the motion, or you can defy the law and grant the motion."

MAKE YOUR OPPONENT THE TARGET OF REACTANCE.

Sometimes you can provoke a little reactance against your opponents. Often you can say, in effect, "Those guys over there are saying you can't do this." Where that fairly captures the facts, consider saying it.

3.8.2 WE DON'T WANT TO CHANGE OUR BELIEFS. INERTIA GROUNDS US.

We don't like to change beliefs. Even if someone comes along with a compelling new argument, change causes discomfort. It feels good to have worked through a question, resolved it in our own minds, and put it away. Even if the content of the existing belief causes discomfort, it becomes part of our identity. Beliefs wend their way through our lives. Changing beliefs means pulling issues back out, facing the prospect that we've had it all wrong, acknowledging that we screwed up past decisions, and going to a lot of mental effort. We resist all that, even when we see the new idea has merit.

We can meet the problem of inertia in two main ways. First, ask an audience for as little change in their beliefs as possible. Show that the view you're offering doesn't differ much from what they already believe. Second, provide motivation to overcome inertia. Show that the change will help listeners solve some problem, will serve important values they now hold, will bring them into line with the mainstream of their community, will keep them out of trouble — or some other good thing. Motivation can overcome inertia.

3.8.3 INERTIA OPERATES WITH SPECIAL POWER WHEN WE'VE PUBLICLY COMMITTED TO SOMETHING.

We feel bound by things we've committed to. Simply for the sake of consistency, we resist abandoning them. The more we express a view, the more we cement our feet in place. That's why it matters that jurors not talk about a case until they've heard all the evidence. The more they've gone on record, the stronger the cement. For that reason and others, you need to know what your judge has said on an issue, how recently, how often, and how strongly.

Handle a judge's prior declarations carefully. A judge will resent an implied threat of criticism for inconsistency. In reminding a judge of prior rulings, emphasize the reasoning and why it applies here, or doesn't. (And get it right. Judges may relish the chance to correct a lawyer's misreading.) In discussing the reasoning of those decisions, avoid language that hints at the issue of consistency. Let that concern work silently.

3.8.4 WE LOOK FOR FAULTS IN IDEAS WE DON'T ALREADY ACCEPT.

Skepticism stands as the third general form of resistance. Fault-finding figures into how attractive the idea seems in the first place, but it also arises as a separately motivated activity. You show me an idea I haven't seen before, and it does not obviously fit in with what I already believe. It feels new, different, unfamiliar. Simply for that, I'll try to find fault with it.

You can sometimes avoid fault-finding problems if you antici-pate them and frame your argument to avoid them. An old story goes: One monk says to the other, "I asked the abbot if I could smoke while I pray, and he said no." The second monk says, "Huh. I asked if I could pray while I smoke, and he said yes."

Apart from framing, you can often preempt potential fault-find-ing. You can't predict every concern a judge or juror will have, and you can't address every concern you do predict. But preempt those that seem serious and likely to arise.

3.9 WE CAN BUILD RESISTANCE TO THE OTHER SIDE, BY PREEMPTING COUNTERARGUMENTS

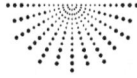

In addition to overcoming resistance to your own arguments, you want to build resistance to the opposing side's arguments. You can do this by preempting them. Preemption creates a more negative environment in which the counterargument will be heard. When you've been inoculated against an argument, you may expect to decide it's wrong, so you look first for the flaws.

Again, preemption requires nuance. Preempt only serious concerns or arguments that the judge or your opponent will probably see on their own. And dispatch them quickly.

3.10 WE GET SUCKED IN, AND MAYBE SUCKERED, BY STORIES

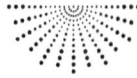

F or most of us, stories allow ideas to slip past our defenses, but they have less power in a legal setting. How effectively a story eludes your defenses depends on how easily you get transported into a story, and that in turn depends on how empathic and imaginative you are. The effectiveness of stories also depends on whether you approach the particular story in a closed, analytical way or an open, uncritical way. In legal disputes, we can assume a critical, analytical audience. Further, we always have an opponent telling a counter-story and saying ours misrepresents reality. Stories do not, therefore, give us a magic elixir of persuasion.

Even so, stories carry substantial power, even in a legal setting. We don't know much about how the ability to be transported into a story varies across the general population or through the legal community. But given the ubiquity of stories in all forms, and the importance of empathy and imagination in social life, it seems safe to guess that nearly everyone has that ability to a substantial degree. Furthermore, while critical analysis may weaken the effect of stories, critical analysis requires mental effort, which we don't like to exert. So stories still provide an important source of persuasion for lawyers.

Take special care with any stories you tell, though. The power of stories intensifies the risk of betraying trust. If you tell a story that affects the listener, and then your opponent shows you've misrepresented reality, the listener may react especially negatively against you. Use stories — carefully.

3.11 STORIES, NOT ARGUMENTS, EVOKE MORAL FEELING

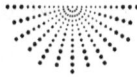

W e don't reason our way to our own moral judgments, and we can't reason someone else out of theirs. You might as well try slapping them out of it.

Instead of making moral arguments, tell stories that draw out the moral feelings you want. Present facts, carefully arranged. Give the audience vicarious experience.

The recent change in public views of gay marriage illustrates the process of change in moral sensibilities. Moral revulsion against homosexuality still exists among some people, but when I was a kid in a nice, midwestern middle-class suburb, no one would look askance at you for using "faggot" or "dike." Many of the kids in both the secular and church-going crowds I hung out with did use those words freely. Indeed, if you flippantly (or earnestly) said gays should be imprisoned, you'd only get mildly disapproving looks (or not).

I recall my first conversation on the subject of gay marriage, about 25 years ago. I thought of myself as friendly to gay people. Still, I laughed out loud when a friend said he favored the idea of gay marriage. I felt no conscious malice toward gays, and I supported legal protections for them. But the idea of gay marriage still felt like an absurdity. It took less than 25 years for a massive change to take place in my own moral feelings on this, and for the same change to occur in millions of other Americans. Today, a small but solid majority supports gay marriage. So great a change, on so fundamental an issue, over so short a time, takes my breath away.

You can consult your own sense of recent history, but it seems to me that this change occurred not because of argument or debate, but mostly because we all became more familiar with gay people. As more people came out as gay, and as TV and movies showed us more of them, we came to see gay people as more or less like ourselves. They stopped seeming weird and scary. They came into view as real, three-dimensional beings. We had something to focus on other than what they do with their genitals — just as we do with our parents and our pastors. It turned out that gays are people, too. And then we could imagine ourselves in their shoes and understand they're not out to cause earthquakes, seduce us into wearing pink feather boas, or whatever. It turned out that they, too, feel lonely, feel love, want to raise children, want to be part of and contribute to society, want the safety and dignity of having their commitments and families recognized by society rather than being forced to live beyond the palings. Exposure to new facts, new stories, new people changed moral judgments fundamentally.

In trying to influence someone's moral judgments, we should speak as modestly and non-argumentatively as possible. Don't step on toes. Don't criticize. Don't moralize. Don't exhort. Don't set yourself up as some sort of seer. Speak as a flawed human being with limited experience and a partial view of the world. Don't state disagreement unless you have to, and then do so frankly but respectfully, stating that your view differs from theirs, but refraining from saying you're right and they're wrong. Speak with as much respect, modesty, empathy, and affection as you can authentically muster. Develop rapport, try to elicit empathy in turn, try to convey your own experience, try to show how things look from your vantage point. This helps create climates of opinion. This helps to counter bad associations with good ones. Otherwise, just stop talking and hope for change.

In a legal dispute, you can structure the perception and vicarious experience of the judge and jury, and thus influence their moral responses. But you can't argue or badger them into any particular moral stance. You just tell a well-designed story, omit or limit your own subjective responses, and hope for the best.

3.12 FURTHER READING

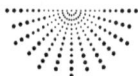

Many of the books and other materials I've already recommended touch on issues of communication and persuasion. I recommend these additional books, too:

- David DeSteno, *The Truth about Trust* (2014).
- Patricia Churchland, *Braintrust: What Neuroscience Tells Us about Morality* (2011).
- Walter Sinnott-Armstrong, ed., *Moral Psychology: The Neuroscience of Morality* (2008).
- Robert Cialdini, *Influence: Science and Practice*, 5th ed (2009).
- Robert H. Gass and John S. Seiter, *Persuasion, Social Influence, and Compliance Gaining*, 5th ed. (2013).
- Eric S. Knowles and Jay A. Linn, eds. *Resistance and Persuasion* (2013).
- Anthony R. Pratkanis, ed., *The Science of Social Influence: Advances and Future Progress* (2007).

PART IV
JURORS AND JUDGES

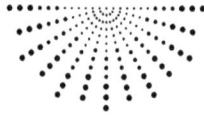

It should be obvious that everything we've discussed so far applies to judges and jurors, just as it does to the rest of us. There are some differences, of course: *First*, in ordinary legal disputes, the decision gets made by nominally impartial decision-makers, after adversarial argument. *Second*, the decision-makers swear to follow the law. *Third*, the decision usually follows explicit, conscious reasoning. *Fourth*, jurors and panels of appellate judges make decisions through a social process of argument and negotiation.

These differences matter. They improve decision-making. Each of these features increases the chance of filtering out irrelevant or illegitimate factors that might otherwise influence the decision. Each of these features increases the chance of getting a well-considered decision.

Despite these features, of course there still remains vast room for bad decisions by judges and jurors. By "bad decisions," I don't mean just decisions you dislike. I mean decisions influenced by illegitimate factors, decisions that don't follow the rules, decisions contaminated by simple confusion, and so on.

I venture here only a few general notes specific to judges and jurors.

4.1 JURORS MAKE DECISIONS AS GROUPS OF STRANGERS — UNDER STRESS, ABOUT MOSTLY UNFAMILIAR ISSUES, ACCORDING TO RULES THEY OFTEN DON'T UNDERSTAND

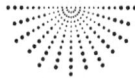

F ew lawyers will need to be convinced that jurors make decisions in more or less the same unruly manner that we all do in our daily lives. We have a smallish but significant literature on juror psychology, but there are only a few big points for practitioners to keep in mind.

First, worldviews — values, attitudes, beliefs, etc. — trump law and drive the inferences from evidence. In short, if the jurors come in with an attitude that doctors should not be held liable for harm they cause even through negligence, they're probably not going to hold the doctors liable. If the jurors believe police officers are authority figures who can or even must be trusted to tell the truth, the jurors will probably accept the cop's story, however thoroughly you impeach it. In this sense, every case is a juror nullification case: If juror worldviews happen to align with the law, the jurors will follow the law. If not, they probably won't. The jurors won't need to consciously reject the law. They'll find a perfectly fine-sounding rationale for the verdict — not that the law requires one — because jurors usually do care about following the law. There's nothing new or surprising in any of this. As I said 100 pages ago:

We believe what we feel inclined to believe, though it's complicated.

This point just brings us back to the golden rule of persuasion: You activate already-existing, favorable thoughts and feelings in the decision-maker's mind, or you lose. And the corollary: All reasoning is motivated, so you have to motivate it.

Second, trust plays an especially strong role in juror decision-making. Jurors usually have no way to understand the details of a case in full. Jurors know this. They know that simple facts of the case — who held the knife — are beyond their ability to know with certainty. Jurors can only listen to after-the-fact testimony by fallible, self-interested witnesses. Lay jurors know that technical or scientific material is beyond them. Jurors know that the judge is withholding evidence they would like to see. Jurors know — or expect — the parties and lawyers and allied witnesses will shade the truth or outright lie. Jurors know that most material assertions will be disputed with or without a good basis, by lawyers and experts trained to make nonsense sound true. Jurors know that lawyers read books on how to appeal to jurors. Jurors know, in short, that at least part of the time, they're being bullshitted. All this creates a fog of suspicion, and in a fog, you need to follow someone you can trust.

There are no shortcuts to trust. The shortcuts you think will get you trusted will get you distrusted. To gain trust, you must show you're trustworthy — actually trustworthy. A convincing appearance of trustworthiness won't do it. Your convincing appearance of trustworthiness is only convincing you. It's not convincing the jurors.

To gain trust, you must come to the jurors with a genuinely good case, and you must be scrupulously, brutally honest about it. No spin. No exaggeration. No smooth excuses. If you don't have a genuinely good case, then you have no business wasting jurors' time. If you can't lay out the truth simply and openly, then you're not trustworthy. If you take cheap shots, if you stretch or spin the truth, if you misdirect or evade, then the jurors shouldn't trust you, and they probably won't.

To gain trust, you must be real. Gerry Spence has hammered this point for decades, and rightly so. Jurors watch and listen to you. If you seem phony, even in small ways, that undermines your trustworthiness. If you are real, authentic, fully present in the moment as your true self — the true side of you that is decent and reasonable — then the jurors can trust you. But in the crucible of trial, how can you pull that off? That's a topic for another day, for other books. (See the trial-practice book recommendations below.)

Third, mere communication is hard. We've already discussed this, but I want to pound the table. It is a big, big challenge simply to get the information into the jurors' heads. Merely keeping the jurors' attention presents a struggle. If you don't have their attention, you might as well not present anything. Then there's the problem of the jurors understanding the information they do pay attention to. And then the further problem of making it stick in their minds. Most of the information that comes out at trial goes in one ear and out the other. Maybe a piece of it makes some vague impression as it passes through. Or maybe it doesn't. Maybe a mass of vague impressions builds up. Or maybe it doesn't. But by far the most impactful information will be the stuff that lodges securely in explicit memory, which jurors can recall and discuss and reflect on.

A thorough discussion of trial communication techniques lies beyond the scope of this book, but a quick reminder of basic principles: We remember stuff that comes with some emotional content. Stories help us remember. We're visual creatures, so use visuals and tangible demonstratives wherever and whenever you can. Good organization helps us remember, by providing a framework to hang information on. Make everything as simple and concrete as possible (while maintaining accuracy). Use language, voice, and body to help the jurors follow, understand, and engage. Develop these skills outside trial, because there's no time or mental space to think about technique during trial.

Fourth, juror deliberation is a social process, and social dynamics shape the verdict. A jury of six to twelve people sit around a table. Some try to persuade others. Some try to avoid talking. Some take bold positions. Some try to find middle ground. Some negotiate strategically. Some just want to go home and will agree to anything, to get out the door. Some dig in their heels and hold out for the verdict they want. Some implore. Some yell and scream. Some conciliate. And out of this messy, unpredictable process comes the decision that matters to you deeply.

The social dynamics of juror deliberation and decision are as hard to predict and influence as they are important. There's little that lawyers can do to influence the dynamics in deliberations, but there are a few smallish things: In juror selection, try for a group of people who seem decent and reasonable. Try to model respectful listening and disagreement — through your own treatment of the opposing lawyers and parties. In closing argument, maybe suggest good processes for the jurors to follow in deliberations — like picking a foreperson whose job will be to ensure that everyone gets heard respectfully. And most of all, make sure you've equipped your advocates among the jurors with a clear understanding of the issues and the evidence, and the ability to cite evidence and argument in your favor.

4.2 JUDGES MAKE DECISIONS AS SEMI-DICTATORS OR IN SMALL GROUPS, UNDER A MIXED BAG OF CIRCUMSTANCES, WITH MINIMAL ACCOUNTABILITY

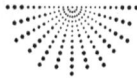

The idea of "legal" decisions by judges lies shrouded in a fog of confusion and acrimony. On the one hand, traditional views of law, and the public rhetoric of law, tells us to think that legal reasoning and legal decision-making is rule-bound, rigorously impartial, and therefore somehow subject to objective certainty and correctness. On the other hand, no practicing lawyer needs to be told that the public rhetoric is nonsense. Maybe the rubes in the general public need to think that's what law is, but we lawyers with appeal papers spilling out of our briefcases know better. And even the general public sometimes knows better. On high-profile decisions, partisans of the losing side accuse the judges of "activism" or ideological bias or simple stupidity.

What, broadly speaking, should we make of judicial decision-making? Again, the basic point is that all the limitations of ordinary human judgment apply in full. But let's add a little nuance to that.

4.2.1 ON FACT QUESTIONS, THE JUDGE'S INDIVIDUAL WORLDVIEW LARGELY DRIVES THE DECISION. AND ALL QUESTIONS ARE FACT QUESTIONS.

Most decisions by judges draw, implicitly or explicitly, on the judge's worldview — the judge's sense of how things work in the world, the judge's values and sense of fairness or reasonableness, etc. Obviously, any decision like that rests on more or less squishy, subjective grounds. The idea of judges making such decisions troubles us — and properly so. Who elected Judge Brown to be King Brown? In a democracy, law is supposed to be made by legislators. Judges are supposed to do no more than apply the law given to them by duly elected legislators.

For the moment, let's set aside any question of frailty in a judge's decision-making. Let's assume a world in which judges always performed with perfect understanding, integrity, self-insight, and self-control. Even in that happy universe, judges' decisions would largely rest on subjective considerations that would and should trouble us.

Press it hard enough, and the ideal of law and judicial decision-making falls into incoherence and impossibility. The democratic legitimacy of judicial decisions is always subject to question. The most we can hope for is to approximate the ideal closely enough that the public can live with the messy reality, without bothering to march in the streets and hold a revolution.

ON *FACT* QUESTIONS, no one minds that a judge's subjective worldview affects decisions. The subjectivity of factual findings is too obviously inevitable. No one bothers to complain about it. To be sure, we may criticize this or that finding of fact. We may suspect the finding was corrupt, or merely stupid. But we're not drawn to a general, principled complaint that findings of disputed fact depend on the judge's subjective view of the evidence. The clear-error appellate standard reflects the broad leeway we give judges on fact questions. All we can ask of a judge is a good brain, high diligence, self-awareness to recognize the illegitimate factors that might influence the decision, the self-control to filter out those factors, and the integrity to follow the evidence wherever it leads on a full and fair evaluation. That's a lot to ask, though, and we can't expect to get it all the time.

Discretionary questions present the same basic situation as fact questions, usually with some values questions mixed in. Will this group of documents likely prove relevant? How much discovery burden is too much? How important is this disputed testimony? Has this company shown a legitimate interest in court secrecy that overrides the public's right of access? Does the plaintiff's history of failed marriages bear any relevance to her emotional distress damages in a medical malpractice case? These questions force judges to look to worldviews that differ, sometimes dramatically, from one person to the next. Here, too, all we can demand of a judge is brains, diligence, integrity, etc. No one is naïve enough to think we can demand objective correctness on a question of discretion.

We do, however, feel pulled to demand objective correctness on questions of "pure law." But there are no questions of pure law. "Purely legal" only means that the trial judge makes the decision, and an appeals court supposedly reviews it on a *de novo* standard. Most "purely legal" questions obviously call on the judge's worldview. At what level of specificity does an allegation in a complaint stop being "conclusory"? Could a reasonable jury decide the case for the plaintiff? If the plaintiff alleges that a mortgage producer sold a group of 2,000 loans, expressly representing that each loan conformed to Fannie Mae standards, but a third of them violated those standards in material ways, does that support a strong inference of a reckless disregard for the truth? When an auto insurance policy uses the term "accidental injury" without defining it, does that include injury you suffer when some guy intentionally rams into your car in a fit of road rage? Does this damages verdict shock the conscience? Does the public policy of this state allow a nondisclosure agreement to shield evidence of a tort? Does the Equal Protection Clause permit states to prohibit gay marriage? Does the prohibition of "agreements in restraint of trade" forbid agreements to buy a producer's entire output — denying any to competitors — even though the buyer will use it all? These are all "legal" questions, but you can't answer any of these questions without drawing on aspects of worldview that differ from one person to another.

Even when a trial judge applies binding precedent to answer questions like this, facts inevitably differ from one case to the next, usually enough to require subjective judgment. "Purely legal" issues are not that much more objective than purely factual issues.

Of course any judge's worldview comes from a limited, partial, biased set of experiences unique to that individual. We hope the judge takes an open, receptive attitude to information brought forward by the lawyers in the case. We hope judges recognize the limits of their own experience. But they can't flush everything they know about the world before deciding a dispute, and if they did, they couldn't do their jobs at all.

Sometimes differences of world view don't matter; sometimes they matter a lot. If the question is whether a criminal defendant may refuse to testify at trial, all of us (in 21st-Century American legal culture) would agree on the answer. We divide sharply, though, over whether a corporation has First Amendment rights, or whether this testimony should be admitted, and so on.

~

NOTHING I'VE SAID HERE ARGUES for legal nihilism — that anything goes and judges should just do whatever they can get away with. Those of us who believe in democracy believe it's vitally important that judges, lawyers, and the public have some shared vision of a restricted function of judges in a democracy. Legal theories attempt to provide a viable vision for that function (usually in a way that deals three aces to the political preferences of the theorist). We need a shared vision, but reality is messy, and human nature irrepressible, so any shared vision of the proper role of judges will necessarily be vague, and eternally subject to dispute.

But while reality does create a problem for the democratic

legitimacy of courts, we shouldn't overstate how disturbing the problem is. Reality betrays all ideals. Growing up means learning to live with that. Living decently together in large societies is hard. It'll always be hard. That's the nature of things. Life isn't about rational coherence and perfection. Life is about getting by together as well as we can. In the end, judicial decision-making just tries to imitate its impossible ideal. If that effort succeeds enough, life goes on. If not, we'll have a political crisis and a recalibration. Public scrutiny serves a vital role in constraining judicial decision-making and supporting democratic legitimacy. So we need more and better scrutiny of the courts. But we don't need adolescent idealism — which ends in adolescent cynicism or adolescent revolt.

Most of all, though, the practicing lawyer needs to dismiss the public rhetoric of law, needs to cleanse the mind of the idea that legal decisions are compelled by the abstract merits of the issue. Anyone who works under the influence of that view is in for a lot of bitter frustration. A naïve faith in the abstract merits of an issue will lead you to ignore problems and opportunities for persuasion. Worldview drives decisions, even decisions by judges, even on questions of "pure law." You can't make good judgments or practice good advocacy if you're kidding yourself about this basic fact of life.

4.2.2 THEN THERE ARE ALL THE NORMAL CORRUPTIONS OF HUMAN JUDGMENT.

Judges vary in their ability to suppress or counteract illegitimate influences — how much they like or dislike this or that lawyer or party, and so on. Some judges are better than others at suppressing such things. Any given judge will perform better at this on some days than on others. So illegitimate factors need to be reckoned with in one way or another, in any dispute submitted to a judge.

It's worth noting, though, that we can't always agree even on whether a factor is legitimate or illegitimate. Suppose the judge's sister was raped seven years ago. Now the judge is sentencing a rapist. Does the judge's personal history provide useful insight into the reality at the heart of the case, or does it create such potential for emotional distortion that the judge should be recused? Or suppose a judge previously ruled, in another case, that a company's employees had essentially committed perjury. Should that bear on the judge's rulings in a later case against the same company? Should it inform decisions about the scope of discovery or the admission of evidence? What if the judge, based on past experience, considers a lawyer to be sloppy or sleazy? Should that affect the consideration the judge gives to motions and briefs? Reasonable answers to questions like these land all over the map.

4.2.3 THE LEGAL SETTING SUPPORTS GOOD DECISION-MAKING.

As I've already noted, in many ways the court system supports good decision-making. The adversarial process goes far toward protecting against distortions of fact or reason. Given good advocacy on both sides, the potential for simple errors or exploitation of biases diminishes. And judges act as professional, independent decision-makers, and they mostly get vetted for competence and integrity before taking the bench. These features reduce the risk of serious error on important legal questions.

4.2.4 THE LEGAL SETTING IMPEDES GOOD DECISION-MAKING.

Some features of the judicial process work against good decision-making. *First*, judges frequently lack the time or resources to fully engage with an issue. Good decision-making relies heavily on the diligence, discipline, and intellectual integrity of the judge. These qualities all consume mental energy, a depletable resource. When we get tired or stressed, or when we work under a heavy load, we become less diligent, less disciplined, more prone to error.

Second, most legal questions carry potential for complication and confusion, which the lawyer with the weaker argument will usually try to exploit. Past confusion, there are simple lies. Judges can and sometimes do get tricked by lawyers who lie about facts or law. There's a breed of lawyer who think that's fine. Those lawyers smell slightly of feces, but courthouses still let them in the door.

Third, judges have minimal accountability. Most decisions by trial or appellate courts effectively enjoy immunity from review. Most trial-court decisions are discretionary. Supreme courts accept few cases from intermediate appellate courts. And politicians and the public learn about only the rarest of decisions. On most issues in most cases, judges act as dictators, and they know it. No one but the parties will ever take any interest; the winning side constitutes half the universe of concerned observers; and they'll almost always defend the decision. (Faced with egregiously wrong decisions during trial, a friend of mine once asked opposing counsel to join in objecting to the error. The opposing lawyer declined, noting that he gets paid by the hour for appellate work just as for trial work.) On most occasions, even the loser won't speak up too harshly, for fear of subtle retaliation by the judge in this or future cases. Besides, the judge has a line of other parties and disputes queued up, and will immediately turn to them. Most of the time, judges are disciplined only by their own intellectual integrity, diligence, and self-knowledge — which are not inexhaustible resources.

Fourth, the makeup of the judge's community will skew the direction of reputational pressure. Most judges come from a community of prosecutors or civil defense lawyers.

Fifth, when people feel powerful, they feel excessive confidence in their intuition. They overestimate their knowledge and skill. Judges have power, and they feel it.

Sixth, many disputes bore or annoy judges and clerks. Depending on the dispute, it can be hard for an outsider (like a judge) to work up much motivation to dig in. When another lawyer tells you about some procedural dispute, how often does the dispute bore you? If it's even 10 percent of the time, you can see the problem for judges.

Finally, inequality of resources between the parties makes for a lop-sided presentation. On rare occasions, judges may mitigate the problem by doing more research and analysis of their own, but they can't do that very often, and it usually won't redress the balance entirely anyhow — especially where the issue turns on fact rather than law. And since judges have less knowledge about the case, and less time and motivation for it, when judges do go off on their own, they're apt to screw something up.

We should keep these features of the system in mind, and try to steer around potential problems.

4.2.5 BENCH RULINGS CARRY THE GREATEST RISK.

The danger of bad decisions increases at trial. At trial, we get snap rulings with little time for consideration. That obviously increases the danger. Furthermore, during trial judges make decisions in a vastly different social and emotional context. The judge is on stage, observed by the jurors, beset by competing advocates. Disputes during trial can implicate a variety of factors that contaminate decisions — concerns about maintaining authority, in-the-moment displeasure with lawyers or parties, desire to save face by adhering to prior decisions, and so on. As you prepare for trial, think carefully about issues to address *in limine*, and other issues on which to prepare short pocket briefs. And try to get on the judge's good side. However self-aware and self-controlled the judge may be in chambers, the judge will have lesser powers when on stage before the jury.

4.2.6 YOU'RE RIGHT TO WORRY ABOUT THE INESCAPABLE SUBJECTIVITY OF JUDGE (OR JURY) DECISIONS.

When you immerse yourself deeply in an issue, you come to think the merits so clearly compel the outcome, that the merits *must* prevail. That's a dangerous delusion. If you let that feeling shape your presentation, you'll pay less attention to the problems that could derail you. You'll look less creatively for ways to draw the judge to the outcome you want.

Do not think the judge's need to write an opinion will cause the abstract merits to compel the conclusion. First, there may be nothing more than a one-paragraph order, or a cursory *per curiam* decision. "*We have carefully considered the other arguments raised by Acme and find them to be without merit.*" But even when judges do write opinions, it's trivially easy to cloak bad reasoning. With a little work, a judge's clerk can always write an explanation that will sound substantive and fair to an outside reader who happens across the case someday on Lexis. The outsider won't know the opinion ducks serious arguments. The necessity of writing an opinion does little to make the abstract merits compel anything.

~

LAW IS A MESSY HUMAN BUSINESS. We'll do better work if we keep the full, messy picture of human judgment in mind.

4.3 FURTHER READING

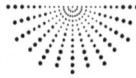

For further reading on decision-making by judges and juries, I suggest starting here:

ACADEMIC BOOKS ON JURIES

- Margaret Bull-Kovera, ed., *The Psychology of Juries* (2017).
- Joel Lieberman & Daniel Krauss, *Jury Psychology: Social Aspects of Trial Processes* (2009).
- Neil Vidmar & Valerie Hans, *American Juries: The Verdict* (2007).

ACADEMIC BOOKS ON JUDGES

- Richard Posner, *How Judges Think* (2008).
- Joel Cohen, *Blindfolds Off: Judges on How They Decide* (2014).

- David O'Brien, ed., *Judges on Judging: Views from the Bench*, 4th ed. (2013).
- Benjamin Cardozo, *The Nature of the Judicial Process* (1921).
- Frank M. Coffin, *The Ways of a Judge: Reflections from the Federal Appellate Bench* (1980).
- Robert Satter, *Doing Justice: A Trial Judge at Work* (1990).
- Karl Llewellyn, *The Common Law Tradition: Deciding Appeals* (1960).
- Stanley Fish, *The Trouble with Principle* (2001).

TRIAL PRACTICE BOOKS BY PRACTITIONERS (MOSTLY PLAINTIFF-SIDE)

- Gerry Spence, *How to Argue and Win Every Time* (1996).
- Rick Friedman, *On Becoming a Trial Lawyer* (2008).
- Gregory Cusimano, David Wenner, et al, *Winning Case Development* (2018).
- David Ball and Joshua Karton, *Theater for Trial* (2017).
- Sunwolf, *Practical Jury Dynamics 2* (2007).
- David Ball, *Ball on Damages 3* (2013).
- Don Keenan & David Ball, *Reptile* (2009).
- Paul Colby & Robert Klonoff, *Winning Jury Trials: Trial Tactics & Sponsorship Strategies* (2002).
- William Barton, *Recovering for Psychological Injuries* (1990).
- Mark Mandell, *Case Framing* (2016).
- Carl Bettinger, *Twelve Heroes, One Voice* (2011).
- Bruce Whitman, *The Inner Jury* (2014).

OTHER RELEVANT WISDOM LITERATURE

- Carl Rogers, *On Becoming a Person* (1961).

- Stephen Covey, *Seven Habits of Highly Effective People* (2013).
- Stephen Covey Jr., *The Speed of Trust* (2006).

PART V
KEY PRINCIPLES &
IMPLICATIONS

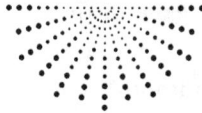

The sincerity of a true heart is the only requirement of effective advocacy. No one wants to know that, because a true heart is so much harder to acquire than a few advocacy techniques.
— James McComas

The empirical findings about people and persuasion hold implications for legal advocacy. The implications range from the very general to the highly specific. A catalog of specific tips and pointers — what colors to use on your Powerpoint slides, how to dress for trial, how to write an introduction to a brief — lies beyond the scope of this book. Here, I go only so far as first principles.

First principles come first, before discrete pointers, because without internalizing the principles, the pointers do you little good. You can't blindly carry tips and pointers from one circumstance to another. Give a man a pointer, and you point him for a day. Give a man a principle, and he can make his own damn pointers.

It's the internalizing of principles that matters, though — not the mere reading of them. General principles always read like flaccid bromides. The thing to do with principles is not just to read them, but to adopt them, to translate them from taglines for inspirational posters into habits of character and action. As reading, even the most useful principles are banal and boring. As habits, they're indispensable.

It's a small minority of lawyers who have encoded the principles discussed here as habits. My own sense of myself, my fellow lawyers, and my fellow humans generally is that most of us act out of a more or less random assortment of habits that have grown onto us like barnacles as we swim through our variously happy and unhappy experience. By virtue of these serendipitous habits, some people seem naturally brilliant at persuading others, and some seem naturally hopeless, but most of us wander about in the middle lands, neither particularly good nor particularly bad. But good, bad, or indifferent, we mostly do what comes naturally.

We are doomed or destined to act mostly out of habits. So to the extent we can, we should mold habits intentionally, on a set of principles rooted in what we know about how people and persuasion work.

The key insights for persuasion are old, simple, and hard. They stem from the over-arching points that we are semi-rational beasts, that we navigate the world with the feelers and instincts of our whole person, and that questions of trust loom large in any interaction between people.

Lawyers lose sight of the basics of being human. We learn how to "think like a lawyer." We learn the virtues of rationality and the vices of sympathy. Professor Kingsfield sneers when we say "I feel" such and such instead of "I think" this or that. And while of course all this gives us something valuable, it also turns us away from our fundamental nature. We remain semi-rational beasts sniffing each other out, but we've lost the primordial sense of our kind. Like an orangutan wearing pants and carrying a briefcase, we ape the disembodied rationality of an angel, poorly. We've forgotten how to behave as proper beasts.

PRELIMINARIES

Before proceeding to actionable principles, I want to suggest an overall understanding of persuasion, provide a quick distillation of the preceding parts of this book, and suggest a couple overarching points to keep in mind as one tries to make use of the principles.

THE NATURE OF PERSUASION

Persuasion doesn't exist, and argument is a waste of time. That's cryptic and stupidly provocative, but let me stick with it for a minute. We think of persuasion or argument as getting someone else to adopt our conclusions. That doesn't happen. What does sometimes happen, though, is that you point out things that lead this other person to form their own conclusion, which happily aligns with yours.

Understanding the difference between these processes affects your behavior, and your success rate. If you think you can get someone to adopt your conclusions, then you urge, you implore, you argue, you advocate, you campaign, you promote, you sell. You approach the other person as you'd approach a customer, a mark, a John. Your skin secretes the stink of a salesman, and your listeners curl their noses. If, however, you understand that people will not adopt your conclusions but will come to their own, then you chat with them as equals, as colleagues, as companions. You learn about them, what they think and feel and care about. You acknowledge and respect those things. You point to the things that have struck you and which might strike this other person, so the light bulb can spark in your friends' minds, maybe. You show how things seem to you, while acknowledging that your companions might think differently. Approached this way, your companions will probably take your views seriously and give them a sympathetic hearing. Your companions may not agree — they are their own people, after all — but this approach maximizes your chances.

You can't persuade, and it does no good to argue, but you can serve as a credible, sympathetic source. In rare moments of grace, a companion may even see the mere fact that you believe a thing as evidence that it's true — because they like you, they see you share a lot of values in common, and they see you care about the truth and have worked hard to find it. Now: If we use the term "persuasion" to refer to *this* process, then we can agree that persuasion exists after all.

∽

THERE'S a fine sentence in *Pilgrim's Progress*: "Then it came burning hot in my mind, whatever he said, and however he flattered, when he got me home to his house, he would sell me for a slave."

How people treat the information you offer depends on everything about you, and how it interacts with everything about them. It's as though you encounter a stranger in the woods. She must decide whether to walk with you together, to calmly go a separate way, or to flee, or to kill you. She doesn't know if you bear good or bad will, if you're a fool or a genius, if you're lovely company or misery incarnate. She must size you up. She doesn't just listen to what you say; for you may be a liar. She takes in your eyes, your face, your voice, your posture, your body movements, which direction you came from, the words you choose, your age, your clothes. Everything she can perceive figures into how she responds.

If she can trust you and like you, then she has to decide what to make of the information you offer. You can't control that. She can't control that. She just sees the information and it means to her what it means to her. If it turns out that the two of you see things in a similar way, maybe she'll walk with you a while.

It's not all about her: It's about you and her together — your relationship, and if that goes alright, then how much your respective views overlap. Tailoring a message perfectly for her does no good if you warp yourself in the process. If you don't believe something, you can't say it with conviction. If you're speaking in person, your body may betray you. Even in writing, the stink of manipulation can leak from the page, like sewer gas from a cracked pipe. If you come off as fake or creepy or weird, what you say won't work, however custom-fitted for her you thought it was.

Persuasion works this way when a political candidate campaigns for votes, when a newspaper writes to a mass public, when a husband tells his wife they should move across the country, when a lawyer talks to jurors or writes a brief to a judge. Each situation has its own practicalities and its own rules and conventions, but in each, first comes trust (or not), then comes the overlapping of worldviews (or not).

The discussion below draws out some of the points that flow from this general view of persuasion.

A QUICK DISTILLATION

This book has tried to walk briskly through a moderately detailed summary of what we know about how people work, concerning persuasion in the context of deliberative decision-making. I organized that discussion to provide a systematic model of human minds — not according to how much practical importance a given point holds for lawyers. So now I want to condense all that prior discussion into a handful of descriptive taglines covering the points with greatest importance for advocates. Each could mislead through glib generality — that's what taglines do — but if you've digested the prior discussion, you won't be misled:

1. Merely paying attention and following a discussion takes work.
2. All reasoning is motivated. Feeling guides thinking.
3. Everyone has a worldview — a partly incoherent mass of thoughts, feelings, attitudes, values, beliefs, etc. — that shapes our responses to whatever we're looking at just now.
4. Only some parts of our worldviews are active at any given time.
5. The unconscious feeds snap judgments to the conscious.
6. Snap judgments come from the interplay of (a) the feelings and thoughts active in our minds, (b) trust or distrust in the source of the new information, and (c) the new information itself.
7. Snap judgments are usually final judgments.
8. No one wants to be persuaded — certainly not by you.
9. Stories and visuals affect us powerfully.

These points yield some practical implications for persuasion. Viewed from above, the whole process of persuasion collapses into a simple-sounding formula:

- Earn trust.
- Enlist existing attitudes, to motivate the decision.
- Justify the decision.
- Make it interesting, clear, and easy.
- Steer around resistance.

Those broad imperatives structure the more detailed principles below. Before that, though, two more overarching points.

FIGHT THE TEMPTATION TO THINK OF PERSUASION AS A MATTER OF PROOF. THINK OF IT AS A MATTER OF PEOPLE.

It takes vigilance to avoid thinking of advocacy as showing the decision-maker that our position is right. That way of thinking comes naturally and tells us what to do: *Our job is to show that the law and facts compel Conclusion X.* This way of thinking — advocacy as proving the rightness of our position — does, of course, capture much of the truth about advocacy. All the same, we should ditch that way of thinking. Its partial truth conceals too much, leads us down unproductive paths, undermines our effectiveness. Better to think of advocacy as a people business that includes not just showing we're right, but managing motivations and the risk of error.

Consider these two questions, and the lines of thought they set you down:

How do we prove our position?

or

How do we get this judge (or these jurors) to go our way?

The first question gets you thinking about the abstract merits of the issue. It tricks you into imagining that the merits can somehow compel a particular decision. As this book has argued at length, that's delusional. The second question reminds you that the decision will be made by particular human beings, and that — as you've known from childhood — human decision-making is messy, unpredictable, and subject to all sorts of things apart from the abstract merits.

Focusing on people, motivations, and the risk of error affects litigation strategy in major ways. I once spent about four months full time drafting a summary judgment motion. We were defending an eight billion-dollar case, so we had the luxury (or curse) of a huge legal team and an unlimited litigation budget. I was tasked with developing what the team saw as the key motion. I did so and lovingly crafted the argument and the brief over months. I was completely convinced we were right. The legal team as a whole was convinced. The client's general counsel was convinced. But David Boies, the lead trial lawyer, nixed the motion. He was convinced, too, but he had been to hearings in the case, and he just didn't believe the judge was ready to kill the plaintiff's case. And because of the nature of the issues, if the judge denied our motion today, he'd probably end up saying something that would harm our substantive position down the road. The decision not to file my precious brief broke my heart a little, but it was the right call. That decision could not have been made from a *how do we prove we're right* mindset. It could only be made from a *what's the judge going to do* mindset.

The impact of focusing on people, motivations, and the risk of error shows up in more mundane circumstances, too. You want to press a discovery request, and under the rules you're clearly entitled to what you're asking for. But the request is unusual in this part of the country, and there's no custom among the judges of enforcing requests like this. If you focus only on the abstract merits, you press the request, full steam ahead. But if you focus on the people, you pause. You ask around about this judge. You look for ways of making your discovery request seem more normal. Maybe you press a narrower version of it.

In my practice, we routinely couch decisions in this language. "We're pretty sure we're right, but even if we are, what's the risk of the judge getting it wrong?" For example, we don't really need an expert for this or that subject, but judges expect to see this subject covered by expert testimony. What are the chances we'll (wrongly) get thrown out on summary judgment if we omit an expert? What would be the chances of fixing the mistake on appeal? Even if we were guaranteed to defeat a summary judgment motion at the trial level, could we avoid spending the time on the briefing, by hiring a gratuitous expert and warding off the motion in the first place? What are the costs of getting an expert we shouldn't have to get? What's the total upside/downside for this particular case?

Similar issues arise with jurors, of course. You've already

presented clear, undisputed evidence on a key point. You've covered it. But what's the risk the jurors missed it? What's the risk they weren't paying attention, or didn't follow the discussion, or didn't register its significance? Maybe you call the additional witness, maybe you don't. What's the full set of pros and cons?

Of course you can never know for sure the answers to any of these questions. These are judgment calls, guesses, and you'll guess wrong often enough. This focus on people pulls you into a constant balancing of uncertainties. But all the same, you step into fewer holes if you're watching out for them.

It's easier to stay focused on people and the risk of error, the more frequently you appear at hearings, trials, and other live decision-making events. That's one good reason to get all the lawyers in your practice involved in hearings and trials. You need everyone around you to understand that law is not an abstract intellectual inquiry, but a business of people, a business of managing motivations and the risk of error. The illusion of abstract merits gains greater power, the farther you get from live human decision-making.

DON'T GET CARRIED AWAY WITH ANY PARTICULAR INSIGHT. THINK OF YOURSELF AS SPINNING PLATES.

Occasionally, this or that insight can hit you like a bolt of lightning. It may be a new insight you've never thought of, or an old insight that suddenly feels poignant because you see it so clearly at work. When you have these lightning strikes, watch out. Handled carefully, they can improve your work. But these strikes create a danger of getting carried away with a single idea. Everything we've discussed in this book works together, more or less simultaneously. The mind has its own ecology. The whole unruly variety needs to be kept in some rough balance. Pull too much on a single thread, and the fabric shreds.

An example: Once upon a time, a plaintiff lawyer in opening statement at trial got carried away with candor — thinking to earn trust by acknowledging the factors that cut against his case. (I read about this guy.) It makes sense to acknowledge some problem factors, but sequencing, selection, and proportionality matter. You acknowledge problems *after* you've done what you can to get jurors moving your way, and then you address only the indisputably material problems (the ones it would be dishonest to omit), and even then you acknowledge problems only as much as honesty requires (which is to say, briefly), and you present the problematic stuff as positively as you honestly, reasonably can. You're an advocate in an adversarial system, and it's your opponent's job, not yours, to make the opponent's case. In this cautionary tale, the plaintiff lawyer put too much stock in a single part of persuasion — the power of earning trust — and lost sight of other aspects of persuasion. One plate kept spinning, but others fell.

In applying insights, pay attention to balance. As part of this, take care with big departures from common practices. It's true that common practices embody a lot of common mistakes, but they also embody a lot of common wisdom. Depart from commonplace notions respectfully and thoughtfully. As you do, keep the whole picture in mind, as well as the particulars. You're spinning plates. Focus too much on just one of them, and you'll have a pile of broken pottery.[1]

PRINCIPLES FOR PERSUASION

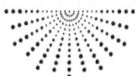

The principles of persuasion provide the granite bedrock that should ground any attempt at advocacy. The following principles apply in most settings outside commercial advertising. They apply particularly in the legal setting — which usually involves extended exposure to the decision-maker, an adversarial process with an opponent trying to poke holes, and decision-making by professional skeptics who view the advocates with high suspicion.

1. EARN TRUST.

Character may almost be called the most effective means of persuasion.
— Aristotle

If you wish to win a man over to your ideas, first make him your friend.
— Abraham Lincoln

Persuasion starts not with hard, concrete, practical actions, but with the soft, simple, character virtues you learned in Sunday School. That's because persuasion is about people and relationships — which is largely to say, *trust*. It's tempting to brush quickly past this, because it's uncomfortably squishy and maddeningly vague. *What precisely are you telling me to* **do***?* I know. It *is* maddening. But all the same, if the decision-maker doesn't trust you, you've probably lost already, regardless of how well you remember your lines and hit your marks.

1.1 RESPECT AND VALUE THE PERSON YOU'RE TALKING TO.

The more we believe people respect us, value us, like us, care about us, the more we credit what they say. That goes for politicians, newspapers, husbands, mothers, and lawyers. When speakers bear ill will toward us, when speakers think we're stupid, when speakers want to manipulate us, when speakers don't like us — then we don't much care what they say. On the other hand, when we feel that people like and respect and care about us, we'll take what they say seriously (if they also seem competent).

In a trial, at a hearing, or even in writing a brief, the jurors or judges will get some feeling, if only subtly, about how you feel toward them. This will usually operate quietly, not fully consciously, but if you pay attention, you'll see it. Watch lawyers conduct jury selection, or watch them in oral arguments, and ask yourself how they feel about the jurors or judges. You'll be able to get a sense of that. It comes through in subtle little things. We rarely focus consciously on these things, but we get a feeling about how others feel toward us. So do jurors and judges.

The only reliable way to show that you respect a judge or juror is to *actually* respect them. If you already know and like the judge, that's easy. With others, you have to actively put yourself into the right frame of mind. We have ways of influencing our own states of mind. For starters, you can just sit in a chair and think up some reasons to like the strangers you'll be meeting at trial, or reasons why the judge you're at odds with isn't really so bad after all. There are other methods, too. Some of the best lawyers have explicit rituals before trial, in which they spend time getting their heads into a space where they feel good about the jurors. Joshua Karton and David Ball offer some suggestions for this in *Theater for Trial* (2017). But whatever you do, do something to get yourself into a mindset in which you respect and value the decision-maker.

None of this means, however, that you should make a special, conscious effort to *display* to jurors or judges that you respect them. That'll probably ruin it. Only rarely can you tell someone, "I respect you," without making them wonder if you're lying. Just get yourself into the right frame of mind, and then focus on the job at hand. Usually if you respect someone, that'll show throw without any special, conscious effort. In the high-suspicion context of a legal dispute, a special smile or a conspicuous show of solicitude usually just makes you seem shifty.

1.2 TAKE POSITIONS YOU BELIEVE IN.

Only argue positions you believe in — positions you *actually* believe in, without self-deception. To the extent you do otherwise, you do not deserve anyone's trust, and you probably won't get it.

If you take up a cause you know to be corrupt, or advance a position you know to be meritless, you weaken your ability to connect with people and gain their trust. Your untrustworthiness shows through. It tends to show up in the content of what you say, and in your person. If you argue a position you don't believe in, often they'll sense you're not to be trusted.

The need to take only sincere, honest positions can pose a problem for lawyers, but it shouldn't. Only criminal defense lawyers who take court appointments should ever face a serious inconsistency between their beliefs and the positions they take. The rest of us get to pick our cases and our positions.

A defense lawyer with a liable or guilty client can help the client through honest advocacy. Help may come in the form of litigation over damages or degree of culpability, in the form of negotiated settlements or plea agreements, and the like. Indeed, dishonest, shoot-the-moon advocacy risks backfiring and exposing the client to a worse outcome than honest advocacy would.

If you have a client (or your client has a liability insurer) who insists on taking a position you believe false or unjust, even after you've considered it seriously, then refuse to take that position. If that destroys your relationship with the client, then refer them to another lawyer. That may come at near-term cost, but selling your integrity will probably cost more over the long run. If you work for a firm that insists you take false or unjust positions, look for the exit.

The idea of the lawyer as an amoral technician debases everyone who embraces it. Lawyers sometimes talk of lawsuits as a game, with all the moral consequence of a poker tournament. Lawyers sometimes say a good lawyer should be able to take any side in a dispute, with equal ease. Maybe that vision of lawyering applies to the few controversies with no moral weight. But in most of our work, someone has harmed another person either carelessly or deliberately — or has been wrongly accused of doing so. We may disagree about what the truth is, but the truth matters. It has moral weight. The outcome will impact people for good or ill. Most of our work sags under the cargo of moral consequence. If we participate in causing or perpetuating an injustice, we bear some of the blame. A bar card does not immunize us from moral responsibility.

The idea of the amoral lawyer also degrades the lawyer's effectiveness. Decision-makers care about making the right decision. If the lawyer arguing to them does not, often the judge or juror will feel the apathy and recoil from it.

We disagree on moral questions, and morally serious lawyers will take different sides on all sorts of issues. Be careful about kidding yourself, though. We want to believe in what we're doing. To deceive others, we first deceive ourselves. But self-deception usually doesn't work completely. Some of the stench leaks out.

We do our best as lawyers and as persons when we approach issues with moral seriousness and act with integrity.

1.3 TELL THE TRUTH — INCLUDING THE ESSENTIAL BAD PARTS.

Even when lawyers take positions they believe in, life still conspires to make lawyers dishonest. Something in us wants to hide from problems in our own case, and from an opponent's good points, so we have to fight a natural tendency to conceal important parts of the truth. Without diligence, we can slide into dishonesty. That hurts persuasion.

Speak honestly, openly, reasonably about the essential information, whether it cuts for you or against you. Treat all the people involved and all the facts fairly. Acknowledge the important facts and arguments that go against you. Don't cheat by addressing a weak version of your opponent's point. Make reasonable concessions. Tell the truth about the real strength of your position.

If you present a one-sided argument, you immediately raise suspicions. Everyone knows that most disputes have two sides. Besides, an honest, preemptive response to important objections builds resistance to the objection. So show that you've tried to do justice to serious, opposing points of view. Show that while you're a partisan, you still care about the truth. Show that you trust us with the truth.

As an advocate in an adversarial system, however, you don't need to — and you should not — address every point the opposition might raise. You should only address the negative points you believe are essential to the issue. If a judge or juror will feel you deceived them by omitting a point, then address it. But if a judge or juror will see the point as just another argument by your opponent, then you should not address it. As long as you engage in no *deceptive* omissions or spin, you won't undermine trust.

Obviously, the best approach to any negative point is to flip it into a helpful point, where you can do so convincingly. If you can't do that, and can't exclude it entirely (as through a pretrial motion), then the next best approach is to put the harmful point into a perspective that drains its power.

Honesty and integrity do not require you to avoid aggressive, bold, or novel positions. Just show they're fair. The more aggressive and unconventional a position will seem to the decision-maker, the greater the need to demonstrate the fairness of the position.

Speaking honestly and fairly requires emotional maturity. Keep a sense of proportion. Don't overstate things. Don't whine. Don't criticize unreasonably. Don't be mean. Don't be snide, sarcastic, or cutting. Don't be funny at anyone else's expense, unless you're responding to an argument that is genuinely absurd. Err on the side of understatement (but not too much). Don't let fear make you sound defensive and harsh. If you accuse the other side of some impropriety, just lay out the facts and avoid subjective characterizations. All this can take real effort and self-control. Especially when the stakes are high, it's hard to be fair to opponents and harmful facts. But you have to do it.

Moral integrity is important in its own right, and it confers advantages in dealing with other people. This is not to say liars and cheaters never prosper. They do, all too often. But over the run of cases, you generally do better with moral integrity than without — even though (or especially when) it costs you to act with integrity. That's particularly true when people encounter you repeatedly or for an extended time, as in most legal contexts.

1.4 BRING YOUR WHOLE SELF — BUT A DECENT, RESTRAINED VERSION OF IT.

It matters who you are. If you present yourself as a shriveled stump of a person — all rationality and no emotion — then you'll come off as weird and untrustworthy. If you present yourself as a weepy hysteric or a raging buffoon, you'll discredit everything you say. Bring your whole self — but the best of your genuine selves.

Whatever the context, tune in to how you respond to it as a person. A closing argument to a jury in a capital murder case will call forth vastly different responses than a brief on the application of clause $2(A)(i)(c)$ of a grain requirements contract. But if you care about an issue at all, then by definition you have some emotional response to it. However quiet it is, listen to it. Then see what you think about your response: Is it apt, appropriate, fitting? If not, then think about why you're overreacting, or underreacting, or whatever. Find the appropriate response that's authentic to you.

Express yourself in a way that suits the occasion. A trial or a brief is not a poetry slam. It's not about you or your feelings or personality. But again, you remain a person. Let the totality of the situation guide you. The look on the judge's face, your history, what the other side is doing, the body language of jurors, what you feel just then — everything influences what suits the moment.

At bottom, you're a person trying to persuade another person. Your chances of success increase if you act like a full, decent person.

1.5 ENGAGE YOUR LISTENERS ON A HUMAN LEVEL.

Especially with live, in-person advocacy — but with written advocacy, too — engage your listeners on a human level. For in-person advocacy, this means simple-sounding things like good eye contact with the decision-makers. It means paying attention to their faces and words and tone of voice and body language. It means responding to what you see there, both in the content and tone of what you say and in your own body language. It means opening yourself up enough to provide a genuine human response. Ultimately, this sort of engagement is possible only by getting into a frame of mind in which you care about and attend closely to your audience — attend to what they're thinking and feeling, attend to their needs in the situation. Engagement means connection; it means empathy.

In written advocacy, the potential for human engagement is more limited and thus simpler. But in writing, engagement again requires empathy, requires thinking about and attending to the needs of the particular judge and law clerk you're writing to.

Of course this is all very banal and obvious, and yet we usually don't do it — at least not much, and not well. Some of us don't do a very good job of engaging on a human level even with our families and friends. But even those of us who perform well as humans in ordinary life do much less well in hearings and trials and brief-writing. The pressures of the circumstances confine and distort us.

It takes practice, and maybe a little group therapy, to become capable of acting as a proper human being under the pressures of a hearing or trial, or even of writing a brief. Practical help with this lies beyond the scope of this book, but again I would point you to the book *Theater for Trial* by Karton and Ball. But serious improvement really takes live practice, preferably with in-person coaching by someone qualified to help.

1.6 KEEP YOUR EMOTIONAL PITCH IN TUNE WITH YOUR LISTENER'S.

Before your language or tone starts to show emotion, be sure you've given your listeners enough facts that their feelings are likely to resonate with yours. Stay in the moment; narrow your focus to the information the judge or jurors have, so you can stay in sync with them. If you get out of sync, you risk losing your connection. If they see you responding very differently than they do, they'll conclude you're somehow alien to them. They can't rely on you. You're dancing with a partner: Get too far out of step, and it falls apart.

1.7 DON'T TRY TO HIDE YOUR AGENDA OR SHINE IT UP.

We know you have an agenda, and that's fine with us, as long as you're honest about it. If it's not obvious, tell us where you're coming from. Don't act like you're neutral if you're not. We can smell manipulation a mile away.

1.8 KNOW WHAT YOU'RE TALKING ABOUT, AND LOOK LIKE IT — WITHOUT PUTTING ON AIRS.

Trust requires competence. You can't fake competence for long. Competence comes mainly from mastery of the subject matter, but appearances matter, too.

No one is omnicompetent, but no one needs to be. So long as you have at least the competence the other person expects you to have, that's enough. You need not engage in self-abasement — especially if it's sham, showy self-deprecation — but you can speak or write in a way that implicitly acknowledges the limits of your competence and makes no claim to anything more. The more competence, the better, if you can wear it gracefully. Put on airs, though, and you're inviting the prick that pops your balloon.

1.9 ABIDE BY VALUES YOU SHARE WITH THE DECISION-MAKER — AND BEWARE THE HAIR-TRIGGER FOR DISTRUST IN HIGH-SUSPICION CONTEXTS.

This final point blends into issues of motivation we'll touch on again shortly, but it's more fundamental than that. You can do everything else right, you can be scrupulously honest, you can exude integrity, and yet lose the trust of judge or juror because your position violates their values. If you don't find a way to make your position appeal to a set of values you share with the judge or jurors, then you become a sort of moral alien. Your professed beliefs and attitudes will seem counterfeit or (if genuine) perverse. Your honesty and integrity will look like a lawyer's trick, in service of a deeper dishonesty.

When judges or jurors draw that conclusion despite your having spoken honestly and sincerely, the conclusion will be mistaken, and it will hurt. When you've acted with scrupulous honesty and fairness but have nonetheless ended on the wrong side of a verdict, it hurts to realize that jurors or judges rejected conclusions you believe in and advanced sincerely. There's no point in saying it's not personal. *Of course* it's personal. There's no more personal rejection than a rejection of your actual beliefs, values, and feelings.

For a lawyer, the need to act from within a set of shared values is all the more important because we face an extremely skeptical audience. Jurors especially, and often judges too, scrutinize us with high suspicion. Departures from the jurors' own attitudes will easily translate into evidence of greed, hypocrisy, cynicism, or dishonesty. This suspicion does not fall on us equally. Criminal defense and civil plaintiff lawyers probably face the greatest burden of suspicion. Prosecutors probably have it the easiest. But we're all lawyers, and we all come under the gimlet eye.

One example: For plaintiffs' lawyers, the biggest, most obvious potential conflict with juror values is money — how much money this client's injuries are worth. You can do everything else right, but if you ask for an amount that strikes jurors as ridiculous, you can destroy your credibility in an instant. In all the time before, you've been fair, honest, and reasonable; but in less than two seconds — the time it takes to say X dollars — that's all gone and it turns out you're just another greedy, grasping lawyer. We have to get three things at least approximately right, (i) the time to talk numbers, (ii) the way we talk about numbers, and (iii) the actual numbers we propose. And what works for *these* jurors in *this* trial won't necessarily work for *those* jurors in *that* trial.

Civil defense lawyers and criminal lawyers have their own special problem issues. Whatever the particular sensitivities of our various practices, we all face an urgent need to understand the decision-makers' values, and to root ourselves within those values in a way that can support a decision for our clients. It may take some digging to find a way to do this, and sometimes it can't be done. But if you don't do the work to find a way to accomplish this, prepare to lose trust and thus to lose the case.

～

YOUR WHOLE LIFE, you've seen lawyers and non-lawyers break their heads against the problem of trust. One image sticks in my mind. I walked out of a courthouse in Sioux Falls shortly after the jurors had returned their verdict. A few yards down, a lawyer sat slumped forward on a sidewalk bench, holding his head in both hands. For just a moment, though he was my adversary and I disliked him, my heart went out to him. An hour earlier, and often through the preceding two weeks, that lawyer had beamed with confidence, seeming almost giddy at how well the trial was going for him. Now he looked like he'd been kicked in the chest by his favorite mule. It was a fraud case, in which the plaintiff had to prove fraudulent intent. And this lawyer, representing the defendants, had put together a perfectly consistent story, a logical argument, uniformly supportive testimony from all his witnesses, all of whom had maintained their composure on the stand, without a single defector. There was no direct proof of fraudulent intent, but only circumstances. He couldn't lose. What this lawyer seems not to have seen was that from their first words in jury selection through their last words in closing argument, he and his co-counsel had shed little tells of bad faith, like dandruff flakes off their shoulders. Their witnesses had done the same. It seems never to have occurred to them that jurors just wouldn't believe a word they said. Now the lawyer sat slumped forward on that bench, short of breath. There but for the grace of God.

THE BEST LAWYERS focus obsessively on issues of trust. "Credibility" is the universal watchword among litigators and trial lawyers — even when honored more in the breach. The best lawyers make strenuous efforts to speak and act honestly, decently, and reasonably. Even many mediocre lawyers at least try to *appear* honest. The best lawyers try to become the sort of people who act with respect and consideration and warmth toward others, always. These lawyers try to work on who they are as people because they understand that in the vortex of trial, you can't reliably pull off an attempt to be someone other than your true self. In short, the best lawyers try to become better people, simply as people. These efforts may include psychotherapy, or religious involvement, or meditation, or other means. These efforts rarely succeed completely, of course, because it's hard to turn creatures of dust into creatures of gold. But these efforts still pay off to one degree or another, depending.

One tiny example that still surprises me: Now and then I'll watch someone else's trial or attend a deposition taken by a lawyer

I'm working with. These days, that tends to be Lloyd Bell, a friend and a splendid plaintiff-side trial lawyer in Atlanta. The questioning goes along in the usual way, and at some point the defendant offers some reasonable-sounding explanation for the negligent conduct. The defendant may express it inartfully, but the explanation sounds reasonable — and thus a threat to the case. Lloyd will say something like, "Oh, I see. You're saying ..." and Lloyd goes on to state the explanation the defendant is trying to give. Lloyd states the defendant's explanation fairly, neutrally or even a shade sympathetically, without arguing against it. This always gives me a little shock. You expect an advocate to argue with the adversary, especially on a point helpful to the adversary — not to seek to understand or to help state the adversary's position. Every argument you've ever seen or participated in — from the kindergarten playground to your last trial to yesterday's quarrel with your brother — has trained you to expect at least argument, and probably cheating. Lloyd violates that expectation. Those moments create a little buzz of surprise, and they do something powerful: Those moments give a gut-level impression that the questioner is honest, fair, and decent. Those moments give the impression that the questioner is unafraid of the adversary's argument — that the questioner knows the adversary's argument is wrong and will be able to prove it wrong when the time comes to do so. (These impressions won't help if in fact you do not have a good answer to the adversary's argument.) Moments like this come and go quickly. Sometimes they pass quickly enough that a juror probably would not consciously register them. But as they pass, these moments deposit little impressions of trustworthiness. Over a couple hours, or a couple days, or a couple weeks, those little deposits of trust accumulate and help to win a case.

YOUR TYPE of law practice can impair your efforts to make yourself trustworthy. If you routinely take positions you don't believe in, that will tend to corrupt you. A civil plaintiff lawyer with a volume practice may frequently end up with bogus cases. You should drop those cases outright. Protect your client's interests as you withdraw, but get out. It's hard to prosecute a bogus case without becoming, and showing yourself to be, untrustworthy; and a reputation of untrustworthiness will trail you like a skunk's perfume. A civil defense lawyer who generally litigates against plaintiff lawyers who select their cases carefully will face the same problem. A criminal defense lawyer will tend to face the same problem. This does not mean, of course, that any particular lawyer is doomed to become dishonest. In any type of work, there are ways to practice honorably. But systemic tendencies can make it harder to remain honorable. It's not every person who will overcome the difficulty. If you've been practicing a while, you'll have run across lawyers who seem dishonest or nasty at their core. They may have been corrupted by years in a law practice in which they routinely faced pressure to take bad faith positions. Over time, contortions calcify into character.

APART FROM STRIVING for decency and personal connection, the best lawyers also obsess over understanding the worldviews of potential jurors. When you talk to a good lawyer about your new case, one of the first questions will be, "What county [or District] are you in?" Or if you're talking about motion practice, the question is, "Who's your judge?" These questions are shorthand for, "What's the worldview of the decision-maker?" The best lawyers, however, do not completely trust their instincts about decision-makers. Thoughtful lawyers do whatever juror-testing (or judge-testing) the practicalities allow — whether through formal surveys, focus groups, and the like (where the money at stake allows it) or through informal means. Don Vinson, one of the early jury consultants who helped create the field, once told me that experienced lawyers make the best clients for a jury consultant. You might think it would be the opposite — that long-experienced, successful trial lawyers would have learned enough that they no longer need case-specific research into juror attitudes. In fact, though, the most successful trial lawyers have learned that life is too complicated and surprising to rely on your instincts about people. Every case requires explicit, focused research into the attitudes of the decision-makers.

A WORD more on the mystery and magic of trustworthiness at trial. Let's assume your position remains rooted in values you share in common with the jurors. Let's assume also that in everything you do, you behave honestly, fairly, decently, and reasonably. It can still go wrong. A trial can function as a distorting lens, like a funhouse mirror. At trial, you work under enormous pressure that can alter your conduct, often in ways you won't notice. And the jurors regard you with extreme suspicion. They expect you to lie, to manipulate, to have a hidden mercenary motive for everything you do. And they expect you to perform your trickery subtly, with a convincing show of sincerity. So they look for small signs of dishonesty, and they'll err on the side of false positives. In this cauldron, you can easily come off as untrustworthy, even when you fully deserve trust.

Look again at the sad lawyer slumped on the sidewalk bench. I said earlier that he shed hints of bad faith throughout the trial. But he also had the misfortune of trying the case against a lawyer, Mike Abourezk, who has mastered the subtle magic of both being trustworthy and letting that trustworthiness pierce the distorting lens of trial. This book is not a manual on that magic, but that feat has something to do with the sort of person you are, and of somehow feeling true faith in the jury, and of somehow maintaining a deep existential calm despite caring intensely about the verdict. This ability probably requires, among other things, lots of practice trying cases — far more than most lawyers ever get. Few of us can get into this Zen state of mind, but for Mike and others who can achieve that (and for their clients), it's a big advantage.

I have only two nuggets of advice on how to let trustworthiness pierce the funhouse mirror (apart from doing your best to become a trustworthy person). *First*, say nothing and do nothing to intentionally make a show of trustworthiness. This may seem counterintuitive, given all this stress on the centrality of trust. But in the crucible of extreme suspicion, anything you do for the express purpose of showing how trustworthy you are will probably come off as manipulative. It will destroy, not enhance, trust.

Second, if you can avoid it blowing up in your face, adopt a smidgen of quasi-fatalism — just enough to counteract your tendency to urge, to implore, to exhort, to strain, to repeat yourself; just enough to show a little faith in jurors. True fatalism is stupid and self-defeating, and if you tend toward fatalism, maybe you should disregard this suggestion. But to be trusted, you must give trust. Jurors must see that you trust them. When fear compels you to repeat yourself and raise your voice, you signal that you distrust the jurors. That can poison your relationship with jurors and convince them that you're so anxious because you know your case is weak.[1] For those of us who haven't overcome the anxiety that makes us urge and implore, the only available remedy may be a modest quasi-fatalism: *I can't make jurors believe what they don't believe. I can only show them the facts and walk through the analysis. Repeating myself and pounding the pulpit will only make things worse.* Even those of us who are not Zen masters can internalize this much, and it can counteract our fear-driven tendency to demonstrate distrust of the jurors.

Tend to trust. Without it, you lose.

2. ENLIST EXISTING ATTITUDES, TO MOTIVATE THE DECISION.

> *People almost invariably arrive at their beliefs not on the basis of proof but on the basis of what they find attractive.*
> — Blaise Pascal

> *If you would persuade, you must appeal to interest rather than intellect.*
> — Benjamin Franklin

One way or another, all reasoning is motivated. To persuade, you'll have to find a way to motivate the judge and law clerk or the jurors. Motivation can only come from the facts of the case, interacting with the decision-makers' worldviews.

2.1 FIND WHAT WILL MOTIVATE THIS PERSON FOR YOU, AND AGAINST YOU.

We need to motivate decision-makers in two different ways: First, just to do their jobs, and second, to make the decision we're asking for. In doing this, we have to preempt or weaken opposing motivations.

Motivating people just to do their jobs often takes work. It's hard for any of us to pay attention and work through the facts and law to figure out the right result. We're all busy. We've all got personal lives and quotidian cares. Here today, sitting in this chair at this desk, or in this seat in this jury box, judge or juror has a lot of other things going on in their work and their lives. This dispute of yours is your problem, not theirs. Except for the lucky occasions when your dispute has both (i) a clear answer and (ii) utter simplicity, you need to motivate decision-makers to do the work.

The motivation to decide in your favor depends on the values that drive the decision-makers and how they perceive the facts. A general discussion of specific motivations lies beyond the scope of this book. However, in legal disputes, motivation comes largely in a few main types:

1. protecting Us from harm
2. punishing rule-breakers (because they endanger us)
3. helping someone we care about, who has been hurt
4. turning away from something or someone offensive or disgusting
5. making work easier for the decision-maker
6. making a public statement about the kind of community we are
7. doing the job well, and being seen to have done the job well.

The last two motivations may be the weakest, but they're worth keeping in mind. For a plaintiff or criminal defendant especially, those latter motivations can become dangerous — because of the jurors who don't want to face criticism at home for a verdict that would seem wrong to those who didn't hear all the evidence. In any case, each of these basic motivations can play out in a variety of ways, and can work for you or against you, depending on which of the various facts in a case come to the foreground.

John Steinbeck said, "If a story is not about the hearer, he will not listen." For any sort of motivation, a lot depends on who counts as an Us for this decision-maker. And also on what norms or rules the decision-maker recognizes, on what counts as a serious infraction or serious harm, and so on. You have to look. You have to learn about the decision-makers and how they see things.

You won't always find a way to activate each potential source of motivation for a particular decision-maker. You won't always find *any* source of motivation that works. But look.

2.2 FIND THE STORIES, SCENES, AND DETAILS THAT FEED HELPFUL MOTIVATIONS AND STARVE HARMFUL ONES.

Motivation grows out of the human stories in the case. Robert Ferguson put it nicely: "Unless it's a story the jury has heard before and believes, you won't win the case." Find the powerful facts, details, scenes, characters. Think through the story of what happened — the values at stake, the good and bad character on display, the struggle, the drama. Think through the alternatives for selection and sequencing of details, to find the arrangements that will make sense to this decision-maker as a true human story. Find the little details that reveal good and bad character, that illuminate good and bad motives. Find the individual scenes to linger over and to conjure vividly, to provide a memorable image that encapsulates important aspects of the story.

In much the same way, find the facts that could trigger harmful motivations, and look for ways to co-opt or preempt or otherwise limit their power to hurt you.

The better the facts fit together into a single coherent story, the better it will likely work. The better the facts fit into the classic structure of a story — conflict between a protagonist and antagonist; an inciting event, a struggle, a climax, a resolution — the better the story will probably work. You needn't obsess over this or despair if the story of your case falls short of the *Moby Dick* standard. But the closer you can match the age-old structure of a story, the better.

To better understand how to turn a pile of facts into a story, read some books on the classic story types and their structures. Every story you've ever heard falls into one of a handful of abstract story forms. Most of us never see the overall structure, because when we read a novel or watch a movie, we get transported into the story and see only the detail, not the abstract structure. We need to read about this stuff. And then we need to watch and re-watch good examples in movies, read and re-read good examples in novels, to see what sorts of particulars fill out the general structures with impact. This understanding won't turn you into Stephen King, but it'll help you develop cases better than you did before.

(If you snicker at Stephen King as a model here, you're missing the point. We're talking about skill in crafting stories — not literary or intellectual merit. King consistently spins out stories that captivate broad, diverse audiences. Prefer James Joyce for literary merit if your taste runs that way, but Stephen King is the better model for sheer story-crafting skill.)

Take care, however, to avoid over-particularizing. A full story does not require Proustian detail. You want to let the reader construct the story in his or her own mind. Too many details can get in the way. How much is too much depends, and you can't really know for sure. But think about it and make your best guess.

2.3 FIND THE LANGUAGE THAT EVOKES THE VALUES AND MOTIVATIONS YOU'RE APPEALING TO AND LEADS AWAY FROM CONTRARY ONES.

As you sift the facts with an eye on the judge or jurors, write down the core values in play — moral values, political values, decent-society values, practical values — and then brainstorm the language we use to talk about those things. Get out a thesaurus. Brainstorm metaphors and analogies. Brainstorm clichés, sayings, proverbs, aphorisms, quotations. Get other people to help. Look at your options and think about what language will work best for this decision-maker in this dispute. However expansive your vocabulary, the resources of the English language, and our legacy of folk and literary wisdom, eclipses it. You won't find all your options without a special effort. (For civil plaintiff lawyers, Keith Mitnick's book *Don't Eat the Bruises* nicely addresses some key language choices.)

Maybe this process sounds like a prissy, delicate frivolity. Maybe it sounds like a long-fingered chef fretting over how to drizzle sauce over the steak. It's not that.

Fretting over language is substantive work. We conduct our conscious thinking largely in words. And the words we use consciously will influence both our own and a listener's unconscious, pre-linguistic thought. The words we use matter to our own thinking and to the thoughts and feelings we provoke in the minds of decision-makers.

Every word carries its own nuance of meaning and feeling. There are no exact synonyms. *Injure. Impair. Prejudice. Mistreat. Abuse.* Those are all synonyms, but they don't all fit your situation equally well. They won't all work equally well with your judge or jurors. In examining word choices, you refine your thinking and the emotional tone of your case. You gain a better understanding of your issue and your audience. You also find power. Mark Twain reportedly said the difference between the right word and the almost right word is the difference between the lightning and the lightning bug. The right word, or the right metaphor or aphorism, carry a punch. They draw on common sense. They evoke feelings that motivate.

Again, keep a lookout for language that will trigger opposing values and motivations.

We can approach the question of helpful and harmful language on two levels: general language choices that apply across all the work you do, and issue-specific choices. Cast a skeptical eye over all the language you commonly use, including language that seems obviously right to you. For example, while I'm a civil plaintiff's lawyer, I suspect my colleagues do themselves and their clients no good when they talk about "justice." When I hear plaintiff lawyers talk "justice," I wonder what's their cut. "Justice" talk sounds to me like a cover for greed. My response may be idiosyncratic, but that sort of question requires thoughtful consideration. There are dozens, maybe hundreds, of such language choices to think about. So get cracking.

2.4 USE COMPARISONS AND FRAMING, THOUGHTFULLY.

We see this in relation to that, so we need comparisons. Pick them fairly but thoughtfully. Show us, for example, what proper conduct looks like, before you show the wrongdoer's misconduct. Show us a normal, expected outcome before showing the botched outcome.

Similarly, consider alternative ways of framing things. Logically equivalent statements can produce very different responses. When you can, frame your position, for example, as (a) preventing the loss of something your listener values and (b) enforcing adherence to widespread norms or other authority.

2.5 MAKE YOURSELF AND YOUR CLIENT AN US TO THE EXTENT YOU AUTHENTICALLY CAN.

Within the limits of honesty and authenticity, align yourself and your client with the person you're talking to. Find where you share experiences or goals or values in common, and let that show through. Find where you share feelings in common, and let that come out in natural ways. To the extent you can authentically wear tokens of shared identity — clothing, speech, gait, whatever — wear them.

Show your client in common roles and situations that judges and jurors can relate to — doing mom or dad or student stuff, going to WalMart, dealing with recalcitrant kids or dogs, whatever.

Obviously, don't fake anything. There's no better way to mark yourself as a lying outsider than to clumsily ape the insiders. A guy who lives and works in Manhattan goes to Montana to try a case. He buys a bolo tie, hat and boots, and rents a pickup truck. Bad idea. Never pretend to be what you're not. Never pretend to believe what you don't. Never pretend to feel what you can't.

2.6 IDENTIFY LIKELY COUNTER-MOTIVATIONS AND DO SOMETHING ABOUT THEM.

We're full of conflicting motivations; so in addition to finding motivations that pull your way, of course you need to make a separate effort to identify other motivations that push the other way — and do something about them. Simply taking half an hour to mull over potential counter-motivations will improve your chances. Yet this is the sort of soft, frou-frou task we set aside for some idle moment during trial prep — an idle moment that never comes. This should be a mandatory, front-loaded step for any exercise in advocacy.

Counter-motivations include both legitimate and illegitimate varieties. Trial lawyer lore is full of stories about ignoble, unworthy considerations that undermine truth and justice — personal like or dislike, identity politics (class or race or gender or regional affiliations or resentments, etc.), crab-pot mentality, physical attractiveness or not, and so on. Whatever the potential issues may be, figure out what they are and what to do about them.

2.7 SEQUENCING: STORY FIRST, THEN ANALYSIS. AND MAYBE BEGIN WITH THE HARM, TO MOTIVATE SCRUTINY OF BAD CONDUCT.

In sequencing a presentation, tell the story before you analyze the issues. We may need the story dissected later, with issues separated and labeled and arranged with logic arrows pointing this way and that. First, though, we just need to digest the facts as a story and find the motivation to do the harder work of analyzing things.

In structuring the story, try out a version that begins with the end, with the injury or conflict that brings us here. This structure doesn't always work, but generally it does two things: Beginning with the end creates interest. *How did we get here? What happened?* This sequence sets up a mystery story that gets people to pay attention. More specifically, and more importantly, beginning with the end gets listeners looking for misconduct. You need them to spot the misconduct when it arises, so prime them to look for it.

2.8 SEQUENCING: ADDRESS ESSENTIAL NEGATIVE POINTS AFTER THE DECISION-MAKER HAS BEGUN TO SEE THINGS YOUR WAY. AND PUT THE NEGATIVE POINT IN YOUR OPPONENT'S MOUTH.

We've discussed the importance of addressing essential negative points. The sequence matters crucially, though. The first thing we see affects how we perceive the next thing we see. If you start your case with the negative stuff, then we believe it maximally, and it taints the rest of your case. So do it the other way around: Start with the things that motivate us to see the issue your way. Only after you've got us started well down that road should you address anything that detracts from your case. You can't always follow this rule, but where you can, do.

This sequencing will not offend decision-makers. Jurors and judges know you're an advocate. They expect you to put your best foot forward, and they give you permission to do so.

Furthermore, getting the sequencing the other way around

(bad before good) probably signals a deep, albeit likely unconscious, dishonesty. An urge to start with the bad stuff probably reflects a desire to show off how utterly, impossibly, world-historically honest you are, how you're so deeply noble that you're really more a neutral than an advocate, how you really belong in the jury box rather than at the lectern and it's just an accident of fate that you're here rather than there. A desire to demonstrate any of that should be drowned. You *are* an advocate — not a judge, not a juror. Pretending otherwise is as dishonest as it is stupid.

IN GENERAL, when you do address a negative point, make clear that it's your opponent's point and you're just preempting it. *The Defense will say such and such.* Or *Plaintiff will respond thus and so.* By explicitly couching your discussion as preemption, you weaken the perception that you think the point is important. By putting the point in your opponent's mouth, you prompt the judge or jurors to apply the discount they always apply to any advocate's self-serving arguments.

By doing this, you maintain your credibility and you inoculate the judge or jurors against your opponent's points. If you limit this to *essential* negative points, you'll avoid shooting yourself in the foot by overdoing the acknowledgement of weakness.

~

SOME LAWYERS SEEM to have cracked the code. They consistently beat the average. Those lawyers have through intuition or effort figured out how to manage motivations with a changing cast of decision-makers. The practicalities of managing motivations play out in a million different ways, at every stage of a case.

In the earliest case evaluation, the first question is what motivations, pro and con, might be elicited — from the entire range of human responses. When I was a pup at Boies Schiller, I had a forehead-slapping moment that has stuck with me. We were taking over the defense of a commodities-manipulation class action from another firm. A team of us had been working to get up to speed on the case, and taking memos and briefings from the prior firm. After a couple weeks of this work, we had a day-long meeting of our team and the other firm's team. In the last hour or so, David Boies came in for the first time. He would try the case if it went to trial. David's first question was, "Who are the class representatives?" Callow as I was, I thought the question all but irrelevant, because the class representatives act as mere functionaries. But as David posed questions and extracted details, smiling here, frowning there, it finally dawned on me how the character and conduct of the class reps might play out at trial. I started to understand that for jurors, the class reps really would *represent* the class. I started to see some of the ways this or that detail about the reps might nudge jurors in this or that direction.

Motivations can work in tricky, obscure ways, and this raises the stakes for even banal-seeming litigation decisions. In this business, we occasionally suffer mystifying, inexplicable losses — when the merits are so simple, so clear, so one-sided that losing makes you feel the ground has dropped away beneath your feet. Assuming you were right about the merits, these losses probably mean you got blind-sided by motivations you didn't see coming.

Consider this a just-so story: A lawyer once lost a summary judgment motion he couldn't possibly lose. It was a simple contract issue. The defendant insurance company raised a strained, silly statutory-interpretation argument to defeat the language of the insurance policy. That effort should have been doomed, because even if the statute applied (which it plainly did not), the ancient, settled law was that an insurance policy can offer more generous coverage than a statute requires, unless the statute specifically forbids it, which this statute did not. This lawyer's brief laid out the law clearly and simply, so that no judge could get this issue wrong. And then a judge got it wrong. More shockingly, the judge decided the issue on a basis not raised or argued by either side. The judge dug into the insurance policy, pulled out provisions that neither side had addressed, and based the decision on those provisions. The judge — who could only spend a fraction of the time the parties had spent on the case — misconstrued those provisions in a way that made nonsense of the policy. This lawyer felt like the rug had been pulled out from under him.

I ask you to treat this as a just-so story, because of course you can't know if our hero was really right. For all you know, the judge was right, and the lawyer was wrong. For our purposes here, it doesn't matter. The point is the trickiness of motivations.

On the assumption that our unnamed lawyer was right, then, how could this summary judgment issue have gone so wrong? There must be a human explanation. We can only guess, but here are some facts that may help:

- The judge had started out as an insurance defense lawyer, defending car crash cases and the like on behalf of liability insurance companies.
- The plaintiff had not suffered great harm. An insurance company had cheated an old lady with dementia out of about $25,000 in assisted-living benefits. But the woman had her own money to cover the costs, so she got the care she needed. The insurer started paying benefits once suit was filed, although they didn't pay the back-benefits they owed. So harm was limited. To see major harm, you had to consider the cumulative effect of the insurer's efforts to cheat people on an industrial scale, using a bogus policy interpretation.
- The judge had a backlog of cases and had publicly fretted about the delays that caused.
- When the judge decided this summary judgment motion, two or three discovery motions remained pending. The discovery issues were complex, and the briefing extensive.
- The summary judgment briefing was not especially complicated, but it was long.

Undoubtedly there are other relevant factors beyond our knowledge. One might guess, however, that the judge found the case trivial and annoying and burdensome, thought the defense's arguments didn't work, spent half an hour or so to come up with another rationale, went with it, and moved on to the next case in the pile.

Some of the motivations involved in this just-so story were beyond any lawyer's ability to manage. But had our hero thought about it, he might have abandoned some discovery disputes, to avoid creating a burdensome pile of work for the judge, and he might have kept the briefs trimmer. Would that have made a difference? Who knows. But I bet that lawyer wishes he had made these changes all the same.

The moral of the story is just that motivations are tricky and always to some degree inscrutable, that we have no choice but to fret over them and make judgment calls as thoughtfully as we can, and that we have no guaranteed outcomes.

AN INQUIRY into potential motivations should begin at the earliest point possible — before taking a case — and continue until the case is over and done. This inquiry should inform the development of the facts, the shaping of a story out of those facts, the selection of characters to focus on, and so on.

This focus on motivations should influence every choice at every stage of litigation and trial. In voir dire, for example, the purpose is to identify whether the potential jurors are willing and able to apply the law fairly. Each voir dire question will reveal something about the case and will set the jurors' minds down some path of thought. Furthermore, even given a fixed set of questions, changing the sequence will change the effect. Ask "has anyone here had a loved one seriously injured in a car crash?" Discuss that for a while, and then, 30 minutes and three topics later, ask "who here is willing to admit you don't always drive as carefully as you should — that sometimes we all drive carelessly?" In that sequence, you get to one path of thought, leading to one set of motivations. Reverse the order of those two questions, and you get to a different place, and maybe a different verdict.

Voir dire is just one random example. In every part of the advocacy process, each substantive choice you make about the presentation of fact or law will, on a parallel track, influence the feelings and motivations of the decision-makers. The best lawyers habitually keep an eye on that parallel track, and choose accordingly.

3. JUSTIFY THE DECISION.

However motivated they may be, decision-makers require some rational justification for a decision. We need to be able to explain our decisions to ourselves and to others whose opinions we care about.

Different people have different requirements for justification. Different people apply different amounts of critical scrutiny. And of course people differ in the knowledge and beliefs they bring to a decision, and the way they reason about things. You may get a cockamamie summary judgment decision rationalized by a nonsense reference to an un-briefed contract provision. You may get a cursory statement that "This Court finds Acme's argument unpersuasive." You may get a jury verdict with no stated rationale. The idea of "rational justification" gets real flimsy real fast. Even so, everyone has some requirement for reasoned justification for decisions.

This book does not address the question of how to develop the reasoned justification of a decision. Law school and other sources cover that topic well enough, and anyone reading this book probably knows how to put together a rational argument. That's the easiest part of persuasion.

But while I feel no need to discuss *how* to provide rational justification, I do want to emphasize a nuance concerning *why* to do so: Rational justification itself plays a motivating role. Earlier, I noted that one basic motivation for decision-makers is to do a good job and to be seen as doing a good job. The presence of a rational justification plays into that motivation.

A juror, for example, typically wants to follow the law, and to be seen as following the law. That's not anyone's only motivation, but it's one motivation. So explaining and emphasizing the jury instructions may both justify and motivate a decision. Plaintiff lawyers probably make a mistake in asking for pain-and-suffering damages without showing jurors the written text of the legal instructions that *require* jurors to assess such damages. The legal instructions may nudge reluctant jurors toward doing their duty, and may give other jurors permission to return a verdict they want to vote for but which they feel uncertain about or fear will open them to criticism.

The rational justification may play a greater motivating role for judges. Judges come up in a culture that valorizes judges for making decisions they dislike, because the law "compels" them to. It would be silly to believe unquestioningly in this heroic image of judges, but the image does carry some truth. Judges do care about doing their jobs well and do believe that the law may differ from their own inclinations.

So of course, lay out the evidence and the law fully, cooly, rationally, dispassionately — after you've told the story that creates the dominant motivation.

4. MAKE IT INTERESTING, CLEAR, AND EASY.

The single biggest problem in communication is the illusion that it has been accomplished.
— attributed (questionably) to George Bernard Shaw

The great enemy of clear language is insincerity. When there is a gap between one's real and one's declared aims, one turns as it were instinctively to long words and exhausted idioms, like a cuttlefish spurting out ink.
—— George Orwell

Your case, your issue, your dispute do not fascinate and engage us as much as you think they do. For years I've wanted to read Marcel Proust's *In Search of Lost Time*, but philistine as I am, I've never quite found the motivation to read a 4,200-page literary novel. Take the lesson: If you want us to pay attention to your case, then make it interesting, clear, and easy.

4.1 USE THE BASIC TOOLS OF EFFECTIVE, EFFICIENT COMMUNICATION.

Your high school composition and speech teachers tried to teach you the basic principles and devices of rhetoric. Those things go a long way. This is not a book on basic rhetoric, but to summarize the key points:

1. Simplicity with accuracy: Make things as simple as possible without sacrificing accuracy. This takes work. It's easy to make things simple if you sacrifice accuracy, and it's easy to make things accurate if you sacrifice simplicity. To achieve simplicity *and* accuracy takes elbow grease.

2. Clear, intuitive organization: At every level of a presentation — from the thing as a whole down to each part of it — the listener needs you to organize the material so it's easy to understand the immediate part, how the immediate part relates to the whole, and the whole thing itself.

3. Say one thing at a time. We can't digest too much at once. At each level of a piece — the whole, the sections, the paragraphs, the sentences — discipline yourself to say one thing at a time. Deciding what counts as "one thing" takes judgment, and it changes from the level of an individual sentence to a three-week trial. Even so, the principle applies at each level.

4. Thesis statements and topic sentences; conclusions that relate back; transitions: We digest things better if you start by stating the point. Again this applies at each level from the overall piece, to the sections, to paragraphs. Similarly, we track the discussion better if you end by restating the point. This principle applies more strongly

to oral presentations than to writing, but it applies plenty even in writing.

5. Short, simple sentences — mostly.

6. Concrete particulars: Keep the discussion tied to particulars as much as possible. Generalities create room for confusion and misunderstanding. Further, intuitive judgment looks to particularities. The abstraction needs a concrete anchor; the suffering throng needs a representative; the corporation needs a face; the statistics need a story.

7. Visuals and tangibles: We're physical creatures who rely heavily on eyesight. Where you can illustrate an important point with a useful image or object, do so.

4.2 IN RESPONDING, FIRST LAY OUT THE TRUTH, THEN DEAL WITH THEIR NONSENSE.

In responsive presentations — cross-examination, an opposition brief, a defense case, etc. — your argument easily grows convoluted, because you have to deal with what the other side has already said, in addition to presenting your affirmative view. Often, the poorer the quality of advocacy on the other side, the harder it is for you to keep your presentation clear. Chaos is contagious.

As a general principle, in responsive presentations, state your affirmative view of an issue first, without any overt reference to what your opponent has said. Lay out the simple truth of the issue clearly, on your own terms — in a way that implicitly preempts the opponent's arguments without mentioning those arguments overtly. Only after you've done that are you ready to discuss the other side's arguments explicitly. By then, you can probably dispose of their arguments simply and quickly. This approach minimizes the risk of confusion.

This approach also makes for stronger rebuttals: In making the affirmative truth clear, you let the listener draw their own conclusion that your opponent is wrong, before you discuss your opponent's arguments explicitly.

4.3 TALK CONVERSATIONALLY AND CONCRETELY, LIKE A PERSON INTERESTED IN CONNECTING WITH THE LISTENER.

We understand conversational language more easily than other sorts of language. Conversational language taps into our feelings and therefore interests and engages us more than formal speech. So speak conversationally, to the extent the norms of the situation allow. Even in a legal setting, the norms probably allow conversational language more than you think.

On a related but distinct point, concrete, sensory language affects us more powerfully than abstract language. The more familiar the language, the better. "On waking, the patient had no motor strength in his right lower extremity." Or, "When he woke up, Duane couldn't move his right leg." The reader will not only understand the second sentence more easily, but will resonate with it more viscerally.

Conversational, concrete speech signals in a subtle but important way that the speaker is trying to connect with us, that the speaker cares about getting the meaning across to us. We engage more with a speaker or writer who seems interested in communicating with us.

Maybe that sounds simple and obvious, but not every speaker or writer seems interested in connecting with the listener or reader. Indeed, I'd guess that *most* speakers in *most* situations do not focus on connecting and communicating. Other desires crowd in front. We want to sound smart. We want to impress. We want to fit in. We want to maintain a noble stoicism. Whatever. These concerns distance and disconnect us from the people we talk to. Whether spoken or written, language communicates your personality and your state of mind as you speak or write, including aspects of your state of mind that you're not aware of. If we speak or write while distanced from listeners, they pick up on that.

Make a habit of speaking in the most conversational language that fits the occasion. That sort of language will weaken your tendency to run around trying to impress people with your lawyerly sophistication. Conversational language will systematically steer you toward connecting and communicating with your audience.

4.4 MAKE IT NO LONGER THAN IT NEEDS TO BE.

It's too easy to praise brevity and to chide people for going on too long. That topic furnishes the most boring jokes at bar lunches. The underlying point is true, of course, but the problem isn't so much that we don't understand the importance of brevity in the abstract. The problem is that we never know how long is too long — *here*, now, in this brief or hearing or closing argument. If they've already got the point, then we don't need to keep going on about it. If they have not gotten the point, then we do. So have they gotten the point or not? Three notes to keep in mind as you make that difficult judgment call:

First, fear distorts your perceptions and makes you talk too long. Or maybe it's your delusional belief that you could guarantee the outcome if only you hit the magic words. So you keep stabbing at it. Whatever drives you to go on too long, it's largely emotional, and usually you don't recognize it in the moment. To make good choices and to work effectively, you need somehow to get into a state of mind in which you trust the decision-maker and reduce your fear and anxiety to a low background hum.

Second, beyond some modest threshold, each additional point, each additional sentence adds to the burden on the listeners and increases the risk they'll run out of capacity to digest what you're saying. The addition may justify the cost. Maybe you should go ahead and say it. You just need to assess the upside and downside thoughtfully.

Third, minimalism is not the goal. Effectiveness is the goal. Those are not the same things.

~

IT'S communication that opens the door to persuasion in the first instance. Without communication first, nothing happens. My own sense is that lawyers — professional communicators though we supposedly are — perform in a pretty sloppy, hit-or-miss way. There are too many discrete types of failures, though, so I don't have a single, emblematic anecdote. One random example will have to suffice: As I write this paragraph, it's been just a few hours since I finished responding to a 17-page brief that contained about one page of operative argument. The rest was citation vomit — a bunch of semi-relevant or irrelevant banalities to pad the brief and to create an illusion of seriousness and merit. I've seen that and a whole sad assortment of elementary errors routinely, from law firms up and down the status hierarchy. Despite generations, and probably centuries, of ridicule and complaints about legal writing, the norm seems almost intentionally bad. Oral communication at hearings and trials seems as bad or worse than brief-writing.

The poor quality of lawyers' communication efforts could seem surprising. After all, the basics have been available to know at least since Aristotle's *Rhetoric*. Lawyers reflexively praise Strunk and White. Everybody takes a composition class and a speech class in high school. And you can't graduate from law school nowadays without at least one class on legal writing (though nothing was required, when I went through, on oral communication). And yet the norm remains depressingly bad.

The problem is not that we're dumb. The problem is that the principles of effective communication are not obvious, the corresponding skills do not come without hard work, and most kids aren't motivated to develop these skills in high school and college — for most of us, the only time in life when the help we need is put in front of us. Those who have made habits of the essential principles of rhetoric mostly did so before they went to law school. Communication isn't taught much in law school. And once you start working law jobs, when are you going to drill and practice and get coaching in oral or written communication skills? For most of us, rarely or never.

The upshot is obvious and unwelcome: If we're to become skillful at communication — whether orally or in writing — we're going to have to make time for focused study and practice. Speech and composition practice isn't just for high school kids. It's for anyone dissatisfied with musty, moldy mediocrity.

OF THE MANY ways we misfire in our efforts to communicate, I do want to single out one issue for special urging — the neglect of visuals. I work with Lloyd Bell, who mainly represents people hurt by medical malpractice. Medical issues get confusing and mysterious real fast, if not presented thoughtfully. Judging from his trial verdicts, Lloyd effectively communicates an understanding of medical issues to jurors, and he does so largely by using visuals. Lloyd uses visuals more heavily than any other lawyer I've seen. Lloyd starts thinking about useful visuals early in case development, and he tries out lots of ideas for visuals, testing their effectiveness with different audiences. At trial, Lloyd's visuals consist of images of actual evidence, drawings or schematics for illustration, metaphors to help understand something, documents annotated by witnesses in deposition, graphics to underscore a point, handwritten notes to emphasize a bit of testimony as it comes out — in short, anything for which Lloyd can think of some useful visual. Lloyd uses a variety of ways to present visuals, from big foam boards to butcher block paper to TV screens.

Lloyd also uses tangible objects, either as metaphors to explain something, or as examples of objects in the case. In a case about a misplaced femoral catheter, for example, in his opening statement Lloyd held up an actual catheter. It makes an impression to see the actual thing. For a lay person, mere talk about a misplaced catheter doesn't mean much. But seeing this long thing and imagining it being fed into a blood vessel in your groin — we can respond to that viscerally, and suddenly the idea of a doctor putting it in the wrong blood vessel means a lot more.

These visuals and tangible objects help enormously. They turn complex, mysterious issues into matters jurors understand and feel comfortable with. That's a high achievement, not possible with words alone.

There's a lesson here for the rest of us, and I do not think the lesson only applies to complex medical issues. If we could get a text-message alert each time we fail to communicate something effectively, our phones would buzz non-stop. Even simple points get lost, even when you're sure they couldn't possibly get lost. Of course not every fleck of information requires a visual, and practicalities constrain us. But we should look diligently for ways to improve communication through visuals.

5. STEER AROUND RESISTANCE, AND BUILD COUNTER-RESISTANCE.

People are generally better persuaded by the reasons which they have themselves discovered than by those which have come into the mind of others.
— Blaise Pascal

Even when the decision-maker sees things your way and is motivated to go your way, you can trip over your feet if you get pushy. That'll provoke resistance. Avoid that. But try to build up resistance to what your opponent will say next.

5.1 EARN PERMISSION BEFORE ANYTHING THAT SOUNDS LIKE ADVOCACY OR OVERT EMOTION.

At some point, you'll need to say something that will feel to the listener like you're advocating, pitching, selling, urging. In some sense, you're always doing that, but the listener doesn't always receive it that way. Often, the listener just feels you're reciting facts in a more or less neutral way. It's squishy and subjective and varies from listener to listener and from moment to moment. Even so, some statements feel like advocacy; some don't. Some expressions of emotion feel pushy; some don't.

Earn permission for anything that may feel to this listener, right now, like advocacy. You earn permission by cooly laying out facts that will justify your eventual advocacy. You earn permission by bringing the listener along. You show them facts that make them want to say what you're about to say. Then you can say it. Maybe it'll be OK to write in a brief, "With any luck, this lawsuit will cause Acme to hesitate a little before lying to the next Annie Mills." But if you ever have permission to say that, you'll only have it after you've already shown — through cold, calm fact — that they lied to Annie and are likely to lie to others.

If listeners feel you advocating before you've earned permission to do so, they'll resist, put their guard up. They'll start thinking of you as a typical lawyer or used car salesman.

In any context explicitly given over to advocacy (a lawsuit, a car lot), the need for permission kicks in at a much lower threshold than over pizza and beer with your friends. You tell a story over pizza about some poor kid who went to school one day and came home with a brain injury. "His mom didn't say goodbye to him that morning, and she never saw that same kid again. He was a different person from then on." Saying that will be fine for your friends drinking beer. Saying that in an opening statement in a personal injury trial probably will not be fine. It'll sound stagey and manipulative. In closing argument, the same statement might work just fine, because by then you'll have earned permission for it.

5.2 DON'T GET PUSHY OR STRIDENT. AVOID SUBJECTIVE CHARACTERIZATIONS. STATE ARGUMENTATIVE CONCLUSIONS ONLY WHEN YOU HAVE TO, AND PRESENT THEM AS YOUR VIEWS, NOT DIVINE TRUTH.

Even after you've got permission, go easy on anything that feels like advocacy. You want your listeners to draw their own conclusions, to own them, to feel motivated by them. You want decision-makers to feel they need to express their beliefs and feelings through action. If you say all that needs to be said, you let the steam out of the kettle.

The more commanding or heated you sound, the more you

come off as a school principal ordering a pupil around. Don't tell us something is clear or indisputable, unless you're trying to get us to say, "oh no it's not." Don't tell us what we "must" decide. Similarly, a little repetition is fine, but if you overdo it, it sounds like (a) you think we're stupid and (b) you're trying to indoctrinate us.

The fewer of your own conclusions you offer, the less we resist what you're saying. For this purpose, anything that sounds like a debatable conclusion is a "conclusion." If it sounds uncontroversial in context, then it's just a statement.

The more subjective a matter is, the more likely your statement of opinion will sound like you're telling us what to think. Tell us something is nonsense or offensive or cruel or beautiful or gracious, and we're apt to hear it as a challenge to find a different view.

We know you have your own thoughts, and it doesn't bother us that you tell us what you think. It only offends us when you tell us what *we* should think. This doesn't mean you must preface every statement with "I think" or "In my opinion." Even without that explicit language, you can talk in a way that makes clear you're stating your view while still respecting our independent judgment.

Obviously, it gets tricky, figuring out how much is too much, right here, right now. No one ever really knows. We can only ever make educated guesses. Just do your best to get into the right frame of mind: trusting, valuing, and respecting the judgment of the decision-makers. Imagine yourself into the shoes of your listeners. Keep them, their needs, their knowledge, their perceptions in mind, and try to stay in sync.

MAYBE THE MOST common mistake of lawyers is to get pushy. The best lawyers consistently do the opposite. The best lawyers usually seem just to be stating plain facts, and when these lawyers do advocate, they undersell. We expect lawyers to push, to urge, to strain; so when they just calmly hold up the facts for us to look at, that makes an impression. That avoids resistance.

The mistake of getting pushy melds with issues of trust and

distrust, and the mistake arises both from a misunderstanding of persuasion and from a lawyer's fear of judges and jurors. The misunderstanding is easy to fix: You can just read a book. But the fear roots itself in your brain where it corrupts your choices, your words, your face and gestures and tone of voice — both in writing and in person. Rooting out the fear takes work. Again, that's a topic for another book, but that work is urgently important for anyone who would persuade.

5.3 PREEMPT AND INOCULATE AGAINST POWERFUL NEGATIVE POINTS.

We've talked about preempting *essential* negative points. This will not only protect your credibility; it will inoculate the listener against those points. Occasionally, it may also be useful to inoculate against the opponent's weaker points, if you can dispatch them quickly, leaving the opponent with empty pockets.

To inoculate, couch the negative point explicitly as your opponent's argument, and keep it brief. *"The Defense will say...." "Plaintiff's counsel will argue...."* Without this sort of explicit labeling (and brevity), you're not inoculating against an argument. Instead, you're just mentioning a harmful point and conceding that it's important enough that you have to address it. You want to administer inoculations, not deliver concessions.

5.4 OFFER CHOICES, WHERE YOU CAN.

We like to make our own choices — at least where we choose from a comfortably limited, prescribed set of alternatives. When the nature of the issue allows it, offer the decision-maker a choice from two or three reasonable alternatives. Every choice you offer must seem reasonable, on its own terms, to the decision-maker. It won't help to offer jurors the option of a $10 million verdict in what's at most a $10,000 case. But often, given a choice of three reasonable alternatives, the middle choice calls to us. Where you can, let us choose among reasonable options.

∾

THE PRINCIPLES I've discussed here won't unlock the gates to
heaven. Employing these principles won't mean you can win
disputes regardless of the merits. It won't mean you'll win disputes
you should lose. It won't even mean you win every dispute you
should win. Life is hard. But applying these principles will improve
your work and your success rate.

Nothing I've said implies that law or the beliefs of individuals
can be molded into just any shape. Quite the contrary. It's hard to
persuade any of us of anything that does not fit with what we
already believe. Trickery is apt to blow up in your face.
Constructing persuasive appeals thoughtfully can help, but it won't
make you a puppet-master. The guy who thinks it does will stub
his toe on a spike.

PRINCIPLES FOR PUTTING
KNOWLEDGE TO WORK

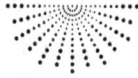

H ere's how it usually goes: You read a book or listen to a lecture or attend a seminar. It all seems illuminating, insightful, and useful. You make a mental note to use these ideas next time you do this or that piece of work. Then you eat dinner, go to bed, wake up in the morning, and in the days and weeks ahead you occasionally remember a fragment or two. You go on about your life and work as before. The valuable ideas you've collected make minimal difference to your work.

The solutions to this problem are old and obvious. Our ancestors a thousand years ago knew the solutions, and we know them today. But that's just more proof of how tenuous useful insights are, how easily forgotten, how hard to implement. So here's a quick review and plan of action.

1. NOTES, BEST PRACTICES DOCUMENTS, AND INSTITUTIONAL ROUTINES

First, take notes on what you've learned and how it applies to your work. Obvious, I know, but also tedious, time-consuming, and a pain in the neck. Too bad: If you want to put knowledge to work, you have to take notes.

Second, create best-practices documents for your own work. By this I mean checklists, templates, models, and other working documents that prompt and guide you when you do any new piece of work. For example: When I write a brief, I create a new document in my word processor, based on a template I've created for briefs. The template contains a set of reminders that help me write a better brief — reminders I'll forget or ignore if left to my in-the-moment inclinations. Some of these reminders are stupidly obvious, but I forget even stupidly obvious things, and I'd bet you do, too.

Third, just as you should use best-practices documents for your individual work, your firm should create explicit institutional routines that embody the insights you find valuable. Lawyers, paralegals, and other staff in your firm should have written procedures to follow, which ensure that good ideas actually get implemented. You should revise these procedures from time to time, as you hit on new, valuable ideas.

As a general rule, any idea that strikes you as routinely important should be embodied in best-practices documents. Otherwise, you won't use the idea consistently, if you use it at all.

2. DELIBERATE PRACTICE

However much we under-use best-practices documents and institutionalized routines, we fail spectacularly at using the other ancient device for improving our work: Deliberate practice.

Our work involves both knowledge and skills. Those are two different assets, and we get and use them in different ways. You can get knowledge and use it just by writing it down and putting it where you'll see it. Easy. Skills are a different matter entirely. You only get skills through practice — deliberate, thoughtful practice.

Actual work on the job does not give you deliberate, thoughtful practice. We want to think it does. We want to think that if we've written 100 briefs, or cross-examined 100 witnesses, we automatically get good at brief-writing or cross-examination. It's not true, at least not much. Questioning a witness in a deposition, for example, involves a multitude of discrete skills. You gain and improve those various skills by focused, separate practice of each distinct skill, taking the time to evaluate after the fact, maybe with feedback or coaching from others, and repeated iterations of the same discrete skill to hone it and make it a habit. In an actual deposition, you can't do that. In an actual deposition, you have to do everything at once, and you can't pay attention to skills. You're too busy paying attention to what the witness is saying (among other things). The actual deposition is the wrong time to practice, for example, generating short, sharp questions. Brief-writing and other sorts of paperwork allow greater opportunities for practice while doing actual work. But even there the opportunities are limited because the substantive content constantly draws attention away from work on general skills.

We should regularly make time to develop discrete skills through deliberate practice. We could probably identify a few dozen skills that any given lawyer should be working on at any given time. But in the press of work and life and going to the grocery, we don't do the practice. We have all sorts of excuses. Accepting them is a big mistake. The excuses make us mediocre.

EPILOGUE

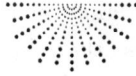

W ho knows why we do what we do? The glib answer is: Most of the time, no one. We put on our thinking caps and our stern-rimmed reading glasses. We sit down to reason rigorously about this or that — whom to vote for, which air puri- fier to buy, what verdict to return. If there are two of us in the room, we come up with two answers. We were both very serious and rational about it, but we came out differently anyhow. We can each explain our answers. We shouldn't put too much stock in those after-the-fact explanations.

You want to move a decision-maker to decide a question in your favor. You want to make me see things this way rather than that, your way rather than mine. What will do the trick? No one really knows. People who say they've got a sure-fire technique are just trying to sell you a book.

The best we can hope for is to identify some general principles that will probably work to some degree most of the time — and to create habits and routines based on those principles. There are no magic beans. There is no way to make just anyone do just anything you want — though there's no shortage of genius-philanthropists willing to take time out from shaping the course of world history to sell you that billion-dollar knowledge for fifty bucks.

After reading a couple hundred pages, you want to come out with a jewel between your teeth. After writing a couple hundred pages, you damn sure want that jewel. But as Carl Sandburg lamented, such a beautiful pail of fish, such a beautiful peck of apples, I cannot bring you now. There are few guarantees in life, and what guarantees there are, are tragic. But you and I learned long ago that life is about nudging the odds a little where we can.

If that's really how it is, though, then we'd better take our insights where we find them, and make the most of them. We're semi-rational beasts. It helps to understand that. It helps to understand that reasoning is motivated, that feelings move beneath the surface and create the currents of thought. It helps to understand the limitations of perception and memory.

Understanding these things can help us write better briefs and put on better trials, yes, but also in various ways understanding these things can help us become modestly better people. Or so I think and hope. I hope you find it so.

ACKNOWLEDGMENTS

I've been lucky in life, especially in the friends I've made, several of whom have helped in various ways in the development of this book. First, my wife, Linda. I've yet to meet anyone smarter or with keener insight than Linda. I don't think there's a single point in this book that I have not discussed with Linda at least twice, and everything here bears the mark of Linda's influence on me (which is not to say she agrees on every point). And then there's the almost absurdly deep and constant support Linda has given me — despite my all too inconstant reciprocation, but to my profound, unbelieving gratitude and love.

When I was looking to leave biglaw and reboot my career, Rick Friedman helped. Rick didn't know me, but he responded to my out-of-the-blue letter with a phone call — which led to a series of conversations that ended with Rick connecting me with Mike Abourezk, which in turn led to a fantastically rewarding sojourn in South Dakota. Rick has continued to help me from time to time in the years since that first phone call — including by reading a longish manuscript I sent him (again) out of the blue, and by supporting the project.

Mike Abourezk (pronounced "aberrant" but with an "esk")

spurred this project along by serving as an exceptional model of a scholarly trial lawyer — and as unpretentiously as one could imagine, whether in a muddy pickup truck or on horseback with boots and incongruous soccer jersey. Mike is a constant reader, and he continuously experiments with ways of applying what he learns. In my years with Mike, I had license to read as much as I could, and I had a living model of the creative application of the principles discussed in this book. I also had a lively, insightful commentary as we drove across South Dakota or rode horses in the Big Horn Mountains. As the Notes partially acknowledge, I've stolen a lot of points, metaphors, and language directly from Mike, with only my brazenness to excuse the theft.

I'm also grateful to my friends Mauricio Gonzalez and Lloyd Bell for encouraging and supporting this project more or less from its inception. At any number of points, it was tempting to shelve the project, and without their encouragement I might well have done so.

Finally, several people — some friends and colleagues, some strangers to me — have reviewed and commented on this book, for no reason apart from their own generosity.

I've been lucky. Thank you all.

— Dan

ABOUT THE AUTHOR

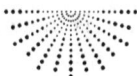

Dan Holloway suffered early frustrations from the disconnect between rational argument and actual persuasion. As a bookish kid, young Danny came to believe the substantive merits of things make the world go round. That let Danny in for a lot of bruising disappointment. Paradoxically perhaps, in high school debate — explicitly premised on an ideology of rational argument — Dan finally started to understand that things other than the mere merits of an issue matter, and often dominate.

After high school, Dan spent four years in the Army, as an enlisted infantryman. There's a lot of downtime in the Army, so Dan always kept a book or two in the cargo pocket of his trousers. In those four years, Dan read a lot of novels, a lot of history and philosophy and economics, and a little psychology. Dan started thinking that changes of mind come after changes of heart, which themselves come from stories.

After the Army, Dan went to college to study history and literature. He wanted to learn about the ways stories work on us. Dan was on the cusp of a graduate program in literary studies, when he decided a career of writing academic journal articles did not match his temperament.

Dan went to Georgetown for law school and then clerked for two years, first on the DC Superior Court and then on the Eighth Circuit federal appeals court.

From there, Dan joined Boies, Schiller & Flexner in New York. While at Boies Schiller, Dan started reading the lay literature on the psychology of decision-making. Dan worked a little with David Boies, and a lot with Bill Ohlemeyer, who had previously served as the head of litigation for Philip Morris, after a career of defending Philip Morris in cancer trials.

In clerking and at Boies Schiller, Dan's experience was that the practicalities of a lawyer's life make it all too easy to focus on the visible intellectual merits of issues while losing sight of the forces moving under the surface. But it seemed to Dan that Boies and Ohlemeyer attended closely to the soft factors at work in a case, factors that might seem irrelevant to the merits.

One obvious difference between Boies and Ohlemeyer on the one hand, and most other lawyers in biglaw on the other, was that Boies and Ohlemeyer spent a lot of time dealing with actual, human decision-makers. In biglaw, because of sprawling cases that consume five or ten years for teams of 10 or 20 lawyers, most individual lawyers rarely interact with decision-makers — certainly not jurors, and usually not judges either. Without that contact, with your eyes focused only on discovery documents and caselaw, it's almost impossible to remember the importance of all the human stuff that stands apart from the abstract merits.

After eight years at Boies Schiller, Dan and his wife moved to the Black Hills of South Dakota. Dan wanted to work on one- or two-lawyer cases that cycle through in a couple years rather than a decade. He wanted to work up close with judges and jurors. Dan joined Mike Abourezk, a member of the Inner Circle of Advocates — an invitation-only group of 100 of the best plaintiff's lawyers in the country. While working with Mike, Dan read a lot more of the cognitive science literature. Dan also went to Gerry Spence's Trial Lawyer's College, which embodies a sort of psychotherapeutic understanding of trial work.

After five years with Abourezk, Dan and his wife again moved, this time for more personal reasons. Dan now works in Atlanta with Lloyd Bell, also a member of the Inner Circle.

This book inevitably but mostly inconspicuously reflects what Dan has picked up from Boies, Ohlemeyer, Abourezk, and Bell (which is not, of course, to say they're on the hook for anything here).

NOTES

PRELUDE: OF RATIONAL MEN & SEMI-RATIONAL BEASTS

1. *Mr. Dooley's Opinions* (1901), p. 26 (available through Google Books).
2. Ambrose Bierce, *The Collected Works of Ambrose Bierce, Vol VII: The Devil's Dictionary* (1911) pp. 196, 274, 277 (freely available through Project Gutenberg, at www.gutenberg.org).

1.1 OUR BRAINS CONSIST OF MANY SPECIALIZED CIRCUITS OPERATING IN PARALLEL, WITHOUT A COMMAND CENTER

1. Photo used pursuant to Creative Commons license. Photo provided by GorissM via flickr.com, at: https://goo.gl/vkHh8x.

1.4 OUR BRAINS AIM TO DO WELL ENOUGH, EFFICIENTLY — NOT TO ACHIEVE PERFECTION

1. Used pursuant to Creative Commons license. Image provided by Valcat96 - Own work, CC BY-SA 3.0, https://commons.wikimedia.org/w/index.php?curid=30894749.

1.5 OUR BRAINS RUN OUR LIVES UNCONSCIOUSLY FOR THE MOST PART, WITH OUR CONSCIOUS SELVES PLAYING A VITAL MANAGERIAL ROLE

1. In, among other places, Mark Twain, *The Complete Works of Mark Twain (Authorized Edition): A Tramp Abroad* (Harper & Brothers 1921), Appendix D, 269-70 (freely available in this and other editions through Project Gutenberg and Google Books).
2. Daniel Kahneman, *Thinking Fast and Slow* (2011), Chapter 2.

1.6 OUR BRAINS GUIDE US THROUGH LIFE LARGELY BY MEANS OF EMOTION — AS AN EFFICIENT FORM OF COGNITION

1. *Descartes' Error: Emotion, Reason, and the Human Brain* (1994), chapter 3.
2. The memo is available through Wikipedia at https://en.wikipedia.org/wiki/Summers_memo.
3. *See* Jay Johnson *et al*, "Potential Gains from Trade in Dirty Industries: Revisiting Lawrence Summers' Memo," *Cato Journal* Vol 27, No 3 (Fall 2007) available at: https://goo.gl/uy7dVA.

1.7 OUR BRAINS ARE BUILT FOR SOCIETY AND BEHAVIORAL FLEXIBILITY

1. Clifford Geertz, "The Impact of the Concept of Culture on the Concept of Man" in *The Interpretation of Cultures* (1973).
2. *See generally* Nisbett, *The Geography of Thought* (2003).
3. Robert M. Sapolsky, *Behave: The Biology of Humans at Our Best and Worst* (2017), ch. 9.
4. Geertz, "The Impact of the Concept of Culture on the Concept of Man," collected in *The Interpretation of Cultures* (1973) (emphasis added).
5. *See generally* Timothy Wilson, *Redirect: Changing the Stories We Live By* (2011).
6. Milan Kundera, *The Book of Laughter and Forgetting* (1979).
7. *See generally* Richard Nisbett, *Culture of Honor: The Psychology of Violence in the South* (1996).

1.8 OUR BRAINS COME PRE-LOADED WITH SOME CONTENT, PROBABLY INCLUDING SOCIAL AND MORAL CONTENT

1. Those who, for religious reasons, reject the scientific consensus in favor of evolution needn't reject the ideas presented here. One could imagine God wiring certain attributes into our brains, to solve the same problems evolution has solved.

1.9 SOME OF OUR DIFFERENCES GO ALL THE WAY DOWN, AND WE HAVE NO TRANSCENDENT ARBITER OF WHO'S RIGHT

1. C.S. Lewis, *An Experiment in Criticism* (University Press edition, 1992), 139-41.

2.1 GENERAL PROCESSES

1. I've taken this point and the example from Douglas Hofstadter and Emmanual Sander's *Surfaces and Essences: Analogy as the Fuel and Fire of Thinking* (2013), chapter 1.
2. This example comes from Richard Posner's *How Judges Think* (2008), chapter 8.

2.2 PERCEPTION AND MEMORY

1. *See* Peter Lamont's wonderful book *The Rise of the Indian Rope Trick: How a Spectacular Hoax Became History* (2004).
2. I've stolen this example (and much else) from Daniel Kahneman.

2.3 IMMEDIATE RESPONSES, CONSCIOUS REASONING, ULTIMATE JUDGMENTS

1. *See* chapter 2 of Klein's book *Sources of Power: How People Make Decisions* (1998).
2. I've taken the cookie crumb metaphor from Mike Abourezk.
3. Again I've taken this example from Mike Abourezk.
4. Via Kahneman, *Thinking, Fast and Slow*, Chapter 5.
5. Tests like the Linda problem obviously depend on how subjects interpret the language of the question. The lesson from such tests may be only — or at least partly — that people read with a variety of background assumptions and conversational intuition, so that in responding to the Linda test they answer a different question than the researcher intends to ask. Thus, in the Linda problem, maybe readers view the phrase "more probable" in the question as asking not about actual, statistical probability, but as vaguely asking only what sounds more true. If that's what's going on in the Linda problem, the experiments carry a different, but equally important, lesson — a lesson about the difficulties of communication. *See* Norbert Schwartz, *Cognition and Communication: Judgmental Biases, Research Methods, and the Logic of Conversation* (2014) and Gerd Gigerenzer, *Gut Feelings: The Intelligence of the Unconscious* (2007), chapter 6.
6. Quoted in Kahneman, *Thinking, Fast and Slow*, chapter 16.
7. I've cribbed the story of D.D. Home entirely from Peter Lamont's marvelously entertaining history *The First Psychic: The Peculiar History of a Notorious Victorian Wizard* (2005).
8. *See* James Randi, "The Project Alpha Experiment," in *The Skeptical Inquirer* (Summer and Fall 1983 editions) (available at https://goo.gl/MEbfK4.)
9. *See* Kuhn's *The Structure of Scientific Revolutions* (1962).
10. Jonathan Haidt, *The Righteous Mind: Why Good People are Divided by Politics and Religion* (2012), chapter 9.

2.5 SOME SUBSTANTIVE CONTENT OR LEANINGS

1. Cited in Kahneman's *Thinking Fast and Slow*.
2. George Lakoff and Elisabeth Wehling, *The Little Blue Book: The Essential Guide to Thinking and Talking Democratic* (2012), 3-4.

3.1 WE COMMUNICATE BY EVOKING THOUGHTS AND FEELINGS IN SOMEONE ELSE'S HEAD — ALWAYS IMPERFECTLY

1. Milan Kundera, *The Unbearable Lightness of Being*, trans Michael Henry Heim (1999).

3.2 WRITING AND READING MAKE THE PROBLEMS WORSE

1. A study by John Bransford and Marcia Johnson, 1972, used in Steven Pinker's *The Sense of Style* (2014), Chapter 5.

3.3 PERSUASION WORKS BY ACCOMMODATING THE DECISION-MAKER'S EXISTING VALUES, ATTITUDES, AND BELIEFS

1. Discussed in Joel Cohen's *Blindfolds Off: Judges on How They Decide* (2014), chapter 10.

3.5 TRUST CONFERS POWER, SO WE GIVE IT WARILY

1. *See* Jared Diamond, *The World Until Yesterday* (2012).

3.6 SOCIAL DYNAMICS PULL US THOUGHTLESSLY AND AUTOMATICALLY

1. *See* Dan Ariely, *The Honest Truth about Dishonesty*, chapter 3.

PRELIMINARIES

1. I've taken this point from Mike Abourezk. I stole his spinning-plates metaphor, too.

PRINCIPLES FOR PERSUASION

1. This is another point borrowed from Mike Abourezk.

INDEX

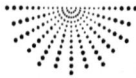

INDEX

INDEX

INDEX

INDEX

INDEX

INDEX

INDEX

INDEX